EARTH'S EMBRACE

The Final Embrace: In Blake's vision the Godhead is an Old Testament
father

EARTH'S EMBRACE

Archetypal Psychology's Challenge to the Growth Movement

Alan Bleakley

Foreword by John Michell

Gateway Books, Bath

First published in 1989
by Gateway Books
The Hollies
Wellow
Bath, BA2 8QJ

Cover illustration by
Sue Bleakley
Set in 10 on 12 pt Melior
by Action Typesetting Limited, Gloucester
Printed and Bound by
Billings of Worcester

British Library Cataloguing in Publication Data:

Bleakley, Alan
Earth's embrace: archetypal psychology's
challenge to the growth movement
1. Alternative society
I. Title
306'.1

ISBN 0 – 946551 – 40 – 5

Contents

Earth's Embrace is dedicated to my late mother and father.

Much love to Sue for the inspiration and perspiration; to Phaedra, Brioney and Sam for letting me learn about parenthood (while getting it right about half the time!); and to Mark and Sue for excellent conversation about much of this material, peppered with a good deal of humour!

Fertility Rites

The lady with red hair wears a red fur
Around her neck, a dead fox.

She muscled me into this world
From between her legs (my first blooding).

My mother's smell is like the musk of the fox.
I grow to love the always-warm pelt —

The fox becomes my familiar,
I flesh the fur and raise it to life;

I give him two penetrating
Eyes, and pristine teeth.

It is March, and I have grown to manhood.
Rain pips the waxy evergreens

By the roadside, where I find the stiff corpse
Of a young fox, fur glossed by the rainfall.

Hardened blood lips the clean white enamel
Of the incisors; one eye is good,

The other closed by matter as hard as resin.
I lift him to look into his good eye.

He has that familiar smell.

Foreword

Alan Bleakley is a distinguished poet, and when poets descend to prose it is usually because they mean serious business. This book is serious about something which most people take lightly, the imagination. The poet's enemy is, as William Blake defined it, "single vision", the literalism which attributes reality to one aspect of the world only, neglecting the entirety of nature and human experience which lies outside it. Alan Bleakley explores the means of expanding from single vision towards a more complete realistic view of human and universal nature. As befits a poet, he works on the level of myths and images, examining those which create and dominate modern conventions and those which are now neglected because they illustrate unpopular or taboo components in human psychology. This sort of activity, meddling with the myths we live by, provokes a strong reaction — as Socrates found out. Yet it is surely the most essentially effective activity that an individual can peacefully engage in. We are here dealing with the material which shapes reality as we experience it. This is a grave responsibility, and the poet is traditionally the proper person to undertake it, as indicated in the Greek word, *poietes*, meaning both a poet and a Creator.

The modern myths which are here scrutinized include those of the New Age, many of them emanating from the materially and mentally fertile state of California. Like every other alert-minded person, Alan Bleakley is attracted by the commodities offered by the New Age philosophers and therapists: high consciousness, glowing health, a commanding personality etc., but he is troubled by their one-sided character. Sunny California has produced a corresponding solar cult, celebrating life's glories and material delights to the neglect of its equal and opposite aspect, the 'night side of nature'. Every field of energy has its negative as well as its positive pole, and it is obviously absurd to regard one pole as better or more desirable than the other. Yet the word 'negative' has acquired pejorative usage, as if it were the natural enemy rather than the complement of the 'positive'. An effect of this has been to limit the popular mythological framework on which are structured the debates, ideas and procedures of everyday life, and because the framework is incomplete, so also is our lifetime experience. If we fail to exercise the full range of our human nature, our world-view grows dangerously narrow and distorted. Nor is it in any way a matter of choice. If it were possible to remake the world in accordance with human whims, by removing death, age, ugliness, the pains and inconvenience of childbirth and all other such apparently undesirable elements, the negative side of nature could justifiably be abolished. This of course is not possible, and those who attempt it by confining their imaginations to the more obviously attractive or 'positive' side of life may be forced into grievous penalty. Testimony to that effect was given by Oscar Wilde in *De Profundis*, written from prison in the years following his disgrace.

"I remember when I was at Oxford saying to one of my friends as we were strolling round Magdalen's narrow bird-haunted walks one morning in the year before I took my degree, that I wanted to eat of the fruit of all the trees in the garden of the world, and that I was going out in the world with that passion in my soul. And so, indeed, I went out, and so I lived. My only mistake was that I confined myself so exclusively to the trees of what seemed to me the sun-lit side of the garden, and shunned the other side for its shadow and its gloom. Failure, disgrace, poverty, sorrow, despair, suffering, tears even, the broken word that comes from lips of pain, remorse that makes one walk on thorns, conscience that condemns, self-abasement that punishes, the misery that puts ashes on its head, the anguish that chooses sackcloth for its raiment and into its own drink puts gall:— all these were things of which I was afraid. And as I had determined to know nothing of them, I was forced to taste each of them in turn, to feed on them, to have for a season, indeed, no other food at all."

The object of Wilde's fatal neglect was the underground realm of the Black Goddess. That is the realm which Alan Bleakley bids us enter. It is an awesome invitation, for the journey takes us through the labyrinthine cave of the Mysteries, where monsters of the imagination and naked images of our own bodily functions have to be encountered before we can return again to the sunlit beauty of the superficial world. The rewards from this experience, however, are very great. The initiate, says Plutarch, "reaches full freedom . . . and gazes down upon the unpurified multitude of the uninitiated who are still in life, abiding in misery from fear of death and want of faith in the blessedness of the soul-life."

Preparation for the ordeal of the mysteries took many years, much of that period was spent on deconditioning the candidate, freeing him from the conventional myths, modes and mores which make social life possible, though at the cost of limiting individual perception. A course of such deconditioning is one of the offerings in this book. It is conducted in the most gentle, painless manner, without blame, rancour, triumphalism or partisan prejudice. Various myths are held up for inspection, together with the attitudes and the subliminal associations which they engender, and with them are exhibited their complements or 'shadows' in the nether world of the imagination. Thus we are given to see, not just one, but a multitude of images arising from every mythic and archetypal theme. Obsessions are thereby diluted and dissolved.

This is a far more subtle and effective method than that of the iconoclast who delights in dutifully smashing people's images of themselves and the gods they have adopted. The author in true pagan spirit (which is also true Christian spirit) accepts the world and human nature as the Creator made them, and has a kind eye for all their manifestations. Though far from uncritical, he does not waste breath in denouncing the immediate, apparent causes of human misery and social sickness. The source of these ills lies deeper, in the inadequacies of modern culture, above all in the limitations imposed on the poetic imagination, producing narrow, distorted, obsessive views of reality. Every modern poet worthy of the name has been aware of the problem and has wished to remedy it.

Robert Graves in The White Goddess encouraged poets to rediscover the full range of imagery belonging to their craft, pointing out that "the language of poetic myth. . .was a magical language bound up with popular religious ceremonies in honour of the Moon-goddess, or Muse, some of them dating from the Old Stone Age, and this remains the language of true poetry. . ." This language, with its wholesome, fulfilling influence on the human psyche, found its enemy in rationalism. The Greek philosophers, says Graves, rejected it in the interests of their new religion of Apollonian logic. In consequence, the balance between the two sides of human nature, male and female, became upset and both

3

grew distorted, the male by glorification, the female by neglect.

"Socrates, in turning his back on poetic myths, was really turning his back on the Moon-goddess who inspired them and who demanded that men should pay women spiritual and sexual homage."

Due homage is paid in this book to the goddess on whom Socrates allegedly turned his back. There is certainly good reason to be wary of her. Provoked by the modern excesses of solar cultism, she assumes her wildest, darkest aspect as Kali or witch-like Hecate, wanton, devouring, manic, goddess of unreason — and at the same time the deepest fount of wisdom. Those who confront her and come to know her, learning her needs and how to answer them, gain freedom from mundane fears and dread of dying. This is the way of initiation. If we choose to explore it, the first requirement is a trustworthy guide, and Alan Bleakley has the right qualifications, beginning with honesty and unpretentiousness. With this author we can safely enjoy the illuminating experience of *Earth's Embrace*.

John Michell

Introduction

"Whoso knoweth himself well groweth more contemptible in his own conceit...Cease from inordinate desire of knowledge, for therein is found much distraction and deceit."

"Know for certain, that thou oughtest to lead a dying life. And the more every one dieth to himself, the more doth he begin to live unto God."

"Nothing is sweeter than love..."

Thomas à Kempis: *The Imitation of Christ*

The inscriptions above by Thomas à Kempis were written over five hundred years ago in quiet contemplation, removed from worldly affairs. Yet his insights are both worldly-wise and absolutely appropriate for our times. They contain the kernel of archetypal psychology's challenge to the growth movement. The impulse of the human potential movement and of the New Age "know thyself" culture embodies a fanaticism — that to know oneself well, to focus always on the personal and interpersonal is considered right and good, while to not subscribe to this perspective is considered to be an illness, a neurotic defence. The desire for personal growth shies away from the leading of a 'dying life', for the self-centred humanistic perspective does not allow the ego to die or relax its hold upon what we value, how we see life, and how we act. Rather, it reinforces ego's tactics of self-reference and assertion. While personalism grips us in this manner, we cannot so easily 'live unto God', and then our experience of love may also be limited.

Contemporary psychology is in a bit of a mess. When I studied

5

experimental psychology as an undergraduate and postgraduate student, I was disappointed to discover that it was not about people, about human relations, but about physiology, mechanics of the mind, 'information processing' models of memory, how rats and pigeons can be starved to below normal body weight, and then made to learn tricks to receive rewards of food (behaviourism), and so forth. When I turned away from this to learn something about people, I found that humanistic psychology was about *nothing but* the 'I', the personal, the ego in relationship. While finding myself tired on the one hand of rats, pigeons and computer models of the brain; and on the other, of self-indulgent and egoistic personal development, and insular, self-referential 'growth groups', there was always depth psychology to counter these surface psychologies. And depth psychology (Freud, Jung and Adler in particular), is often true to its name, providing images of deepening to soul, a logos of the psyche.

However, it is the orthodoxy of scientific, empirical and experimental psychology ('University' psychology, where Jung usually constitutes no more than one session on a 'Personality' course) that dominates current psychological inquiry. And, coming up strong on the inside track is a growing interest in the 'growth' or humanistic psychologies (now even infiltrating the Universities), especially within fields such as management and personnel training, where strong egos and polished interpersonal skills matter, in a tough world of economic 'reality' where winners are praised and promoted and losers go poor. Both psychologies are explicitly secular — they rarely concern themselves with religious questions, with issues beyond the tight confines of personal ego. Neither has as its explicit aim a returning of soul to the world, a making of soul. Experimental psychology values models and theories about humans that carry the shadow of social engineering: control and dominance. Growth psychologies value personal experience and contact, celebration of the self, that carries the shadow of conceit and inflation. Neither may lead to a psychological reflectivity that honours and celebrates God rather than person; that returns soul to the world or recognises the presence of the gods (transpersonal encounters), rather than the cultivation of more polished personal encounters.

Earth's Embrace is a psychology book and a book about psychology, that attempts to inquire through the values and perceptions of the poet rather than the academic psychologist. Here is an inquiry into soul at play in the world, and its language of

6

imagination. There are no mechanical explanations here, no answers, cures, explicit tips or directives on wellbeing. Rather, there are metaphors prompting new ways of looking at the world; images for educating the archetypal eye; challenges to established dogma. Where contemporary psychology has neglected soul in its quest for mechanics of the mind, functioning of the body or transcendence through the spirit, then its shadow of neglect shows as a symptom — a study that stays in the shallows, on the surface, with literal description, and then avoids the depths, interiority, the underworld perspective that leads to a 'dying life' so that we begin to live again with a fresh eye, informed by metaphor and myth.

Moving into the depths is a move away from utility-thinking (what can be used now, quickly, is disposable, fashionable, consumer-oriented, does not tax the imagination) towards aesthetic imagination. The aesthetic outlook wants to see beauty in the world through a beautiful eye, wants to cultivate things of value, and wants to restore animation to the things of the world, considered by materialistic, utility-thinkers to be 'dead', disposable and open entirely to human whim. Such thinking is not simply focused upon the 'inanimate' resources of the Earth such as minerals, but contaminates what science calls the animate world. Plant, animal and human groups are just as likely to be disposed of by those motivated by greed and personal power, in the name of utilitarian philosophies. In the free market economy of the post-industrial world, losers are dispensable, for human relationships are built on utility also — people abused in employment for example, where they are simply a work-force, slave labour, commodities to be bought and sold. There is neither love nor beauty in the extremes of utility-thinking, as Greek myth tells us, where Hephaestus the blacksmith god of utilitarian outlook was dogged by his ugly appearance and manner, cast out by his mother and rejected by the other Olympians; and was crude, ungainly and unlucky in love.

Every myth has more than one side, and Hephaestus has much to teach about skill with the hands, and judgemental attitudes towards physical appearance; but here I am speaking of the overall manner, expression of the value system that shows through utility-thinking — the aspect of Hephaestus' character that makes him unable to appropriately value and care for the embodiment of beauty in Aphrodite, his partner. When we cheapen love and beauty because we have forgotten how to invoke them, how to respect them and call up the presence of these values in the world, then we land ourselves with a world that is surfaced with cheapness: crass dictators who love themselves and money, in that order; cheap politicians who crave power, and paper the cracks with surface talk; a surface education that leaves the majority of children as examination failures from their schooling.

Fifteen years ago, I taught biology for a short while in a secondary school. For the first time, 'ecology' had been introduced to the fifth-and sixth-form curricula as a subject of study in its own right. Now ecology has common currency, popularly associated with conservationists, the 'greens'. 'Ecology' is derived from the Greek, and means literally a study of the house (as habitat). Ecology is then putting one's house in order. Where the world is our bigger house, then ecology involves our relationship to all things 'natural' and 'man made'. When the Greeks put a house in order, this would mean creating a temple. The house not simply a utilitarian shelter — a roof over the head — but a place of worship, where the gods of the household may be attended to. House-'work' is then a devotional act — the domestic rubbish given over to Hecate for example. A house of God is not built as a place where people can shelter from the rain — it is specifically made as a place of worship and devotion to love and beauty. An archetypal ecology's project is to treat the world as a place to which soul may be restored, in devotional act that is both loving and beautiful. Then the supermarket, the highway and multi-storey carpark are places of soul, just as the green lanes and village ponds, the churches and stone circles.

Yet we so often build a world of ugliness, again based on economy and utility, rather than aesthetic. A house of God such as a Renaissance church may have a beautiful painted ceiling, because this was an image of the sky that opened out to angelic realms. (The word 'ceiling' has three possible roots: as sky or heaven; as engraving or carving; and as a screen of tapestry. Whichever root we accept, what is implied is a decorated surface, whose images lead one beyond the room.) At the College in which I work, and many similar institutions in which I have taught, I often point out the ceiling of the rooms to my psychology students. These are built not for the students' eye — so that they may look up and see an inspirational and imaginative sky — but for the maintenance staff: the electricians, plumbers, cleaners. The ceiling is made as an object of utility, where ease of access to wiring, plumbing and basic decorating take precedence over aesthetic, appearance, over the ceiling's value as an image of the sky, or tapestry depicting a landscape.

The ceiling then has no value in the original sense of the word, as a vault to the sky or out of the room. Not only is it then simply a cover to keep the rain out, but also a barrier to keep us contained within the room, to lock us up and to keep the imagination contained. The room is then certainly not a place of devotion. How can students learn to return soul to a utility-built world so de-souled, so under-valued, so lacking in beauty? It is no wonder that the world is taken for granted, treated as a place to plunder, to pillage, for there is no stimulation from our surrounds, and so we respond in a deadened manner, and do not make soul in the world. But we know that bored schoolchildren, locked in dull class-rooms, escape through the imagination in day-dreaming, gazing out of the window — so a vault is made. And in imaginative schools such as good primary schools, the walls are covered not with information posters (more utility), but with the products of imagination — paintings, wall-hangings, images of the world that beautify the containing room and breathe life into it.

Earth's Embrace is about returning soul to the world and reclaiming value in things, through confronting our value systems and stimulating our imaginative capacities and possibilities. I feel that New Age values, as I argue throughout this book, do not address this project of returning soul to the world because they do not begin with psyche in its perspective of depth, but confine themselves to metaphors of surfaces (for example the ecology movement dealing only with the literal green surface of the Earth and the immediate atmosphere, and not with the metaphors of the under-earth and the back of the sky that we will meet especially in chapters 1 and 2). Also, rather than deepening or moving out-back, or returning to source in a reflection and revisioning, the New Age impulse is upwards with spirit with no looking back, everything fresh and vital, that includes the developmental/inflation fantasies of 'growth'. This finds its expression especially in the new therapies that cultivate a 'growth' of person, mirroring the 'growth' of the economy based on the pillage of Earth's resources, where both views seek an impossible ideal, a utopia free from shadows and a person free from symptom, clear of misadventure.

9

Soul: An Explanatory Note

Soul (Greek *psyche*, Latin *anima*) is the proper subject of study for psychology, which is a logos of the psyche. Soul itself is the medium through which we are able to reflect on our existence, although contemporary psychology would reduce soul to 'mind', or further, to physiology, to functioning of the brain. James Hillman, the leading figure in archetypal psychology, has provided a summary definition of soul, most recently in his *Archetypal Psychology: A Brief Account*. In essence, Hillman says that soul is an unknown component that makes meaning possible. Soul gives life and death meaning and purpose, the purpose of life being the recovery of the perspective of soul. Soul 'works' through the metaphor of deepening, deepening events into experiences; and has a special relationship then with the mythical underworld and with death. Soul is communicated in love; is at the heart of religious concern; and is the imaginative possibilities in our natures — the ability to experience through reflective speculation, dream image and fantasy. The language of soul is image. Soul is the 'middle ground' between body and spirit/mind.

I would add to Hillman's outline that soul is that which is motion. Plato says that the soul is capable of self-generated motion. Proclus says that the soul is kinetic or has "perpetuity of movement". The soul's motion may be ordered or chaotic. Proclus says that the soul often shows through number, rhythm and periodicity: the soul "must move in periods", and "what moves perpetually will return to its starting point, so as to constitute a period." Proclus also says that, "every soul is indestructible and imperishable." The followers of Plato said that soul is the unknown factor that makes memory possible. Christ called the soul his "bride": "out of love for thee, I am fastened to the wood of the Cross." Psychology is then properly the giving of meaning and speech to soul, where we live in imagination, and restore soul to every thing, 'making' soul in our imaginative responses to the world.

Part I
Backpacking Through Hades: Forming a Relationship With the Underworld

Chapter 1

Several years ago I took a tour through the various body therapies
of humanistic psychology, such as Rolfing, bioenergetics,
Reichian massage (which I look at in more detail in chapter 5). In
retrospect, they did little for my body but a good deal for the
therapists, who, on average put on ten 'pounds' per hourly session
(perhaps cheap by today's standards)! What I do remember clearly
is the common obsession of these therapists with 'grounding'. As
somebody who finds many of the transpersonal therapies such as
psychosynthesis far too transcendent or unworldly for my taste,
and much of the 'New Age' thinking and posturing a defence
against both the common senses and sensuality, one might have
thought that I would applaud the 'grounding' of the body-workers.
But I do not, because their version of 'having one's feet on the
ground' is literally that. The body is treated literally, as if it were
a machine or hydraulic apparatus, and imagination is avoided.
This is a defence against the imaginal body, and the body of the
Earth as metaphor, as we shall see in the following chapters. For
me, grounding is to make a closer relationship with death and the
energies that depress or force us under. And this means making a
relationship, not just with the surface ground of Earth, but with the
world's under-earth, the mythical underworld. This is quite
different to, say, the vision of bioenergetics, which wants to get
energy up, and wants us to live in a world of wellbeing, on top of
things.

Now I also plump for health and wellbeing, but only when
visioned through the dark — the shadows — of the vales of life. For
when we face the sufferings of soul then we do not so easily inflate
on the highs of spirit and become blinded by the light of our egos.
In embracing the shadow or interiority of the world in
imagination, we do not so easily act out this shadow in literally
destructive, violent or malevolent behaviour.

The Fool Embraces the Earth

A man dreams that he is with a crowd of people. Someone in the crowd has a unicycle. Although he has never ridden one before, the man (the dreamer, or dream ego) has a desire to ride the cycle. He is completely confident of his success. He jumps onto the cycle and instantly gets the knack of riding it, impressing the watching crowd. He even starts to do tricks, confident that he will not fall off. The cyclist has perfect equilibrium.

Another man dreams that he limbos under a piano, only inches above the floor, again in front of an appreciative crowd: "I am almost horizontal . . . I am not sure how I am going to get up, but an energy field (spirit, or ghost) reverses the whole action and I am on my feet again."

He has another dream the same night, in which a woman parachutist descends upside down, righting herself just before she lands on her feet. "She sheds her parachute, tips her hat and walks off, to applause."

The following night the same dreamer has an idea that he can "climb into the sky. It involves a stairway of glass or crystal . . . The idea works beautifully and I climb the staircase which reaches a great height . . . When I reach the top, I jump into the water hundreds of feet below." There is a sense of the presence of a crowd.

A third man dreams that he is in a bookshop in an upstairs room. He sets off to find a book downstairs. There is a "very tall ladder". He finds himself almost at the top of this ladder, descending, when somebody shouts "stop". "I look down and a gang of roughs (undesirables) has put two lumps of explosive on the ladder. They want me to shit from where I am so that the moisture in the shit will set off the explosive . . ." thus killing the man. But he makes a daring leap to safety: "I pause a moment then make a frantic leap for the safety of a thick plank at the top of the ladder." (Thus leaping upwards.) "It is thick enough to stop bullets. I pull myself onto the plank and below the roughs let off some bullets but seem to be subdued by the presence of a large crowd. I am out of danger."

These dreams of daring exploits; of crowd-pleasers; of suddenly acquired equilibrium and poise, and of tremendous verve and skill, show the presence of the puer, the high-flying youthful spirit. (The dreamer who limbos under the piano, then reverses the action, is helped by a "spirit or ghost".) The puer/puella has an

16

| 0 | THE FOOL | 𝕾 |

The Fool as Puer, living close to the edge

17

heroic edge, but his or her daring deeds do not endanger or hurt anyone. The figure climbs high; leaps from heights; leaps upward, seeming to play with danger and death, living close to the edge, righting herself just in time, playing to the audience.

The puer is illustrated as the Fool of the tarot, who begins his journey at cliff's edge. What will happen if he steps out? He looks confident, not a care in the world. Youthful folly cares not for the next step, being brimful of public confidence, like the heroes and heroines of the dreams above. There are no boundaries, no constraints of wiser (senex) authority, no rules for the fool. The world, Earth, is his oyster, and he is open to accept her embrace. He may not have a care in the world, but he does have a care for the world.

Each of us is born a fool into this world, seeking the peaks of experience. And, having known the world, having also spent time in the vales, is born again at death. So the fool and the world are, using James Hillman's[1] metaphor, in tandem, as spirit and soul, peak and vale. In most tarot representations, we see the peaks of the mountains behind the Fool, who stands perhaps on a peak, with the valley below. He often holds a plucked rose; wears a feather; and stands under the sun. These images are of air and fire rather than water and earth; of rising with spirit rather than deepening to soul. And the bag he carries over his shoulder may be a bag full of air, a windbag. He is a type of intoxication in the image of competence, like the drunken driver. In this sense, he is an aspect of Dionysos and Bacchus, gods of intoxication. But his wine is the ferment of youth, the rushing river of new growth — the rising sap. And a sap is a simpleton with a 'skull of sapwood', in short, a green or innocent fool. As the counter to the over-seriousness of wise authority (the older, more experienced person who sets limits or rules), the fool is the court jester or joker.

The puer as fool has many faces — there are as many fools as there are people! Paradoxically, one of the faces of the fool is an old man, a senex character — the foolishness of the aged. It is often said that in growing old we begin to recapitulate childhood. The Jungian developmental view tends to place undue stress upon the wisdom of maturity, in the image of Jung himself, as a learned, grand old man. In this we may miss the character and value of childish foolishness in later life.

Through Jungian eyes we would also, perhaps compulsively, search out a four-fold characterisation of the fool — a mandala, as wholeness of character (rather than perfection). This four-fold nature should then include the youthful puer, whom we have met;

the ageing fool (a senex aspect); a feminine personification; and the fool's dark side, or shadow nature. Indeed, the fool has four such aspects in traditional pantomime, stemming from late sixteenth century Italian characterisations, as: Clown (youthful puer); Pantaloon (senex); Columbine (feminine aspect); and Harlequin (shadow figure). 'Panto-mime' is a word with its origin in Roman theatre, but its roots are in antiquity, in the primal drama of human relations. It means actors expressing themselves by dumb gesture. Gesture, the root of spoken language and number, is the animal form of human communication.

The wise old fool in harlequinade or pantomime is Pantaloon — also a bitter and sometimes vicious person. He is recognised by his loose and puffed-out clothes that make him look ridiculous, especially his trousers, the pants of a loon or stupid man. But, as we have said, there is a wisdom in the foolishness of the aged. Pantaloon has a daughter, Columbine. Her name means 'dove-like in gentleness' and she is invisible to mortal eyes. Her lover is Harlequin, also invisible to mortals, known by his triangulated black and white tights, and his black mask. Harlequin carries a magic wand like Hermes, the bringer of waking dreams, and Hypnos of the underworld, the bringer of sleeping dreams.

'Harlequin' has its root in a family of words that describe the

The Fool's brush with Death (Harlequin)

black horsemen of Hell, who ride by night. He is the night-mare demon, yet he comes as a gentle lover to Columbine. He is a sophisticated aspect of foolishness, closer to tragedy. This reminds us that the fool who steps into the world may be a high-flying, confident puer, who takes risks only because he has an intimate relationship with death. In Gerald Massey's words, his "starting point is on the night-side of phenomena". Our foolishness in the world is sometimes a nightmare, but we can also laugh at our extreme stupidity and our enormous risks. Death's presence is sometimes a rib-tickler, more so when the danger passes and we see how close our brush has been. Harlequin is attractive, and entices. A brush with death, a close shave, makes us look twice into his face, once in agony and once in relief.

Harlequin has a rival for Columbine's affections — the doltish knave or Clown. He is the flip-side of the knight in shining armour. The clown is traditional court jester to the king. He makes a literal living from this, because if he fails to make the king laugh, he is killed. The king must remain the butt of his taunts and jibes, so the jester treads a dangerous path. The clown frustrates harlequin, who has not learned the deceptions and strategies of the worldly-wise ego. Because harlequin has his roots in the night, he is not caught by the perceptions and distorted moralisms of upperworld ego. His is the dream ego, uncontaminated by the worldly ego's inflated deceptions and guile. Like the masked crusader of comic books, or the masked man of many disguises in folklore (Robin Hood), Harlequin is an outlaw who fights for justice, out to expose the trickery of clowns such as knavish politicians, businessmen and court advisors (law lords). The masked man who fights in a naive way for justice has become a central part of our culture. Contemporary versions include the Lone Ranger and Batman. The Caped Crusader's 'familiar' is a creature of night who flies 'blind' — by sonar. The bat is also a familiar of the black, underworld goddesses, rulers of the unseen. Justice herself is such a goddess from the under-earth.

The Lone Ranger uses silver rather than golden bullets, showing his allegiance to the night's moon rather than the day's sun. The personae of these comic-book heroes suggest an underworld origin in the employment of the under-earth or black goddess who is blindfold, representing a perception of the interiority of things, the 'hidden' faces of phenomena. One of her more familiar forms from myth is Ananke, Queen of depths, whom the Orphics equated with the Greek Persephone. Persephone surfaces for part of the

Batman, the masked helper in modern guise. The Caped Crusader dresses like a bat and lives in a cave. He is an outsider in the tradition of Robin Hood and the Lone Ranger.

year — the dark coming into daylight. And the harlequin is chequered white and black, day and night, as the two faces of the night's dream: pacific and disturbing.

The Front and Back of the World and Gravity's Call

It is currently popular to think of the body in terms of two faces — left and right sides — related to the right and left hemispheres of the brain cortex; and to think of the left side as feminine and the right side as masculine. In the ancient mysteries, the basic observation was that the cycle of the day split into the light and the dark, day-time and night-time, and this was applied to the human body not as right and left, but as front and back. The unseen part of the body is the back; the seen, the front. The back of the body is then the dark part, while the front is the light.

Earth herself has two fundamental faces, dances to two basic tunes. For those in the northern hemisphere, the back-side of the sky is the northern arc, where the sun and moon never pass, but where darkness is the bringer forth or the birther of the seven stars of the Great Bear constellation. This is seen throughout the year, revolving about, and pointing to, the still pole star, which is traditionally the tip of the world-tree, or axis of the world. This is also the mother who births time cycles, as well as bringing forth the light of stars from darkness. The southern arc of the sky, where the sun passes in daylight, is seen as the masculine side of the sky, as the son of the mother Bear.

When psychologists talk of the unconscious, they usually mean that which is not yet acknowledged by consciousness, or is out of awareness. It is also, from the perspective of consciousness, both unresolved and unseen potential. One face of unconsciousness is the dark, interior life of the body, that is always in shadow — the senses within, but also the unseen back of the body. When we close our eyes to sleep and dream, or drift into reverie, in relaxation, then we move explicitly to the inner nightsky, where stars are birthed as our spontaneous dream images, lit by an intrinsic brightness that comes out of the dark and allows us to 'see' the images with our inner-eye.

The front of the body is in light, always seen and recognised, and is easily defended against hurt. But the back of the body can only be seen wholly in a mirror, or described by others, and is less easily defended against physical or psychic hurts. It is unseen, but

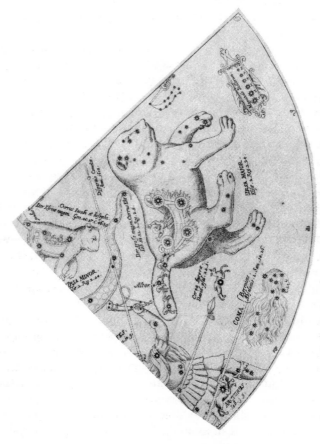

Great Bear Constellation: The Mother of Beginnings

felt, open to the more primitive sense of touch. The body's back-side, night-side, must then be seen as a natural carrier of shadow. In evolution of our upright stance, where we come to face the world with our front, which then naturally becomes active, guiding and seeking, we have had to develop compensations for carrying such a large brain and heavy skull on an upright frame. The work of the neck and back muscles in particular, that allow the head to rest at the top of the spine, works against the pull of gravity, which would otherwise collapse us to the floor, to our deaths, to return to earth.

This pull of the world's gravity is then the challenge for the foolish puer, who would wish to deny gravity, to pull clear of earthing and grounding; clear of senex duty and responsibility. And to pull away from contact with the literal soil, the clays that are common dirt. The transcendental spirit does not wish to be spoiled by mundane matters, and denies the value of rooting in the shadows where the white sunlight of solar consciousness and clarity may never reach. A woman embarking on the 'spiritual' path of self development, a devotee of New Age 'awareness', of moving towards the Light, is disturbed by a dream where: "I feel something splat on my left leg at the calf. There is something on my feet, especially the left foot. It is mud or dark blood or shit. I can see it down my left leg, but not the source. I want to roll away from it. I am quite put off and shake my feet to try to get it off, but it seems to be stuck."

What is 'stuck' is the 'I' in the dream, the dream ego sticking to its borrowed perspective from waking ego, that is anti-mud, anti-dark blood and anti-shit. This is working against the soiling, as a transcendence of the dark body of earth. In another person's dream, the dream ego sticks to its morbid business in a different manner, readily accepting the pathos of the dream, the under-world's logic. A social worker, openly critical of some of her colleagues' and friends' interests in New Age awareness, dreams that one of her clients has died sitting up in bed. There is a large and growing blood stain on the bedclothes, from an open stomach wound. There are several other people in the room and they are panicking over the man's death, and cannot understand the calm and accepting way in which the woman (the dreamer) is accepting the man's death.

With the first dreamer, the dream ego attempts to moralise, censor and control, but, as the dreamer discovers, the psyche 'sticks' irritatingly to its sinister business. The second dreamer accepts the sinister, the dark side, the morbid, without moralising. She benefits through gaining a closer relationship with death, the under-earth, which, in the dream is paradoxically comfortable for her — she readily accepted the open wound and the man's death. Jung[2] was at pains to point out how western culture had opposed the spirit and body of earth, then invested 'high' spirit with a moral superiority over 'lowly' earth: " 'Spirit' always seems to come from above, while from below comes everything that is sordid and worthless. For people who think in this way, spirit means highest freedom, a soaring over the depths, deliverance from the prison of the chthonic world, and hence a refuge for all those timorous souls who do not want to become anything different.''

As we have seen, the moist earth that sticks in the dream is repulsive to the moralising and transcending dream ego that has not shaken off its upperworld guise and its puer ambitions, to avoid facing the decay that inevitably accompanies ageing. I remember attending a Psychosynthesis training group some years ago, where the fundamental model of the psyche suggested was one where all so-called 'negative' qualities (such as jealousy, fear, anger, hate) are *distortions* of 'positive' qualities (such as joy, wellbeing, love), and hence do not 'exist' in their own right. I wondered how Psychosynthesis followers dealt with the shadow of such a viewpoint, and, considering that they claim Jung as one of their greatest influences, via Assagioli, whether they had read passages of Jung's such as that quoted above, and really taken these in.

Traditionally, the morbistic perspective, that faces the issue of change through death, and of the unseen shadow of the world's imagination (and then unseen forces such as gravity), has been personified collectively as the Black Goddess. She has many styles (such as the Greek Hecate and Persephone; Hindu Kali; Buddhist Green Tara; Celtic Morrigan). She also governs our night-time, our dream-world, and our undiscovered potentials. Some of this potential is now being researched, such as our ability to communicate via pheromones or ecto-hormones — chemical messengers that cannot be explicitly seen, tasted or smelt, and hence involve non-conscious senses.[3]

The Black Goddess also reaches into the realms of the wider use of our more primitive, animal senses of touch, smell and taste. She then attempts to return us to union with the natural forces of the Earth, a union that we have lost (as William Blake was at pains to point out) in our reliance upon the five outer senses, and the cultivation of sight as the primary sense. In passive visual perception, we judge the world in terms of the visible light spectrum, without the benefit of imagination. For Blake, the five senses must be informed by imagination, otherwise they are like a prison, containing us within a narrow view. This visible, explicit world is traditionally personified collectively as the White Goddess, whose styles may be seen especially in the vegetative, growth goddesses such as the Greek Demeter; Roman Ceres; Celtic Brigid; Scandinavian Freya.

The White Goddess gives life and resists death. She leads us to expand our senses and to dominate in an outward sense, as we have done with radio, television, computer technology and satellite communications. The world of the White Goddess is that of birth, of fruiting. The world of the Black Goddess is that of inner expansion, of change through deepening to previously untouched areas of potential; of the inner births of children of the imagination; and cultivation of the eye that 'sees through' the phenomena of the world, the eye that perceives interiority. She rules the as yet unseen, and unexplained.

We are in danger here of erecting an unnecessary opposition between two overall styles, which can lead to a moralism that one style is superior to another. The White and Black Goddesses can, rather, be seen as a tandem. Also, we must never lose touch with the wide range of styles by which we can discriminate the presence of, for example, Hecate, as opposed to Proserpine; or Demeter as opposed to Artemis — a rigorous discrimination of the style of the particular deity behind the experience; and, more so, the aspect or particular face that deity presents at that moment (reflected in that god's epithets).

We have talked of something which seems to be known, but is generally 'unseen' or not yet revealed. Let us now explore the notion that revelation of the hidden face of Nature depends upon educating our perceptions, changing our attitudes and values, to allow what is already there in phenomena to show through. What stops us visioning the world or seeing its interiority, is, as we shall explore, the blinkering by the ego, that is anti-imaginal, or denies imagination in the world. A simple example of this is the way in which our post-industrial culture divides the world into 'live' (animate) and 'dead' (inanimate matter), as if a cliff-face or a pebble had no vibrant soul in its self-presentation; and as if the wonder of the world were invested in our response to it, rather than its beautiful presence. (This view drives us into the ridiculous philosophical position that the tree is not there if it is out of our awareness. Then the beautifying presence of the tree is also not there.) It is actually the light of the White Goddess that blinds us to the deeper perception of interiority, to a deepening to soul through this perception, for she is ally of passive perception through the five senses, that is limited by the person's ego concepts and values of how the world should be (that Alfred Adler calls our "guiding fictions").

Archetypal psychology[4] stresses that an archetype is not a thing, but a move one makes; and an image not a thing, but a way of seeing, of re-visioning. With the current popularity of the 'inner journey' of guided imagery, and the conquering of inner space (set in opposition to the outer space-race), we have restricted the world of image and imagination. The image is not simply interior, it is in the phenomena of the world as such phenomena present themselves.[5] However, we must learn to sense through imagination, which is to sense the *interiority* of the thing as it presents itself (which is also a hearing through, to echo).[6] As Blake said, we then get out of the limitations of passive sense-perception. We re-educate ourselves through imagination to re-cognise or re-know the face of the world, in seeing through that face as it reveals itself. The perception is then a revelation.

Jung talked of the persona — the 'face' and bodily expression by which that person is known and recognised — as an archetype. The persona is then the image into which we grow, and by which we are known — the characteristic way that we act in the world, by which others characteristically know us. It is in a sense invariant. People say 'you haven't really changed after all these years' because they recognise the archetypal persona. When we use phrases like 'let's face it', or 'you have to face up to it', we are talking of archetypal reality — putting a face to something so that we can recognise it. This face is character, which comes from a Greek word meaning to make marks or scratches with an instrument. The face is etched, marked, in a characteristic way, and it is these markings, the outward face, that we recognise as invariant.

This is the manifest, not the hidden or latent. But we literalise this manifest content — we caricature it — if we do not see *through* it at the same time as we see it. This is to see the world through imagination. Then, as the neoplatonists would say, we would see the 'genius' that shines through the person and reveals the true essence. Petrarch talked of this transparent genius as the *aria* or

A person's essence or 'tonus' is revealed in physiognomy. Leonardo was a master in capturing the soul's expression in the individual's face.

characteristic form; and the art critic Gombrich, as the "tonus", ". . . that invariant that normally survives the changes in a person's appearance", which is an ". . . unwritten and unwritable formula. . . "[7] This essence is revealed then in image, in the way in which we have seen; and is archetypal, for we have made a move of deepening, of event turning to experience, in this seeing through. At that moment of seeing the person, we are in soul or Blake's Imagination, seeing with the imaginative eye that is, traditionally, a vision, wisdom, or thinking of the heart. And then, simply, yet paradoxically, we see the world for what it is, we see the thing in its self-presentation as we hold it in the heart. We see beauty with the eye of beauty.

Hillman[8] says, in an essay on this direct perception of the heart, "All things as they display their innate nature present Aphrodite's goldenness; they shine forth and as such are aesthetic. Here, I am merely restating what Adolf Portmann has elaborated. . . : the idea of self-presentation as the revelation to the senses of essential interiority. Visible form is a show of soul. The being of a thing is revealed in the display of its image."

Note that Hillman talks of display of "innate nature", not inner nature. Hence we do not fall into the trap of opposition between inner and outer. The faces of things are 'given', and the given is archetypal in its revelation, as we see it unfolding in the world. And what we see is the person or phenomenon in its self-presentation unfolding within a myth, a guiding fiction or fantasy, a character. The Black Goddess in her many guises comes basically with a morbistic guiding fiction; while the White Goddess comes with a developmental fantasy.

Just as the perception of the heart should not be tied to the literal organ, but is a metaphor, so we have been using the word 'see' not in the literal sense of vision, but of re-knowing the world. We cannot see our backs, we feel them, and the way in which we sense them grows out of the image we have of our backs, which is part of what Jung called the persona. As our more primitive sense of touch does play second string, or is considered inferior to sight and hearing, then our back-image is inferior or dark, and we are kept in the dark about it.

Gravity, a non-conscious force, would want to collapse us, to return us to our natural changer the earth, to release us from being trapped in a narrow range of sense perceptions that deal only with the most immediate surfaces of things, uninformed by the seeing through of imagination. This potential collapse is frightening

29

because it is an invitation to the under-earth, which is unknown. It is no wonder that the ego defends us against such collapse and collaborates with the impulse of the youthful spirit to rise away from the ground. But this defence has its limits, and we must be taken by under-earth if we are to deepen to imagination, that is the capacity to participate in soul-making.

As we shall discuss in more depth later, the body has its unseen capacity, which Blake called Tharmas, our undiluted and cleansed (imaginative) senses. Our necessarily wounding changes, that are living deaths, are redemptions of Tharmas, an awakening to greater capacity for touch and taste. In Blake's drawings and paintings, again and again we see figures with arms open in a characteristic pose that precedes embrace. Some are reminding us of the waiting embrace of Earth at death and in life; others that we may be foolishly waiting for embrace like innocent children, unable to open ourselves to Blake's "Jesus the Imagination", and hence waiting forever, with closed senses. This is the paradox that the archetypal fool addresses. Experience is the active education of the archetypal eye, not the passive hope for the lost innocence of children. The latter tends to cultivate a transcendence of the world's suffering, rather than an informed and imaginative addressing of the suffering, a dialogue.

Blake's vision confronts our self-defeating and narrow systems that only see the world in one way, and turns us around to take in other realms of beauty through as yet unexplored avenues. In our upright stances, facing the world, looking and listening, we ignore the back, for we cannot swivel our heads that far. Also, the thickening of muscle that keeps us upright reduces sensitivity in the back, so that touch sensation is paradoxically masked, or not given high profile. Our up-right egos similarly mask the beauty and variety of the psyche's possibilities, and dulls the sensitivities of the imagination.

The more primitive senses of touch, taste and smell are especially important in intimate contact — in lovemaking; in contact with children; in care of the sick and elderly; in the balm and energy that is created simply out of deep concern and empathy — the special magic that is created in therapy when somebody is really listening.

Female animals present their backsides or rumps for intercourse and the male enters from his front. The words front and back have roots which reflect the assertion that the back-side of the world is feminine, the unseen realm from which healing occurs, while the

Blake's 'The Dance of Albion' is a characteristic pose — the naked and
vulnerable man open to the embrace of the world

masculine is the front-side, the arranger of after-care. (Remembering that there is a masculine element in every woman, and a feminine in every man.) And the back-side or under-side of the woman both receives (in sex), and gives (in birth).

'Front' comes from the Latin *frons*, a projection or swelling. This is the White Goddess as fruiting mother, pregnant with child, breasts ready to produce milk; and also the virile, erect male. The word 'back' is derived from the Old English *baec*, and Old High German *bach* or *baccho*, from which we also get the word bacon — the pig's haunch or rump. The sow is traditionally the animal sacred to both White and Black Goddess, full moon and dark moon, as she has large litters (is extremely fertile), but also is notorious for eating her young. (The Black Goddess as Kali the devourer, reflecting the menstrual pole of the woman's cycle, which is the devouring of the potential child that is now given back to, or eaten by, the world.)

Rump, romp and rampant are all derived from the same root, which means to crawl or to creep, and the Middle English *rampen* means a sexually bold woman or girl. Hence, the back-side, the rump, the unseen, is creepy and crawls, or makes the flesh crawl, a reversal from our reptilian days when we crawled on the belly. Now it is our backs that crawl, for we are afraid of what may be creeping up on us. Hairy Pan, unbridled lust, is said to leap onto the back with no warning, when least expected, at midday's light. The stab in the back comes when we are off our guard, or relaxed. When we cannot face fear, or give a face to our fears, then we turn our backs on it. This is repression, a dangerous business when we consider that by turning our backs and not facing our issues, we are inviting those issues to attack us from the rear, to make the wound or vulnerability even greater, although now out of consciousness. This is a sure way to chronic psychosomatic symptom. When we attack the symptom only, the seen, this is a White Goddess maneouvre. Therapy should be an active deepening to what is at first unseen, the realm of the Black goddesses.

The Front and Back of the Brain

The aftermath of the second world war left us with a legacy resonant with the 'split brain', and a caricature of lifestyles — capitalist west versus communist east; the right-hemisphere, liberal and creative 'free' world, versus the left-hemisphere, rigid and dogmatic communist regime. The world, however, now divides more clearly into north and south — post-industrialised, overfed, conspicuously-consuming north; and pre-industrial, underfed, overpopulated south. This is of course a gross simplification, but a useful metaphor. It reminds us of how the right-left, west-east split has dominated popularised accounts of brain functioning, at the expense of the back-front, north-south split:

The Apple Fall and the World Orchard

Here is a polarity in the apple fall—
A cobble of tops glazed by rain looking
As clean and waxy
As they would in their blue tissue wraps,
Selling by the pound.

But kick them over and the rotten halves sing out
With a heady odour of cider:
Pulp under firm top-flesh.

The apple fall mirrors the world divided
North to south, toned muscular front
And pulpy ferment.

Another month and the apples will be wholly mulch,
Top-frosted by the crisp nor'-easters.

Lateralisation models ascribe discrete functions to left and right cortical hemispheres as:

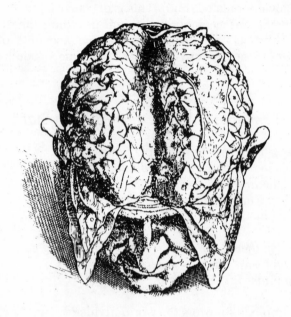

The brain, like the modern world, split east to west, rather than north to south: hemisphere lateralisation

LEFT HEMISPHERE
(To right body)

Verbal arts
Rationality (Thinking)
Discrimination (Valuing)
Symbolic verbal
Causal
Self-criticism
Discrete particle
Logos (meaning)
Senex authority
Waking ego
Focusing
Time
Apollo

RIGHT HEMISPHERE
(To left body)

Plastic arts
Irrationality (Intuition)
Direct perception (Sensation)
Spontaneous non-verbal
A-causal (synchronicity)
Self-pity
Wave function
Eros (relating)
Puer/puella youthful folly
Dream ego
Peripheral vision
Space
Dionysos

Such models are within the guiding fiction of oppositionalism, and necessarily flawed. Lateralisation is challenged by those cases where damage to an area of right- or left-hemisphere cortex is compensated for by an area in the opposite, undamaged hemisphere recovering that function. The cortex then has an holistic temperament, as it were.

Although still within an oppositionalist guiding fiction, we can view the brain sagittally, front to back, the antero-posterior plane of the body. Stan Gooch[9], in a sequence of books, argues that the cerebrum and frontal lobes are in tension with the back-brain cerebellum, which itself has two hemispheres like the cerebral cortex, and, although it is much smaller than the cerebrum, actually has a surface area that is three-quarters as large as the cerebrum. Also, women have larger cerebella than men. He presents evidence that at one stage in our evolution, the cerebellum appeared to be developing along with the cerebrum, and may have become the major organ of consciousness. This seemed to reach a peak with Neanderthal peoples, who appeared about 100,000 years ago, and survived for 70,000 years.

Neanderthals had a far bigger cerebellum than modern people. Then evolution seemed to take a U-turn. Neanderthal peoples had disappeared by 30,000 years ago, to be replaced by Cro-Magnon types. Gooch argues that Cro-Magnons wiped out Neanderthal peoples, while inter-marrying with some. Modern *Homo sapiens sapiens* is the product of the Cro-Magnon line. From Neanderthal burials we can deduce that there was an explicit sense of ceremony concerned with the passage of the dead. For example, a grave was discovered in northern Iraq where the dead person had been laid out in a bier of wild flowers and boughs of pine.

In brief, Gooch argues that cerebellar functioning is intimately connected with dreaming and visionary states (rather than the right hemisphere of the cortex). It may also be the " . . . originator and controller . . . " of paranormal phenomena such as telepathy, while the cerebrum's concern is the waking ego. Neanderthal consciousness was rather a living in unconsciousness, in the imaginal and symbolic worlds; where Cro-Magnon consciousness is waking world, ego-inspired. Hence we ascribe inferiority to the back-side, the dark-side, the north, the underworld of dream, because we are the direct descendant line of Cro-Magnon victors over Neanderthal outlook.

Neanderthal, cerebellar consciousness is then the world of imagination as Blake views it, the world seen in a visionary state where the tactics of the ego are seen through. Cro-Magnon, cerebral consciousness is the world seen only through the five senses, conceptualised by ego and uninformed by dream, by imagination. It may be that the currently popular left-right model, set within an oppositionalist conceptual outlook, is distracting attention away from the perhaps more fruitful front-back, cerebrum-cerebellum tandem. The loser in this is not the less dominant right hemisphere/left body; but the radically inferior (from our cultural perspective) back/north of the world, sunless, moonless, dark and star-bright. Night-world and dream-time rather than day-world ego; soul and vale rather than spirit and peak.

James Hillman[10] subscribes to this sagittal view when he talks of the dominant Protestant, cold psychology from north of the Alps (including Jung); as opposed to the inferior, dark, but warm Mediterranean psychology of the Greek pantheon, and the neoplatonic revival within the Italian Renaissance. The former is spirit-oriented and impelled by guiding fictions of monotheistic growth to wholeness (wellbeing, health, individuation, balance at the centre of the mandala), within logos (understanding). The latter is soul-oriented and impelled by guiding fictions of morbism, pathologising, and polytheistic possibilities (splintering), within eros (relating). Here, the literal geography is reversed in the metaphor — Protestant north is front (south sky); learning by effort, guided by utility. Pagan south is back (north sky); learning by love, guided by beauty.

The Celtic Imagination and the Lovers of Albion

One cultural imagination straddled the Alps, and the opposition suggested by Hillman between monotheistic and polytheistic psychology. This is the Celtic imagination. The Celts not only colonised much of modern-day Europe, where they are evidenced today in the north-western fringe — Ireland, Wales, Scotland, Cornwall and the Scilly Isles, the Isle of Man, Brittany; but they also sacked Rome (c.390 BC), and pillaged and desecrated the Greek Oracle at Delphi (279 BC). The Celts traded with Italians, Etruscans and Greeks. Although they are still perhaps stereotyped in popular imagination as 'barbarians', as opposed to the civilised Greeks and Romans, it was the Celts who introduced soap to the Mediterranean peoples!

The Celtic outlook was polytheistic, where the freedom of the

Stylised bust; Celtic head from County Durham. For the Celts, the soul
resided in the head

individual is paramount. There is a dual ignorance and romanticism concerning the Celtic outlook within the current day Celtic
fringe, which calls for nationalistic identity. Rather, the Celts were
passionately anti-political, and never had a unified culture. As
Frank Delaney[11] says of them: "They exercised a philosophy
which saw truth as a diamond, many-faceted and precious. And
thereby they celebrated one quality of life vital to them —
personal, spiritual freedom. But they also cut off people's heads,
offered human sacrifice, burnt men, women, children and animals
alive *en masse* in enormous wicker effigies."

The Celts also saw physiognomy as direct expression of soul.
The head contained the soul, and was revered for its features, but
not in a literal sense. Rather, the genius shone through the head. In
Celtic art, the head is not represented in a naturalistic manner,
which would flatten the voice of soul through literal representation. Rather, the head is stylised to allow the voice of the soul to
speak through.

The British have traditionally retained a Celtic strain that is both

37

polytheistic in outlook yet honours the individual soul. It is a strain that worships the garden of England, the green land, the soul that shows in Nature. It is a truism that the British have a special love affair with the countryside and the garden. Since the industrial revolution, the public interest in this love affair has waned however, as Blake predicted, where the island of Britain has fallen asleep on itself, in response to its unconcerned inhabitants. Traditionally, Brittania is the mother-island, a sacred garden, personified as a goddess. She is the Celtic goddess Brigantia, of whom Brigit is a local variant as keeper of wells, the source or spring of wisdom of the isle.

In Blake's mythology[12], Brittania is wedded to Albion (the first recorded name of Britain is Alba), where Brittania is the vegetation on Albion the slumbering giant, who is the rock itself. They have twelve daughters and twelve sons, the original inhabitants of the isle. Albion's emanation, soul or anima, is Jerusalem, the indwelling soul of the land, which inspires humans to re-spect the landscape, to look again with an eye to re-animating the land. This is to return soul to the world, to re-enliven the slumbering country as *anima mundi*. It is the world ensouled that teaches the human directly, that inspires the human to creative art and science. In Blake's vision, the world ensouled is the realisation of heaven-on-earth, of the new Jerusalem.

Any person interested in the British spiritual heritage (that has become known as 'the Matter of Britain'), would want to seek answers to the following questions so that he or she may reconnect with the anima of the isle: i) Why is St. George the English hero, and why does he slay dragons? ii) What is Albion? iii) What is Avalon? iv) What is the Grail? v) Who is Arthur?

George may be derived from the Greek Ge-orgon, meaning tender of the garden of Ge or Gaia, the mother Earth.[13] If George is the gardener of the Earth, why does he 'slay' dragons? Traditionally, the dragon is an active and eruptive aspect of the serpent of the earth, who, in some Creation myths, is central to the birthing of all things. In the Orphic Creation myth, the serpent Ophion wraps itself around a silver egg, warming the egg until it hatches to release all of creation.

The silver egg may be seen as the moon, and the serpent, the moon's changes, mirroring the monthly changes of the woman. The serpent sheds its skin and is seen as a symbol of menstrual change in the woman, and of the shedding of the mantle of vegetation by the Earth as she moves into her dark time of winter.

The serpent is close to the earth, crawling on its belly in humility, and is associated with death and the underworld, or banishment. Associated with menstrual change, the serpent of the earth is naturally feminine in antiquity, but in many cultural outlooks gradually becomes masculinised.

The dragon is a special kind of serpent — fire breathing and therefore of deepest earth, volcanic. George is the tender of this earth-serpent as the deeper, more eruptive changes and rhythms of Nature, and his 'slaying' of the serpent may be to fix it so that he can more readily converse with its changes. The rhythms or currents of the Earth have their manifest expression in the electro-magnetic spectrum, a part of which we have immediate access to through our five outer senses, but most of which is hidden from us, is dark to us. We know more than we immediately sense, and so we symbolise the current of the Earth in her dark, unseen, or as yet unknown aspect, as 'dragon lines' (the Chinese *feng-shui*), or ley-lines.

These are words that describe a mystery that may be a repressed commonplace experience, as a direct knowledge of earth energies. For example, a registered sensitivity to small faults in the earth's crust; or an underground flow of water; or to the earth's magnetic field. Robin Baker[14] has suggested that such sensitivity to the magnetic field of the Earth is a human 'sixth sense', a sense not immediately conscious and perhaps mirroring the homing device of pigeons, and the facility that allows birds to migrate.

The word 'ley' may have the same root as 'lustre', something which shines. The brightness may be the spark of inspiration that occurs in the dark of dream time. If the forces of the Earth are dark or unseen, then a vision of them (or a feeling for them, as in dowsing), would indeed be lustrous, shining, brilliant, like the minerals of the Earth illuminated from within, deep underground, from the intrinsic light that darkness always holds. In a dream we see images in the dark of our active souls by their brilliance, their intrinsic light, which is also their worth or value, Hades' 'Unseen Riches'. The more worth or value we ascribe to something, the more beautiful or shining it becomes to us. As Professor von Hardwigg, leader of the expedition to the centre of the earth, in Jules Verne's novel, suggests, "...as we approach the Centre, I expect to find it luminous..."

This shining, this brilliance of something interior to body, and body of Earth, is what Blake saw as the sleeping anima of the land. It is the vision of illuminated trackway that Alfred Watkins 'saw' in the Hereford landscape, that birthed the idea of leys. Also, the nerve network under the skin of soil that Katherine Maltwood saw as the Glastonbury Zodiac. In each case, the active eye of the *mundus imaginalis*, in which we participate, is at work.

As the moon shines with its peculiar quality of brightness out of the dark nightsky, so this interior-light-made-plain of the inner earth is a brilliance of a similar quality, derived from the depths. This is an animating of the sleeping rock Albion, whose name derives from Alba, a version of the shining silver-white goddess. She is the moon in her changes, the land in her seasons, and the woman in her monthly cycle — where even the dark pole, the invisible moon, shines, is known by her phosphorescence, and is personified as the brilliant underworld angel Hecate.

This brilliance is also the earth-dragon's essence as the molten core of the planet, who shows in volcanic eruption and in earth tremors, earthquakes, landslides and so forth. Perhaps George's heroic reputation was enhanced in that the dragon in Britain seems under control to some extent, with an environment that is singularly free from major extremes — a pleasant garden, but also conducive to slumber!

The tender of the Earth, George, has the special opportunity to vision the dragon awake, to be taught by her how to see in the dark, how to regain use of his neglected powers or hidden potentials such as the ability to dowse water or minerals, or to extend sense perception to make conscious the knowledge of orientation to a magnetic field. The particular illuminative quality of this vision — its phosphorescence — derives from the quality of relationship to the landscape: how much one values or ascribes worth to the landscape and her interiority. This section began with the British love of the countryside, and now we must deepen this to a special relationship — an erotic one. Eros was a dweller in Hades, the underworld, and yet was the god of love and life, and of eroticism. So he brings the special phosphorescence of relationship born out of a wedding between the hero who is not afraid to descend to the dark and expose his vulnerabilities, and the particular Woman who teaches him there.

'Relationship', a word which did not enter the English language until 1744[15], comes from the earlier 'relate', which means 'to tell'. This descent and acceptance forms a literal 'telling relationship', for the man must confess his deep ignorance of the feminine.

The Greek pantheon includes the erotic Dionysos, tender of the vine, and his associates: Pan as Nature in her raw and animal state;

40

Bacchus the god of intoxication by wine; and Priapus, the essence of male potency and virility, with his exaggerated penis. Of these, Priapus is specifically the gardener, a tender in particular of the pear tree, and a pruner. The clan of Dionysos have then an erotic relationship with the land, that is the archetypal basis for the love between gardener and garden, and gardener/ gamekeeper and lady of the garden (lady of the manor) as Mellors and Lady Chatterley, in Lawrence's novel.

Such an erotic connection will of course bear fruits, and, in the first instance, the lover of the Earth who is also asking to be taught through her embrace (the seeker after 'Earth Mysteries'), is concerned with her outer display, her fruiting, her immediate presence as landscape beauty. This aspect of Albion is the visible White Goddess, the ovulatory pole of the woman's cycle as the child-bearing capacity. Here, the Earth is personified as fruit-bearer, as the grain-giver Demeter (Ceres, Brigid, Kwan-Yin, White Buffalo Woman, Isis).

There is a danger here that the admirer gets caught just in the outward beauty of the fruiting, an anima fascination that becomes a voyeurism, a tourism, and this only. Such a relationship must be deepened beyond surface physical attraction. Robert Graves'[16] description of the Black Goddess (as greater Muse) implies three levels of initiation of the tender of Earth to a personified goddess, where the special erotic relationship described above is deepened at each stage.

When we are young, we are in the service of the Grandmother (Hestia in Greek myth). At this early stage we learn orientation to the world — how to stand up on her — how to find our way. The feeding mother is the omphalos, from whom we venture a little more on each foray. As children we are innocent of the powers that allow us to orient in space and time, such as the deep reliance upon the more primitive senses of smell and touch, and the unacknowledged senses such as an ability to orient in space via a sensitivity to the Earth's magnetic field. This is an orientation to the hearth of the Grandmother, a finding our way home, for the hearth or heart of the planet is a molten iron core which generates the very magnetic field to which we unconsciously orientate.

As we grow up, our orientation may be to relationship and possible children of our own. This is to form a union with the White Goddess who rules childbirth and the battle of the sexes. We must go through this warring initiation of the White Goddess in order to relate as men and women at a deeper level than the battle

41

of the sexes, a level of exchange. As Graves discovered, service to the White Goddess carries an enormous shadow. Firstly, as Jung pointed out in criticism of dogmatic exoteric Christianity, a seeking of perfection is imbalanced where it leads to repression of the shadow. Acknowledgement of shadow is a seeking rather of completion, the alchemists' *unio mentalis* — the grain of dirt aggravated over time forms the pearl; and the original blemished particle is not forgotten. Completion is the coming-to-fullness (at any moment in time) of a phenomenon, as its self-presentation in the world: this particular pig, that lime tree; this spontaneous feeling, that ageing face. Things in their image. And things do not have to be grown up or adult to be in their fullness — this is the trap of the developmental perspective so loved by the New Age. Such a perspective keeps us as undeveloped children — as long as we are 'growing', or participating in self-*development*! And, as lost children, we will then seek developed father-and mother-figures — authorities — such as the guru, or charismatic therapist.

Secondly, concentration on the fruiting pole only of Nature's cycle brings with it an obsessive orientation to growth, a life-subscription to the developmental fantasy. Then we are concerned with childbirth and its shadow in over-population; with gross national product, economic expansion, and its shadow in inflation and unemployment; with exploitation of natural resources, and its shadow in ecological problems and imperialism. And when the whole cultural child has been overfed to an obscene level, become too gross, too cumbersome, our thinking is still expansive or more-for-less, as we move into the microchip revolution and slimline designer fashion. But the shadow of heart disease — from a whole culture being overweight — has already struck. And this reflects a paucity of an imagination of the heart.

This subscription to development or growth is a mania, character-istic of Hercules' Labours. The growth movement in psychology suffers this mania and its shadow, as we detail in chapter 5. We are trying to keep Nature at bay as we try to control her; and as we engage in a growing need for her material goods, and a growing fear of not possessing the latest designer model. What we fear in the White Goddess of material productivity is her drying up.

An example of the culture that has dried up, or become devoid of beauty, is Los Angeles. Punning on the sound of the words, the loss of beauty is right there in the name: the city of 'lost angels'. We would guess that the underworld Hecate would explicitly show her face here, as she is lady of the compost, of all our rubbish,

42

our cast-off and worn-out, our consumed. Los Angeles has lost its soul, like many cities, through an explicit ugliness. And there is the conscious knowledge that California rests on a major geological fault-line. But the prevailing fantasy is live-now-pay-later, in the hope that science will some day bring under control not only rampant viruses, but even the tremors of the Earth herself. In this uneasy relationship, we are oriented only to outer manifestation of the landscape rather than her inner-soul, her feelings; and only to utility — what we can get from the Earth, rather than what we give back or can appreciate. We may treat the scenery as voyeur rather than lover. Then we do not see the interiority of the land, or feel the spirit of the place. And so we become parasites and global tourists resting on the Earth, rather than geomancers existing with her.

Another aspect of the shadow of development is pollution. Fruiting and growth leads to its own natural decay, but a forced and unnatural level of fruiting and consumption distorts the ordinary process of decay, and it is precisely at this point of stench, amongst the rubbish-tips of culture, that our relationship with the Earth must be tipped towards the shadow-sisters of the White Goddess, the Black goddesses such as Hecate, who rule over the alchemy of composting.

We say alchemy, because facing the rubbish through Hecate is very different than facing the rubbish with material consciousness. Hecate demands that a person gains dialogue with her own interiority or shadow nature before engaging with the shadow of a culture. Indeed, the choices humans make about the beauty of their environment or the way they treat fellow humans, are products of the myths or guiding fictions in which the person is embedded. In archetypal psychology, one faces first the myth, then the person, for the person is embedded in the myth. Material outlook attempts to change people's habits without ever considering the collective issues, the myths that guide us, which is a back-to-front, utilitarian, patchwork process, in which we apply the sticking plaster before the wound has had a chance to speak. And we shore up an ugly culture with more material, utilitarian ugliness, rather than addressing the lack of eros, of beauty.

A movement to facing the underworld issues can lead us away from reliance on our five outer senses as the realm of the White Goddess, to our unseen, unacknowledged senses, or sense of interiority of things, as the realm of the Black Goddess. Here, in the vales and creases of the world, is a deeper level of initiation. The battle of the sexes is dissolved in the discovery of a circulation between partners which is rooted in an honouring of the woman's menstrual pole of experience, the dark side.

Our deeper erotic relationship with Earth, her embrace of us, must include this respect for her dark side, aspects of which we already label, from the White Goddess perspective, as 'natural disasters'. Then we are still in a battle of the sexes as technology vs. Nature, throwing pans at each other across the continents. We over-farm, she throws back a dustbowl; and now the beautiful, alluring, lush goddess has dried out to old hag, and we turn away from her, abandon her, right where the suffering needs to be re-spected, re-viewed.

If we work through the battle of the sexes to this deeper level of erotic relationship, we begin to talk with the Earth where her powers are most concentrated — we get to know her currents. In Blake's terms, this is a redemption of the zoa or quality of Tharmas, of body, a discovery of the potential of the body in a wider sense experience than the five outer senses. Then we discover and restore the whole imaginal body of the Earth, the *anima mundi* or world soul. In a dialogue with the unconscious, we are ensouled; and in a dialogue with the soul of the world we are released from the mania of 'growth', and the seduction of material 'solutions'.

In this move, Albion, the sleeping giant, may be ensouled to awaken Jerusalem, which is Avalon, Britain's spiritual heart and animated expression. Avalon connects both the seen and unseen of the world, as she is a place of 'mystery' in the original sense of the word — to see with the eyes closed, with the borderland senses. She is the between-world of inspiration, where seen and unseen are felt as a unity. The descent to the underworld that results in a permanent binding to its force, a recognition and honouring of the Black Goddess, is facilitated in Greek myth by the pomegranate seed, and in Celtic myth by the apple.

We have seen that *Avallen* in Celtic tongues is the apple-isle or apple-garden. So Avalon is the twilight country, where upperworld and underworld meet in both fruiting and decay. The apple is the fruit of memory, the five-pointed star at its centre a body of woman, one half in seed, the other without, as the ovulatory and menstrual poles of experience. Avalon is a folk-memory of the animated body of Britain as the full anatomy of the body of the goddess, in both light and shadow.

We began this section by asking five questions. We have talked

44

of St. George, the tender of the garden of Earth; of Albion or Alba the White Goddess who is the vegetative earth, and of her dark twin, the Morrigan/Hecate as the composter; and of Avalon, the apple-isle, where the apple leads us to the underworld, to conversation with the Black Goddess. Our fourth and fifth questions concern Arthur and the grail. Arthur means 'son of the bear'. He is the heroic son, lover and consort to the Great Bear sky goddess who points to the navel of the northern hemisphere at the pole. The bear is the major cult animal of northern peoples. Arthur is the waggoner or charioteer who drives the Great Bear around the sky, and then is the overall masculine component in the feminine rhythm, that Jung termed the animus, which must be searched for its many faces, its many self-presentations, or archetypal presences.

As stellar time-keeping gave way to lunar and solar time, so each outlook carried with it a new set of myths.[17] These tended, more and more, to emphasise human control of, and distancing from, Nature, with a consequent loss of direct knowing. Arthur is the knowing hero who loves Nature to death, who could lead men back to knowledge of the grail, that in one sense is this felt erotic connection with feminine Nature. (The Celtic scholar Eleanor Merry[18] simply equates the grail with the body of the Earth.) To achieve this embrace with Nature, Arthur the wandering fool is destined to meet his dark twin, his shadow nature, and must descend to its root.

The Knights of the Round Table are twelve in number — Arthur is the thirteenth, reconciling solar and lunar time, as there are thirteen lunar months in each solar year. Their quest is to discover and apply the grail's secret that will restore the ailing King and his land, fallen into sickness. The king Amfortas of the wasteland is Arthur himself, and the ailing land is Albion. The quest is to re-member the body of the land, to re-animate the country in honouring its rhythm. This is to return soul to the world, thus ensouling humans. The aim of the quest in these terms is to regain the respectful erotic union with the land — a deep love for, and engagement with, the world — that was enjoyed by the Ancestors, as birthright, who learned this love from the animals.

The grail in older texts is described as a tree, not a plate (like the placenta, the twin we lose at birth), or a cup (like the womb in its changes). To re-member the inner-sense or interiority of the body of the land is to recall the teachings of the trees, such as the Celtic tree alphabet.[19] Then we see the trees in a new light, and want to recall them, fall in love with them again. In a new relating to the land, we acknowledge the grail as 'king and land are one'. The grail is realised when this erotic union of masculinised will of person and feminised unconditional love of Earth is restored. The kingly and queenly natures in each of us must re-animate the world in order that we can learn from the Earth what we must do with our royal natures. The work for this begins with whatever has been spoiled or desecrated, where beauty may be restored. The human body is identified with the body of the land in a return of soul, pursuing the alchemical circulation between consort and Queen.

In this erotic connection, we re-member both topsoil and subsoil, both outward scenery and interior current, in an awakening to our neglected capacities. We remember also the dark of sky and sea — the terror of the world is respected — and we are taught of a more intimate relationship with death. Each respectful moment with the land, each re-looking with a new eye, is to deepen in the looking, for we are now viewing not with the spectator's eye, but the eye of interiority. If we look with the eye of Hercules, then we rape the land. We do not see or respect world soul, we are in materialistic outlook rather than imagination. If we spectate, as tourists, in the passive style of Demeter/Persephone, then the land takes us unawares, rapes us in a turbulent descent to the underworld. If we allow ugliness to grow around us and with-hold responsibility, then that ugliness will engulf us, swallow us whole to face the Black Goddess unprepared.

In his story "Heart of Darkness" Joseph Conrad shows a third way to relate to Nature, neither in hostile activity and control, nor in detached passivity. Rather, Marlow, the hero of the story, sets out on a journey to specifically test himself. He consciously chooses to make the descent, so that he might change in aware-ness, in the style of Homer's Odysseus or Virgil's Aeneas. These heroes accept Earth's embrace and are flexible to its gifts — despite the dark face that Nature chooses to sometimes present — as opposed to fighting off the embrace in the style of Hercules, or being taken unawares, in the style of Persephone. The latter is the naive innocence that Parsifal shows on first viewing the grail procession, being unprepared for deepening to his nature at that time.

Conrad's own experiences speak through the hero Marlow, who 'followed the sea'. His wanderlust is a vocation, a calling, in which he finds his voice, his individuality. The training of the shaman is also about discovering this unique voice, that is under nobody else's control. Such a voice answers to a specific aspect of Nature. Marlow's answered to "the mystery of an unknown earth"; "the dark places of the earth"; and more, to "the sea itself, which is the mistress of (the seaman's) existence and as inscrutable as Destiny." Then, specifically, to the blank space on the map that was Africa's interior: "True, by this time it was not a blank space any more. It had got filled since my boyhood with rivers and lakes and names . . . It had become a place of darkness. But there was one river especially . . . resembling an immense snake uncoiled . . . The snake had charmed me."

After making the journey up-river to meet the anti-hero Kurtz, and to face the horror of Kurtz's vision of life, Marlow is changed forever, for this is "the farthest point of navigation and the culminating point of my experience". Within the depths of darkness and terror is a supreme height. In the valley of the soul, and the body of the snake, is the condition for a peak experience.

The Celtic world saw the western isles, where sun and moon both set, as the blessed isles of the dead. Hence the large number of burial graves in west Penwith and the Scilly Isles. The great figures of Arthurian drama are those who teach directly of conversation with the dark serpent of the world — the sleeping dragon that is Nature in her unrevealed or Black Goddess aspect — so that they do not themselves act out this darkness literally in life. They are not attracted to the darkness because they want to utilise this force in life, but to avoid its unconscious acting out, where it has never been faced.

The facing of the dark is a night-sea-journey, and those intimately associated with darkness in Celtic lore are often of the dark waters by name, of the tarnish of the silver sea in which the island-jewels of Britain are set. 'Mor' is the Celtic root for sea. [20] Mor-vran, sea-raven or cor-mor-ant, is said to be the ugliest, most blighted man alive. Mer-lin is the magician who teaches Mor-gana, Arthur's sister. Arthur's dark twin, his half-brother, is Mor-dred. And the Celtic goddess of the underworld, Annwn, is the Mor-rigan.

Our erotic connection to the world is to her whole current, and we should not be afraid of making love when her dragon or serpent is stirring, at her dark time. A young man has a dream where he is holding the globe of the Earth between his hands, at the south and north poles. He could feel into the north pole, which became a woman's vagina. As he pushed his fingers inside, he felt warm blood. He took his hand out and looked at the blood, suddenly feeling an overwhelming love and humility in the presence of the world, that made him burst into tears both within the dream and in the re-telling of it.

The Fool on the Hill and the Valley of Tears

So the Fool is the young Arthur brought up by people close to the earth — his step-family — who lives for an erotic reunion with the mother from whom he was estranged; and for guidance from his dead father as to the nature of his work or vocation. He must descend from the hill and the magical certainty of never losing his balance before an appreciative audience (which is the same innocent confidence that allows him to believe he can draw the sword from the stone). As king, he must realise his adult vulnerability and foolishness. He must become Pantaloon, as the waste land grows in inner-nature and outer world.

Now he must enter the valley of soul with its inherent imbalances, its pathos, which he can no longer transcend; and here he puts on the black mask of Harlequin, to regain a new innocence. He must re-vision his persona as he dons a dis-guise, an underworld face that faces the underworld, and appreciates or gives a face to the unseen. He also puts on his Harlequin pants, to show his dual nature, ego now overshadowed, black checking white. Now he faces the spectres of his dead parents; the woundings of others; and finally, his own vulnerabilities. He reclaims innocence as a state of grace, for the senses are open, perceptions free from judgement, as in a dream. The potency of the interfering ego is eclipsed.

In descending to the underworld to meet his ancestors; in facing the aspect of Nature that most terrifies yet most attracts him (such as Marlow's sea, "inscrutable as Destiny"), and may take him at death, the fool, Arthur-in-everyman, begins to write a Book of the Dead in the traditional manner. This is, paradoxically, a life script; for coming to love the dark earth provides a rich humus for worldly growth, a redemption of the waste land (that is loss of soul). And he deepens to what he must face or put a face to, as the persona and character, now recognisable to others as his signature. The auto-nomous psyche then expressing itself through personal auto-nomy, or style, that is also a spiritual nobility.

Chapter 2

I have talked of a relationship to the world that respects the interiority of things, or looks at the self-presentation of the world through the senses informed by imagination. It is clear that in our culture, touch is greatly undervalued as a way of knowing the world. The skin is the largest organ of the body, and it is through touch that we instantly connect to the mother's skin at birth. Let us now consider the underworld of touch, aspects of its pathology or dark side, for it is from this perspective that we may better know how to use touch fruitfully, imaginatively.

The skin carries symptom of the soul's sufferings. My daughter suffers from eczema, and she has taught me a lesson about suffering and homeopathic approaches to relief. When her skin itches, she says, it is as if she is on fire. What she then most craves is a balm for the sulphurous skin, and often, as we live near the sea, this would be immersion in the cold ocean. The relief is immediate — followed by an even worse agony as the sea water evaporates, leaving a crust of salt on the skin. Rubbing salt into the wound is then a literal suffering for her, but also the homeopathic treatment that the body itself calls for, where fire treats fire:

Swimming

We are re-made in a round
Mirror of water, assembling
And dis-assembling at will.
A high cloud steps back,
The sun moves through us
And hits the water, shifting
Opacity to transparency,
Revealing a torrent of small

49

Silver fish into whose
Trembling gills the sky
Has collapsed whole,
Is eyebright and lipgloss
For those creatures who have
Fallen into the paradise
Of Davy Jones' open box.

My daughter folds into the water
To relieve an issued hair-shirt
Of eczema, treating same with same,
Prickly rash by salt-burn,
Returning her itch
To the round of rubbing water.

She surfaces through the froth
Of her dive — Aphrodite
With eyeliner — eyes pencilled
With Proserpine's coal
To better see in the undersea dark,
And for the boys to better see
Her darkness, by which means
She will in time effect a skin cure.

Artemis, Anorexia and the Weight of the World

The body a tub of blood; a moveable casket, a canopic jar in life carrying the soft tissues and organs. And a bag of skin wrapping an arrangement of bone. The body as information playing itself out through time as an electromagnetic field. And as a torquing muscle, the frame ready to spring, electricity providing the impulse. The body growing into its form; and, as a microcosm of the planet herself, each person's body a small Earth. Or each body merely a standing, sitting, crawling whisker on the curve of the world, held by gravity and sustained by the world's breath.

The realisation of our being on the body of the world comes to us through touch, at first, as we have said, through contact with the mother's skin at birth. In touching the skin of another we immediately become both engaged and self-reflective, aware not only of who we touch, but how we touch. What if this touch were to be consciously denied; what if a life were to be cultivated that worshipped distance only — and distancing — the space between things? Then the greatest pleasure is found away from gravity, that pulls one body to another; away from density, from material, towards a feather-lightness and ultimate disappearance. In the suspension of gravity, whose field embraces us and keeps us in embrace with Earth, one would never reflect on one's literal contacts: the lover's touch, the child's kiss, a hand of a friend.

A nature of this ilk, that would never touch or be touched, would also never be violated, or acknowledge the pathology of touch. She would remain inviolate, clear, pure, raw and virginal. The dirt of surfaces, the smell, taste and touch of closeness; the disturbing yet necessary shock of the close-up would be avoided, despised; and there would be a forced innocence of the sexual and sensual, that demand touch.

Everything that tied the body to the greater body of Earth would be anathema: everything that brought the person into contact with the dirt of the ground, with the primal Adam — whose name means 'red dirt', and who was said to have been moulded by a creatress from clay mixed with menstrual blood. Anything that tainted the purity of the body would be abhorred; the body's natural functions and orifices ostracised. Blood especially would repel as this is the material tie to the sustaining greater body of Earth, whose oxygen reddens the blood and gives life.

What we are describing is the world of the anorexic, hater of food and density; but also, following Jung's advice that the ancient gods will find their expression in the symptoms and disease of modern people, we are sketching aspects of the Greek goddess Artemis (Roman Diana).

Otto[1] says of Artemis that she can be the cruel yet untainted side of Nature — the purity and chastity of unfettered Nature, undisturbed by people. She is "transparent and weightless", has transcended base Earth which has now ". . . itself lost its heaviness and the blood is no longer conscious of its dark passions". Artemis is lack of "reflective sensitivity"; a nature out of touch with its blood course, which is completely overwhelmed by an obsession with the upward-striving sap of youth, the spirit of the puella as eternal child, who we met in the previous chapter.

Kerenyi[2] sees her as an eternal nine-year-old, Artemis *parthenia*; virginal, untainted by experience. She is Nature left to be, given distance. But Nature, like the little girl, needs to embrace and to be embraced. She needs to know the skin of others. Artemis is the spirit of the hunt — the killing of animals at a distance, rather

Artemis as the cruel hunter, killing Actaeon

than the close, loving embrace, taking up the animal as familiar. When Artemis' animals turn on humans, there is the toughest kind of literal contact — an extreme violence — but they are distanced from any loving concern. Actaeon's hounds rip him to pieces at Artemis' request; and her scorpion's sting kills Orion, who was said to be "the handsomest man alive". Artemis, like her brother Apollo, coolly calculates from a distance, by eye, rather than valuing through touch and contact. There is then no potential contamination, no dirtying of the body, and no body of dirt or earth to be reckoned with.

'Jenny' is twenty-two but looks fourteen; weighs ninety-one pounds and is desperately trying to get down to eighty-four. She is a cool, distanced observer of others, but unreflective about her own experiences. She has forced the blood away from body and mind. Her skin is pasty white and she is seriously anaemic. She hates blood, and dirt of any kind; ritualistically washes many times a day; and abhors food, especially pork, as pigs are seen as filthy. She will eat at home, and sometimes in company, but only to avoid argument; and she immediately visits the bathroom after the meal to vomit it up, knowing she has done a good job if she also brings up blood. For the food must be disgorged before it is digested, otherwise she will fatten. Her stomach lining has ulcerated from this compulsive vomiting.

Every ounce of excitation is at her skin surface. She is jumpy and irascible, taut, like a scared animal. She hates to be touched, or to touch herself (masturbation is especially dirty). Her favourite fairy tale is "The Princess and the Pea", where she empathises exactly with the Princess' dilemma. Her inturned skin, the gut lining, is also acutely sensitive — she feels the pressure and weight of every morsel of food in her stomach and either does not want it to be there in the first place, or makes herself vomit to relieve the sensation. She is losing sensation in other places. She will masochistically cut herself, and prod deep into muscle with sharp objects, claiming to feel no pain.

She cuts herself, she says, as a reminder that she is still alive, although she would prefer to be dead. Her emaciation is seen as a 'lightening', a thinning out to nothingness, so that she can transcend earthly realms, can exist as a living phantom, a wisp, an occasional wind. Weight, body and density — like blood, sex and bodily functions — are dirty. Men touching her anywhere are only after one thing. By nature they are dirty-minded. She compulsively washes off the taint of others in accidental touching. She has a routine of washing which cannot be broken. Vomiting after any food is also a cleansing and part of the routine, which must be kept holy, a sacred ritual.

To have a child would be unthinkable — childbirth is also dirty — yet she likes young children, and gets on especially well with her sister's baby boy. Like Artemis herself, she is a virgin. As *Eileithyia*, Artemis is also the goddess of childbirth. But her patronage has a cruel edge, for she is said to bless the mother with the pain of birthing, and can, at a whim, kill mother or child in the process.

Jenny's lower intestine is so untried that she gets constipated easily. She has vitamin mixes to drink, but tends to vomit these up as well. So little nourishment is getting through that she is always tired, and cannot concentrate, is open to infections, and needs constant medical attention. She is slowly killing herself and says that this is what her being desires. She has attempted suicide twice before, but now feels that this is not how she would wish to die. Rather, like Artemis, she wants to become "transparent and weightless", to pull herself out of the field of Earth's gravity, to become as thin as the wind.

Home life is a series of arguments. Her father has given up talking to her, out of frustration, for he cannot get her to change as he wishes. Her mother consistently gets angry and shouts at her. Jenny says that they never understood her. As a child she could only speak to her maternal grandmother. She does not menstruate, and has not done so in nine years. She started her periods when she was thirteen, in September. She remembers it clearly because at the time she was a keen swimmer, and was horrified to discover herself suddenly bleeding, for this meant that she would not be able to swim. She felt she would taint the water. Her mother had not prepared her, merely handed her the necessary sanitary arrangements when she first bled. She was confused and horrified, but fascinated by the blood. She could talk openly about her feelings only to her maternal grandmother, who set her mind at rest that she was at least not diseased. By March of the following year, she had her sixth and last period. She had willed them away.

She remembers a dream that came during her first period, which has recurred: she is being menstruated upon from above. A great globule of blood completely encloses her — it is sticky, messy, she cannot breathe or get out, she hates it. She now dreams often of silver or bloody globules floating in the sky, as disconnected parts of a skeleton.

In this account, we have suggested that Jenny's guiding fiction within her anorexic symptoms is under the shadow-nature of Artemis, drawing her away from her relationship to touch and earthly human contact, and touch with herself — care for herself. This is clear in her neglect of her own rhythm, the monthly cycle which has died on her, as she pulls away from contact with the dirt or surface of the Earth, where the bruised and neglected serpent lives in permanent contact. Again, as Otto says of Artemisian outlook, "... the blood is no longer conscious of its dark passions". With the symptoms comes an unreflective attitude towards the necessary binding of our lives to Earth, our host.

To be effective in life, a guiding fiction or value must have an aesthetic reality that returns something to Earth, or ensouls. The value must be of value. Otherwise, the fiction of life [3] one writes for oneself, one's life story, is too youthful, too transparent, too transcendent — giving nothing to the ground of Earth in the way of a creative gift. Transparency and weightlessness need the ponderous and often depressive or melancholic body of artistic endeavour, the saturnine aspect of imagination.

We often use the phrase 'figment of the imagination' in a

disparaging manner — putting down imagination (in opposition to 'reality', that is then judged as better, in a moralism). Figment is seen as a fancy, not a concrete, useful thing (which is to be caught in both a *material* fantasy and a *utilitarian* fantasy — the former in the image of the earth-mother(s); the latter in the image of the worker Hephaestus and the inventor Daedalus). Now a figment is something fashioned or fingered, from *fingere*, 'to mould'. A figment of the imagination is then the material fantasy discovering its liberation through images that can be touched, and touch us with their worth. Images can be held close, and have presence. This closeness, fingering, making, fashioning is alien to Artemisian outlook.

Like working with clay, figmenting is to get the hands dirty; is to soil the skin or bring the skin into contact with soil. For imagination is returned to Earth herself through our aesthetic endeavours. Fig was Roman slang for haemorrhoids, and the fig-hand sign says I don't give a fig (a fuck). Fig is also slang for the vagina. So here we return to those despised orifices, and that secretive dirt compulsively washed out by the anorexic, who equates food with future excrement; who would not want to soil the earth or herself with that excrement, and so keeps a distance between herself and the soiling. And then she avoids the sensual, the left hand path that rejoices in body and the body of image.

In this avoidance of the sensual, the golden presence of Aphrodite, the anorexic has not only starved herself, but also the world, in not returning soul to the earth. She has not given soul due respect in recognition of its intrinsic dirt, which is its worth, its value or filthy lucre. Rather, she has transcended such concerns, wasting away her time in ritualistic and compulsive avoidance of the soil of life, literalised in a wasting away of her own earth, her body, in emaciation.

In *Starving Women*, Angelyn Spignesi[4] argues that it is precisely the above sort of moralism, or judgement, that does not see through the values of the anorexic — that her choice to waste away questions the over-emphasis (to the point of caricature) that western culture places upon the succouring and feeding aspects of motherhood. In the latter outlook, the mother is seen only as the feeding earth-mother, whose presence is material (the White Goddess). Hillman[5] points out that the materialistic outlook is a block to appreciating the no-body of the spectre, the image, the phantom. Hercules, Aeneas and other heroes discover this to their disconcertion when they raise their swords against spectres, in the

Halls of Hades, that are no-bodies, that cannot be attacked as if they were material.

While empathising with this aspect, we must see through its guiding fiction, which ignores the sensual perspective of Aphrodite. From Aphrodite's aspect, the self-imposed wasting away of the anorexic is not a seeing through of the material perspective in a movement closer to the spectres of death, but a plain transcendence and defensive avoidance of sensual touch, a masochistic feeding of the spirit of perfection that in itself is a terrible phantom and oppressive ideal.

Artemis' greatest enemy is Aphrodite, goddess of earthly sensuality, over whom, the *Homeric Hymns*[6] tell us, Artemis has power and control. Artemis (from the perspective we are arguing here) needs both a loving mother and father to hold, to remind her of touch, of sensuality, and to teach her directly of the rhythm of the Earth, that gives a self-regulatory form to Nature (just as Jenny was told the truth of the woman's rhythm only by her grandmother). Artemis' mother, Leto, whose name means 'stone', is said to have given painless birth to her daughter, and maybe then to have not fully felt Artemis' presence at birth, or to have given birth in a stony manner. And one of both Leto's and Artemis' epithets is *parthenos*, 'child of an unmarried mother', which means that they both may not have had the touch of a present father.

The lessons of myth are often paradoxical, and we must not tie ourselves to a single facet only of Artemisian character. She is a goddess of the moon, and so rules gorging and starving, as the moon alternately swells to full and starves to dark. If we challenge the dominant ovulatory cultural values of the nourishing-mother (full moon), we may see the dilemma of the anorexic. The dark moon, the darkness of dream-time, may constitute the sustaining 'food'; while the full moon is starved because it reflects light rather than absorbing it in self-reflection. Starving for the anorexic, as a paradoxical but necessary lunacy, may then be a royal road to self-reflection. As Spignesi reminds us, this may be an honouring of the imaginal world rather than cultivating a materialistic perspective at the expense of the imagistic.

Angelyn Spignesi uses Hillman's[7] differentiation of levels of the earth — Gaia splitting into the material Ge-Demeter and the spectral, underworld Chthon — to show that the anorexic is serving the deeper chthonic realms rather than the nourishing surface. She is then starving herself in the service of death, and is not in need of literal food as this underworld perspective sees through literalism and materialism.

But there is a deep anima fascination at work here, that is likely to lull us into a transcendence of the common senses, for Spignesi puts forward an argument that literalises the morbistic perspective. The call to death of the anorexic (a slow suicide of self-imposed starvation) is to literalise the call of soul, which calls rather for a *relationship* (as opposed to an *identification*) of the ego with death; or a perspective in life that is close to death, is morbistic, as a *preparation* for actual bodily death. The psyche's call in such instances may not be for a literal death of the body. It is the ego which literalises such a call. The psyche is calling for a death of the ego; a desubstantiation and suspension of the ego, so that psyche can be heard in its call for the ego to see through itself, or relativise itself. Russell Lockhart[8] reminds us that "Separation from life is not depth". And it is the ego that needs to deepen to psyche in life. The ancient books of the dead call for people to cultivate a varied and healthy life in order that death is put into perspective, and time is generated by which fate can be contemplated. (In Ingmar Bergman's film *The Seventh Seal*, the hero, a knight who has returned home from the Holy Wars, plays a protracted game of chess with Death, who has come to claim him. This buys the knight time, in which he can contemplate his fate).

If Artemis is an important face of anorexia, then the anorexic, like the goddess herself, is arrested in her development: a puella or eternal nine-year-old. Guggenbuhl[9] suggests that such an arrest is characteristic also of a psychopathic personality, and is a move brought about to resist potential change and upset created as we enter new rites of passage, new developments. This is a kind of immunity to experience, reflecting the virginal, the anti-sensuality of Artemis. As Hillman[10] says, "We are each virginal when we are preserved from experience".

In psychically moving back, arresting development and resisting rites of passage, we see the puella, the spirit that avoids through ascending, though transcending; avoids a grounding and a deepening to the changes of the grounding monthly cycle of the woman's body; avoids a grounding in relationship. This makes the anorexic deeply conservative — afraid of change — and in this sense she is tied to the staidness of Athene, Hebe and Hestia as much as the virginal Artemis.

Spignesi[11] calls the anorexic "...a child of Hecate..." in "...her intercourse with the imaginal realm..." Here, "...the anorexic might recall her ability as a borderline being to nurse underworld presences". We would suggest that a stronger underworld association may be with Ananke, goddess of Necessity, for the anorexic reminds us so directly of the soul's pathologising; and then, as Hillman[12] suggests, of the necessity of abnormal psychology. Hillman points out that Ananke is called the Great Lady of the underworld; that the Orphics identified her with Persephone; and that Homer calls Persephone "virginal", "holy" or "pure", as is Artemis. Ananke does not have a nourishing, surface-of-the-Earth nature, for she is of the deepest place, and ties us to that part. But we have suggested that it may be the ego that wants to literally starve a body to death by choice, in order to visit that deepest place; rather than the soul giving a means of seeing through the material body, so that a relationship to that deepest place may be respectfully cultivated in life. One clue to the anorexic's compulsive avoidance of forming such a loving, worldly relationship to the depths (which would be mediated through Eros), is the lack of a dark humour (or any humour of depth). A dark humour is Eros' uplifting presence in the morbistic outlook[13] that keeps it from becoming compulsive, burdensome.

However, within the familiar stereotypical Olympian character of Artemis is a chillingly engaging side, a reminder of our life-long engagement with destiny. As a death-dealer, through her hounds, and her lioness that takes life at birth, we could argue that Artemis does indeed deal directly through touch, but of a kind we ordinarily prefer to deny. In this death-dealing guise, she has been appropriately compared with the underworld angel Hecate. Like Hecate, a ghostly messenger of death, Artemis is phosphorescent (as *phosphoros*, the light-bearer), or shines with that eerie light that illumines the dark of the dream. Now this deathly touch is a chilling caress that ripples up the body from the inside and raises the hairs on the skin. We talk of it as 'somebody just walked over my grave'.

Also, Artemis has a life-affirmative aspect as the nourishing many-breasted Diana of Ephesus. Indeed, Graves[14] calls her an "orgiastic goddess" in her pre-Olympian form, in which her virginal aspect is not read literally, but as a woman tied to no man, as temple prostitute, or Queen who chooses her consorts.

We have tracked differing faces of the symptoms of an anorexic, emphasising the anti-sensual whilst appreciating the paradoxical presence of Diana of Ephesus. We have also attempted to see through what has already been seen through — to recover the body of the anorexic that is, in a misplaced desire for perfection or absolute purity and through a masochistic asceticism, slowly destroying itself in its fascination with underworld and the peculiar nourishment of the spectres who inhabit that place. This recovery, or saving, of the body rests on the notion that while the literalising ego translates the call of soul into actual bodily harm, then the soul's move to bring death to ego, as a desubstantiation of ego, is resisted. Here is a literally destructive displacement of psyche's purpose by ego.

Our description of the condition of anorexia stresses the relationship between weight, density, body, dirt, and the desire to transcend these. We suggested that the aversion to food is an aversion to potential faeces, to the dirt which food becomes, or the latent quality of food. The body as a microcosm of the body of Earth ties us to the planet's surface and hence brings us feet first into relationship with soil. Soil and earth are the bodily expressions of soul in both life and death aspects — body as nourished in and by soil, and soil as decayed body. Tomb and womb in the one process.

The anorexic's body is dirty when full because it then has to defecate. Her body is dirty when pregnant because this is a product of sex; of contact between bodies, of soiling by the man; and the body is dirty when menstruating because it is full of bad blood. It is best then to stop menstruating; to not have sex; and to avoid food, all of which become taboo in a ritualistic cleansing and purging. Vomiting food and blood from the stomach is preferable to releasing excreta and menstrual blood from below, because the latter are closer to the earth and hence more contaminated. The anorexic wants to waste away from such close contact with earth — in fact, to be free from body altogether, which can be dumped, paradoxically, where it belongs, rotting on the soil, in mocking embrace.

The Loving Hug

Although Artemis' familiar is the bear, this animal would seem to not fit the anorexic's symptoms, for the bear loves to touch so much that he would hug us to death! The bear, only in recent times extinct from Britain along with the boar and wolf, is seen by Joseph Campbell [15] to be the traditional totemic animal of the shamans of the northern hemisphere: "Of the Palaeololithic traditions that spread west-to-east, the bear cult is almost certainly the oldest, dating, as it does, from Neanderthal Man's veneration of the cave bear . . . When the bear has come forth from his long winter sleep, he is frequently seen walking on his hind legs like a man. What sustained him during those months of hibernation?"

The same question may be asked of the anorexic. What sustains her during those self-imposed starvations? We have found Artemis behind the self-imposed starvation of the anorexic, who is obsessed with the discomfort of bodily fullness. The bear gorges, then sleeps it off in hibernation. The anorexic gorges, then vomits it up in consternation. In honour of this goddess, in ancient Greece nine-year-old girls would dress in saffron clothes and participate in a ceremonial animal slaughter. They were called *arktoi*, or young she-bears.[16]

Although the child's teddy bear was said to be named after Theodore Roosevelt, and then only current this century, this comforter and familiar has its roots in antiquity. It is no coincidence that the child goes to sleep cuddling the bear, for the animal has always been regarded as a keeper of dreams — a dreamer itself because of the long period of hibernation. The she-bear also stands for supreme motherhood and care through fierce protection of her offspring (an Artemisian characteristic, for Artemis loves young children).

Pythagoras called the Great Bear and the Little Bear constellations the "twin hands of Rhea", the Mother-of-beginnings. The bear was said to lick the formless mass of the cub into shape, beauty and life, as the world forms us. The bear was displaced onto the great constellation of stars that takes her name, not because this configuration looks like a bear (in fact, it is more popularly known as the waggon, plough or dipper), but because the Great Bear circles the north pole annually without ever disappearing below the horizon. (Homer speaks of her as "the only constellation which never bathes in Ocean's Stream"; and in the *Egyptian Book of the Dead* she is called the constellation that never dies). She is then in constant motherhood, vigilance and attention for her offspring, the Little Bear within her orbit. She was called by the Egyptians *Ta-Urt*, the Mother of Revolutions, as the first time-keeper. The Egyptians also knew her as the animal thigh (because birth is from between the thighs). She was seen as the great dreamer who brings alive all the stars at night from a source at the north pole, beyond the north wind. But the bear has also been brought to earth, for she symbolises the mothering body of the world, which dreams all life into being, touching us with her hug that deepens our life events

Contemporary soapstone carving of eskimo killing the totem animal

into experiences. And while she cares for us, she also chills, for the stars only come out in darkness, as a revelation; and the revelation of the green Earth is her sinister under-belly, the dark underworld.

The Great Bear circles the north pole with the Little Bear in her orbit whom the Celts saw as Arthur, son of the Bear, within the caer or castle beyond the north wind — the ever-turning castle of the northern stars. In the poem ascribed to Taliesin, "The Spoils of Annwn", or the glories of the Celtic underearth, the underworld is truly beyond deepest earth; displaced to farthest sky. The Greek Tartarus, deepest underworld, is said to be an airy place where the four winds meet in an ever-present chill, and this is precisely the Celtic description of the otherworld Hyperboreas, that is the depths of Annwn. This is a place beyond the nourishing realm of the earth-mothers, the vegetative goddesses who would keep us as eternal children, at the breast, or tied to their apron-strings (which keeps them, like some mums we know, as eternal motherers). In the poem, Arthur sets out to visit seven sacred caers — castles, circles or centres of increase, holy places. These are the seven stations of the mother bear, her seven stars clearly visible to the naked eye, the most striking feature of the northern sky. The final station points directly to the centre of the sky, at the north pole, which, in the Celtic tradition, all souls must visit.

In this journey of the soul is the traditional grappling with the serpent, and this is *Draco*, the dragon, a string of stars that wraps itself around *Ursa minor*, within the orbit of *Ursa major*. The seven stars of the Great Bear are the mother in her ovulatory or child-bearing, fruitful aspect; the dragon is the menstrual snake, the flow that moves against life. These are also the two hands of Rhea. It is conversation with the serpent-hand that the hero seeks on his way to the interior, or in seeking the perception of interiority.

In journeying to the centre of the Earth, Jules Verne's trio of heroes discover and are threatened by the product of the Age of Reptiles — the dinosaurs. The journey of the soul in this life is more than a regression to the mother's womb — it is a regression through our phylogeny, our evolutionary history, where we grapple with the part of us that is reptilian and serpentine. This part is our instincts, so slippery to conscious control, and so cold-blooded. Techniques of bodily control, of mind over body, such as the yogis cultivate, are ways in which the instincts are brought under conscious control. [17]

People are often afraid that they might just lose themselves if their instincts were to take over. Patients in therapy often say that their greatest fear of looking into themselves is to discover some horrendous buried secret, or to get completely out of control — a control that they will not be able to recover. This fear of going crazy, or of discovery of the unbearable repressed secret, is a fear of facing that which is most deeply instinctual — the archetypal presence, and the faces of the archetypes, for archetype deepens, and it is the depths which frighten us. It is easier to keep things at surface level, unruffled; to keep the lid on, and to gain cathartic release by proxy — through soap operas, which reinforce the surface outlook, the trivial. We talk of 'opening a can of worms' — fear projected onto the very animals that make soil of our remains; a bunch of tiny snakes.

Perhaps it is the repression of feeling that leads to skin symptoms such as eczema — as expression of the repressed snake at the skin surface, for the snake is a skin-shedder, and eczema forces a breaking and peeling of the skin through scratching the irritation. As the skin-shedder (like the renewing of the womb's lining), the snake is one of the faces of the woman's periodicity and rhythm, and we have argued here that the man need not be a dragonslayer as solar hero, but may converse with the serpent, as lunar consort. The moon and darkness are in constant battle — the moon slaying darkness when waxing, and darkness winning as the moon wanes. Sometimes the dragon can spontaneously devour the whole moon, in an eclipse. So the dragon or inner serpent of darkness must become known to the woman and mother. She then reveals its potency to the lover and consort who is willing to learn, to open to this embrace.

As we detail in a later chapter, there is a myth still held in hunter-gatherer cultures such as the aboriginals of Australia, that is said to be universal.[18] A story now withheld from women by men, because it tells of a time when the women were the sole keepers of sacred knowledge. While women menstruated and ovulated together on a cycle synchronised between themselves and in phase with the cycle of the moon, they held this knowledge. This was symbolised as the Rainbow snake, a serpent that could live below ground (within the womb and earth), or above ground (as the rainbow).

It is said that the men stole the knowledge from women by guile, by splitting the women up, then preventing them by force from meeting together (forcing them to parturition huts for menstruation, or to go off alone to give birth). The men then imitate the women's bleeding and birth-giving capacities in secret-society ceremonies. Here, they attempt to gain the more intimate body-knowledge of the women, of which they are jealous, by wounding or thinning the skin. They also distort her myths in their favour, to make her appear a temptress or seductress, or a terrible destroyer, thus avoiding the hidden facets of the Black Goddess, who bears gifts in disguise. In the co-operative learning of woman and man, symbolised by the twin snakes of Hermes on the caduceus, the woman helps the man to face the Black Goddess that he will surely discover in his descents, so that he may converse with her, and better understand the many faces of Anima in the world. [19]

Changes in the Weather

Arthur's knowledge comes partly from his association with Merlin, the Druid or wise visionary. Merlin is in the sky at the Little Bear's side as an aspect of *Draco* the dragon, for *druic* (a feminine noun in Cornish) means 'dragon'. This serpent at the crown of the world inhabits the realm of the seven caers, and is the source of thunder and lightning. The patriarchs say that such weather is the crackling beard of the sky father — Indra, Zeus, Jupiter, Thor, Dagda — who thunders when he is angry. But the mothers say it is the issue of the rainbow snake who is turning herself inside out in her changes, casting off the old skin that dries and crackles as thunder. And the lightning is the illumination provided by such changes, available to everywoman.

At the back of our own worlds, the shadow-side of our nature and physiology, is also our own source of thunder and lightning. This is the weather we create in relationships: the local climate of the household, or place of work, perhaps the habitats we frequent the most — and then we both create and become students of this ecology. This weather is a product of the relationship between electro-magnetic fields and chemical (pheromonal) exchange, each person's field fluctuating with their mood. Within this weather we can call up changes, just as the medicine woman or man, the witch-doctor, can synchronise with weather changes in the larger world.

To call up such changes, and to know how one could appropriately respond to another's changes, we need to develop a more intimate body-knowledge, and, as we have said, the woman is gifted with the deeper possibilities of such a knowledge. It is this

The Druic or Druid, the Celtic high priest

bodily knowledge that the anorexic seems to repress, that Artemis desires to transcend, and this results in distancing in relationship and an inability to deepen to emotional contacts. Then the local weather goes unnoticed, and worse, cannot be predicted or acted upon appropriately.

There is a Chinese myth that tells of a dragon devouring nine maidens, one after the other, and of a woman who collects the bones of these maidens and reconstitutes first the skeletons, then the flesh of the maidens, bringing them back to life. This is a recreation of the oldest burial practice, where the bones of the skeleton are daubed with red ochre to reflesh them for a rebirth. Such practices were followed by attempts to embalm the body. Also, when a woman is pregnant, the menstrual change as serpent is repressed, or devoured, for nine months or nine moons (the nine maidens); and is recovered, or the body of the cycle is restored, after breast-feeding. The wandering bones that need to be re-fleshed (a reconstitution of the body of the cycle, a calling back of the blood) reminds us of the dream of the anorexic girl, where bones were seen floating in a disconnected way in the sky. Perhaps her lost periodicity needed to be recalled, the bones needing to be refleshed. As indeed did her own body, to recover the feminine nature she had lost or was repressing, and with which she was now punishing herself. Also, she was 'menstruated upon from above' — which could not have been the sky father, but rather the Great Bear's own serpent, drawn out of the darkness.

Stalkers and Dreamers: Hunters' Clubs and Magicians' Wands

The body may be literally repressed through a wasting away as in anorexia, a feminine pattern. The body-politic of men is character-istically a muscling-up, and is repressive of the bodies of others through clubbing or warfare, in the style of Hercules: kill first and ask questions later. Further, this clubbing comes out of taking the body literally ('pumping iron', the health-club culture), which may club the imaginal body to death. The thick musculature then screening, shielding and repressing the more sensitive body, or the body's wider sensitivities.

In the southern arc of the nightsky we find the seven major stars of Orion the hunter, with his belt of three stars pointing to the brightest sun of the night heavens, Sirius the dog-star. Orion is a hero in the style of Hercules. As we have seen, he gained his place in the heavens through a bite from Artemis' scorpion. Bearing in mind that Artemis' animal is the bear, and that Artemis can be cruel to men, we find Homer commenting perceptively in the *Iliad* that, "...the bear...(is) the only constellation which never bathes in the Ocean Stream, but always wheels round in the same place and looks across at Orion the Hunter *with wary eye*". (Emphasis mine.)

The machismo hunter begins as arch-enemy of the feminine, but eventually comes within her circle. Thus Hercules is made to wear a dress as he serves Omphale, and Orion is made to swirl in the heavens forever around the navel or omphalos of the skies. On the *Strength* card of the tarot, Orion or Hercules is sometimes shown opening the lion's jaws, instead of the woman. This merely adds to the stereotype of the hunter taming the animal through brute force (Arthur does not draw the sword from the stone by force, as the other knights attempt to do, but by faith); where the woman, correctly depicted, charms the lion, is mistress of the animals. Homer calls Artemis Lady of the Wild Beasts, and recounts that she lifts a lion by the scruff of its neck. Indeed Otto[20] says that the lion is the favourite of Artemis even over the bear.

Sirius yaps at the heels of the hunter in the sky. Taken to be Orion's hunting dog, it is more likely that this is one of Artemis' hounds, sent to worry Orion, to keep him within her circle, just as the scorpion that killed him is assigned to the sky, to always follow him. Orion is also mirrored by Arthur in the northern sky, who has already come within the circle of the Great Bear, as the bleeding Fisher King. He has learned how to hug rather than club. Then he also knows how to call the great hound of Artemis, as a Lord of the Animals such as the Celtic Cernunnos, and Kynon the old man of the forest, who have conversation with and loving care for the animals, or knowledge of the instincts (the animal face of archetype).[21]

The dog and bear are in particular relationship. Anorexics refuse food, as if in hibernation like the bear. Bulimics cannot help gorging themselves in massive binges, as if preparing for hibernation, but then compulsively vomit this up to lose weight. The voracious appetite of the bulimic is matched by that of the dog, who will eat until it is sick, or has a morbid hunger. The hunger of the bulimic is called a canine hunger. (Because the dog will never let food go to waste the ancient Egyptians took the animal as a preserver, and embalmer, and then a guide to souls in their

The Strength or Fortitude card of the Tarot, where traditionally a woman opens the lion's jaw, as Lady of the Wild Beasts, but sometimes a man is depicted as Orion the Hunter (here the Magus in Herculean disguise)

passage through eternity. The jackal Anubis became the Greek Cerberus, guardian of the underworld).

Anorexia and bulimia are different sides of the same coin. The ravenous dog and the hibernating bear are different sides of an anorexia-bulimia complex.[22] The dog, as familiar and helper to the bear goddess, never turns on her in her bear guise. In Artemis' realm, beast rests with beast, but humans are treated with indifference, for their tragic conviction that the animal kingdom is without soul. In the human realm, dog and bear have been set one upon the other as sport. Bear baiting was the favourite spectator sport of the Elizabethans, a time when, paradoxically, we had an Artemisian queen on the throne — the pale-skinned but fiery 'virgin' Astraea — Elizabeth the faery queen. In the nightsky, Sirius the dog and the bears face each other, but do not fight. They are fixed in their devotion to the centre around which they revolve. The queen they serve, however, is not the light-skinned Astraea, but the dark of night, Elizabeth's shadow-sister, a black Virgin (Catholic Mariolatry includes a cult of the Black Virgin). Elizabeth I was said to parade "...through London in her coach with a dark Jewish beauty beside her,"[23] with whom she had a deep fascination.

This other queen is a radiant black sister carrying her own illumination or intrinsic worth, which is an eros. Artemis herself,

68

as we have said, carries the epithet *phosphoros*, light-bearer. The black beauty does not need to bask in the glory of the throned queen Elizabeth. The Great Bear is a night-time goddess, a dreamer and hibernator, but carries eros, the strongest of loving hugs, that will hug us to death, to eros' origin in the underworld, where we discover an illumination. The black bear goddess is beyond the sun because she is with all suns, the stars themselves at the back of the sky. She forces us to see through, to reverse things, to turn the world upside down and inside out, to look at the world anew. All these elements come together in a man's dream of "a large black bear with the sun behind her, bottom up, head down. I cannot see the sun but its light makes a halo around the bear. A feeling of great beauty. I want to make contact to get to grips but am unable to get closer; and the bear, although very much alive, stops moving."

Maybe the dream bear with the aura of beauty was frozen in its tracks (as was the dream ego): eclipsed. Or maybe it lost its animation because the impatient dream ego starts wanting, instead of waiting; wanting 'to get to grips', instead of allowing the hug of the bear (which is its characteristic) to come in its own way. (Although the dream bear does not necessarily behave like the dayworld 'natural' bear — to assume so would be to apply the perspective of upperworld nature to the substance of the dream. Hillman calls this the "naturalistic fallacy".) This may be a kind of clubbing of the image within the dream by the dream ego, that de-animates, stuns, and then denies touch, for the dream ego, like Hercules in the underworld, demands contact on its terms, and will not let the bear be in its own image.

Orion and Hercules carry a club, the instrument of change through physical dominance (where the wand is the symbol of psychological Will. Exercised will can of course be as cruel as a physical battering, but holds so many more possibilities, whereas the club has only one purpose — to bring to submission by force). The Orion aspect of the future rounded hero such as Arthur, then needs to learn how to substitute wand for club, or must learn how to apply a developed will in an appropriate manner. [24]

The magician's wand, like the sacred pipe of the Oglala Sioux, is said to bring the universe into relationship with the person, where we ask for embrace by the world. The wand takes many forms, such as the parliamentary mace. It is not an instrument by which the magus exerts the power of will over Nature (as it is popularly seen, more as a conjuror's wand), but a signal of readiness, given for the world to come to us. The wand represents the

| 1 | THE MAGICIAN | ב |

The Magician or Conjurer: Hercules' or Orion's club is now the more subtle
magic wand (see ill. p 68)

will in the sense of preparation for what the world has to offer. It is a signal of personal authority, a taking responsibility for cleansing the doors of one's own perceptions, for learning to see the interiority of the world, or adopting an archetypal perspective. Then we are ready for the revelation of the world as she is.

This is the core of the preparations for revelation in mysteries such as the Greek Eleusinian rites — a cleansing of the senses in order to receive the fullness of the death-dealing bear-hug. A re-orientation via the embrace of the world through her everyday face and self-presentation, for whose far-reaching beauty we are ordinarily unprepared, de-sensitised or under-adapted. The temptation in the face of the unknown in Nature is to avoid her embrace (as in the reception of a dream, which is for many people instantly and purposefully forgotten, disregarded as of 'no use'). Then we distance Nature by an heroic clubbing, an avoidance of her images, of the world in her own image (as she is, warts and all). When faced with the unknown or the 'unreal', the herculean hero attacks first and asks questions later. Both Herakles and Odysseus in Greek myth, and Aeneas in Roman myth, are armed when they enter the underworld. Verne's Professor von Hardwigg astounds his nephew and companion Harry by wanting to take rifles on the journey to the centre of the Earth — the implication is that a confrontation is expected, hence one goes on the journey armed. This creates an expectancy that the journey will involve dangers that can be defeated rather than conversed with. In the Sumerian myth of the descent of Inanna, and the rape of Persephone in the Greek story, no weapons are involved. There is rather a focus upon the awe of the innocent initiate.

Inanna descends in order to know her dark sister, her shadow-nature, Ereshkigal; and later Tammuz, her son/lover/consort, also descends to meet this black goddess. Tammuz is initiated by Inanna prior to his descent, so that he is prepared for the awful vision.[25] Christ's death on the cross and his resurrection may be seen as a descent to the underworld prior to his ascent to heaven. (See my poem "Awareness-through-movement" at the end of chapter 5.) In John's gospel, the first person he sees at rebirth is the dark Mary Magdalene from whom Christ had previously exorcised seven daemons, who became one of his disciples and apostles, and in some apocryphal accounts, his wife. Christ and Tammuz descend without weapons.

The club prevents us from using our hands, in touch. The wand is an extension of the hands, not a substitute for them, and is soon dropped in those acts of magic we call healing — in a laying on of hands, or the simple loving touch between parent and child, between lovers; or the healing handshake or hug of forgiveness.

What is felt from the hands of a healer is authority and truth. The hands do not lie and the healer does not inflate, otherwise the healing gift dissolves. When such truth-in-beauty is coming through, it is as clear for the pen of the poet or the brush of the artist; for the hands of the potter, surgeon or gardener as for the hands of the healer. Truth is in the beauty of the fingering, the making, the concretised and translated figment of imagination, of which we spoke earlier.

In the political world, the wand is traditionally the rod of authority (for example, the parliamentary and Queen's mace), as a symbol of truth in the resolution of disputes. The wand is the rod, sceptre, trident, crozier, mace, magician's and conjuror's wand, conductor's baton, staff of life, and, as we are suggesting, the absolute refinement of the hero's club. Hermes or Mercury, as the patron of the magician, has two wands. The rhabdos is the enchanter of the dead; and the caduceus, a guide to the living. Hermes' rhabdos conducts the vision of the little death — the penis, clitoris and fingers are wands that 'fight' to the 'little death'

Hermes contemplates his wand

72

of orgasm, and may bring a vision through senses cleansed in the depths of the erotic embrace. Then Hypnos' wand brings the healing rest of sleep and dreams, where, in dreaming, we know that the clitoris and penis are both erect, whether or not there is explicit erotic content in the dream, for Eros resides in the dreamworld, the underworld, and there his wands come and go in attention and rest, in the cycle of dreaming sleep and dreamless sleep.

As the rod of Hermes, who connects upperworld and underworld, the wand is the *axis mundi*, the world tree, figured in our spines. When we need self-authority, the spine is straightened. Taking a rod to the back cancels out this opportunity, in punishment (many people take a rod to their own backs in self-criticism). The *axis mundi* is the tree of measure (a rod is an old English measure), the roots of the wand nourishing its top, which flowers and fruits in creative endeavour. The magician's wands are then trees, groves of native trees that teach the wisdom of the annual tree calendar and tree alphabet, the core of Druidic wisdom.

The wand of the practising magus is of hollowed wood with a metal core, magnetised like the Earth herself, and then truly the axis of the Earth. The best wood is yew or hazel, the witch-trees. Yew for longevity and resilience; hazel for suppleness, flexibility and sensitivity. The wand must bend, but should not break or remain permanently bent. Self-authority is like this — as the bludgeoning club of Hercules it is ego inflation. As the bent rod, it is self doubt, where the body is bent and assumes the posture of the question mark: ? — this is the 'hunch' that is never applied, the intuition that is never grounded in act; the withheld inspiration, which becomes a back-breaking burden. (Personified in the figure of the hunchback of Notre Dame, who is treated as inferior, low and loathsome; but who loves and feels in the deepest way, through his wounding, his burden.)

Hyperboreas: the Land Beyond the North Wind

At Cerne Abbas in Dorset is a large, chalk hillside figure made by cutting into the turf, and exposing the white chalk below. It is a giant with a huge erect penis, holding a club in one hand and said to be carrying a cloak over the opposite arm.[26] This figure is readily identifiable as Hercules or Orion. Walter of Coventry in the thirteenth century reported that the god Helith was worshipped in the district of Cerne; and Stukeley reported in 1764 that the Cerne giant was called Helis. Helios is the Greek god of the sun whose sacred animal is the snake, having his Orphic personification in Priapus, the gardener who also has a giant erect penis. Helios was said to have horses that rested on the islands of the Blessed, at the western extremity of the Earth, where they browsed on a magic herb. Now this is Celtic talk — the western land of Britain being the jumping-off point to the Otherworld, and Avalon being the blessed apple-isle.

We have talked of the two sides of the world — front and back, the white and black goddesses; and of Blake's Albion and Jerusalem. This is giving soul and imagination a *topos*, a geography and locus, a place to rest; just as we have previously talked of giving a face and

The Priapic Cerne Abbas Giant in the characteristic pose of Hercules or Orion with his club

a personification to image. The Celtic soul rests in a number of imaginal loci — Avalon as the nourishing apple isle with its underworld aspect in Annwn. The caers as the turning crystal castle of stars at the pole of the sky. And Hyperboreas — the land beyond the north wind.

Beyond the north wind implies the *Arctic* circle (which means the 'place of the bear'), but Hyperboreas was given a specific location (by the 4th century BC Greek commentator Hecataeus of Abdera), which sounds like the British Isles. This was endorsed by Pliny, who said that Hyperboreas was the birthplace of Leto, mother of Apollo and Artemis, and is visited by her children.

In the Pelasgian creation myth [27] — the oldest of the Greek myths concerning the origin of the world — the north wind, Boreas, is at the back of the creatress Eurynome, as she faces south. She turns to face the wind, and, rubbing it between her hands, creates the serpent Ophion, and begins to dance with him. Ophion then couples with Eurynome, who has become a dove, and fertilises the bird, who lays a silver egg. Ophion coils around the egg until it hatches to release all of creation. Ophion is then the wind that fertilises, the vulnerable fool as a windbag, embraced by the world (Eurynome) and embracing her in return.

The Celts called the world soul that animates all things, the "wind of purposes". Access to paradise is at the back of this wind, paradoxically, as we have seen, in deepest earth. Here the golden apples grow that facilitate the entry and return to and from the underworld, also effected by the golden bough (mistletoe), and pomegranate seed. The dark paradise that is deepest earth and farthest sky, illuminated by its own intrinsic phosphorescence, a balmy starlight and moonlight, is reached via the apple, mistletoe and pomegranate because each of these is part of an imaginal complex of the underworld that is a guide to travellers. Not a literal geography, a map of a literal place, but a metaphor, a locus for an image, a way in which an image may be given a place. Then the traveller may return the image to its place, in a revelation of its fullness, which is to restore soul to the world.

At the centre of the apple is the five-pointed star that reminds us of the five rivers running into the underworld. In Greek myth these are Phlegeton, Acheron, Lethe, Cocytus, and the better known Styx, across which Charon the ferryman is said to guide souls. The five-pointed star is a map of the human body, arms and legs outstretched, head as the fifth point. The rivers to which we are connected in the womb, the umbilical vein and twin arteries, give over after birth to what the psychoanalyst Francis Mott[28] calls the "umbilical affect", discussed in more detail in a later chapter. When the umbilicus is cut at birth, we are severed from the placenta (whose origin is in the growing ovum), as well as the mother. In other words, we are severed from ourselves.

Mott suggests that this severing from the placenta is highly traumatic, because the affect or emotional connection related to the physical coming and going of blood through the umbilical arteries and vein, is suddenly in limbo, and now needs to find new ground, new connection. It is as if a river were suddenly picked up from its course and set down in a new place — it would have to now find its new route, its reconnection with the ground. The umbilical affect has the potential to find its course in five directions at once — to arms (embrace), to legs (grounding), and to head (the force of rationality), and may eventually be drawn back to its centre at the heart, as the organ of love. Mott suggests that in childhood, the umbilical affect, seeking direction, is a five-way energy that first spreads from the navel, down through the legs, out through the arms and up through the spine to the head.

This affect, an emotional energy or disposition, reconnects us with the placenta we lose at birth, through connection with the greater placenta: the Earth herself; and through connections with substitute placentae — emotional connections to others. (Wolfram's[29] description of the grail, as a flat dish and food-dispenser, points to its symbolic relationship with the placenta).

Thus, we can ground on the earth through the legs, or through the hands in a making and fingering. Or we can choose to fly from her, as the puer/puella, and never feel the sensation of rooting. In this rooting is the beginning of a deepening to life through taking responsibility for ourselves. We can choose to ignore or transcend relationship through seeking spirit only (logos); but then we again shirk a responsibility to ground through deepening, that Earth presents as a challenge. Finally, our fifth point is to the head, where the Celts said that the soul rested. The affect that reaches the head brings the courage to take on the responsibilities of deepening at all. The affect to the head, 'rising' from the navel, joins heart and head, and brings consciousness to bear on the unknown, and the opportunity to generate a way of seeing that returns us to the mysteries rather than remaining within the prison of the five senses. This is to accept and live within Imagination.

The move outlined here is a response to gravity's calling, by taking life seriously. This is not to become overbearing, rule-

bound, but to break from the innocent, childish perceptions that
are unreflective (an aspect, as we have seen, of Artemis *parthenia*).
In gaining reflectivity, we loosen the ego's grip that would keep us
unreflective, caught in a perception without imagination. By re-
specting gravity's call, we move out of the grip of the surface earth-
mothers (realm of the White Goddess), who, as we have said,
would want to keep us as children; and we descend to the 'greater
Muse', where a relationship with death may be formed. Here is
forged our individuality and adulthood.

Pigs and Pearls

We saw in a previous section that the word 'back' has the same root
as bacon — the pig's haunch. There is a folk tradition that only
pigs (and goats) can see the wind. Also, that mares can conceive by
turning their hindquarters to the north wind. When the north wind
is personified, it has serpents' tails for feet, and may also be half-
horse, as the swiftest of winds. The Hobby 'Oss May dances, of
which Padstow's (in Cornwall) is the most famous, are fertility
dances in honour of the serpent/horse/human that dances with the
north wind and is fertilised by it to release all of creation.

The skirts of the 'Oss hide the feet of serpents' tails. The
reptilian part of us is then closest to earth, the mammal and
primate rising from this as horse, then man. This is like the African
creation myth that tells of a time when God, in attempting to make
humans, first makes a frog (reptile), then a bear (mammal), and
only then is able to mould the human primate.

The particularity and peculiarity of this place beyond the north
wind, Hyperboreas, is what the Greeks understood by *kosmos* —
that everything has its place in the universe, or is placed in
imaginal space, as in an Art of Memory.[30] Each location is a
particular resting point and gathering point of soul — a centre of
reflection — that gives a particular quality, aspect or face to soul
making; and everything is re-membered (given fresh body, or new
outlook, which is to say that we re-vision the phenomenon, and
catch its interiority) according to the place it occupies. For the
hyperborean, "The boy who is born when the wind is from the
north", says an ancient Irish poem : "He shall win victory, but
shall endure defeat./ He shall be wounded, another shall he
wound,/ Before he ascends to an angelic Heaven."

In these trials, that are paradoxes of opposites to be held in

The Obby Oss May Day celebration: an ancient fertility ritual, still enacted
annually

creative tension, the boy becomes a magician, complete with lightning conductor or wand; because to win and lose, to be wounded and to wound is to discover the vales and peaks of human nature and personal will. And his ascent to angelic Heaven is to greet the stern Ice Queen Arianrhod, and the bearded Dagda, the personifications of lightning and thunder, whose origins are at the back of the north wind. There he may learn that Dagda is guest at the queen's court, and a potential usurper of her knowledge. Just as the bearded snake Zeus *chthonios* (Dis, Hades or Pluto) usurped the underworld Black Goddess, so the sky-fathers move in with give-away beards (like our previous illustration of the bearded Druid, looking like a Jewish patriarch), masculinising the whole of heaven. They have replaced the feminine dragon — the *druic* or druid who is priestess of the nightsky — the slippery, coiling changes and the red rain of blood, whose period or time cycle marks the arrival of thunder-and-lightning weather, the eye of the storm at the birth-place.

The god's anger is said to cause the storm, his crackling beard the thunder and lightning, where the storm was once not a product of rage, but a celebration of passion. And the apprentice magician must remember that, in his search for the centre of learning in Hyperboreas, in the great star-lit library within the turning crystal castle, it is the lowly sow in the backyard munching at waste and excrement rejected even by the other animals, who actually sees the north wind, and so learns directly from it. The apprentice must converse with the swine before he can even dream of casting pearls.

Chapter 3

We have seen how touch can become pathologised in a hatred of sensation, leading to a starving of touch; and in a manic touch that is a clubbing, an herculean aggression. We have seen also that the therapeutic touch of the world, the twin hands of Rhea, can paradoxically be imagined as a breath, as the air of the underworld (perhaps the quiet breathing of the silent watchers Persephone and Hecate). This metaphorical cold air at the centre of the world and at the back of the sky is the chilling presence of death as an ally. So now we are far removed from the mothering and homely warm soil, from the New Age's idealistic Eden of a sugar-coated, fruiting Earth. If we are to make a realistic connection with the Earth, then we have to recognise her shadow. We must reclaim inner-earth. Not the literal soil of Nature, but the image of a ghostly white earth, an angelic world; and an arresting under-earth that wishes to embrace us. In this chapter, our primary guides to this realm are the visionary poet and artist William Blake, the poet Robert Graves, and the Elizabethan magus John Dee.

Shaking Hands with Aphrodite

In *Creative Mythology*, Joseph Campbell[1] makes much of the differences, but possible marriage, of the right-hand path of ascetic spirituality, and the left-hand (tantric) bodily-based path of spiritual concern. He does not explicitly detail the third way, the between-ness of spirit and body, that is soul. The opposition between spirit and body is familiar within a western culture that denies soul. On the one hand the transcendentalists and the ascetics explore spirituality through control of the body and instincts in meditation, relaxation, breathing, yogic techniques, visualisation, martial arts, so readily taken up by the Aquarian Age. On the other hand the tantrics explore spirituality through sensuality, sexuality and, as we critically explore in chapter 5, humanistic bodywork (in muscular and emotional release). This so often leads to prescriptive and manipulative techniques concerning 'correct' posture, breathing and lifestyle.

On both hands, as it were, is the third way — a seeing through of the opposition between spirit and body, that is a soul-making. Pythagoras, as we have seen, talked of the metaphorical twin hands of Rhea (the greater and lesser bears) at the pole, as the guiding force of the world, as soul, personified in a mothering goddess. Zen talks of no hands at all (or the sound of one hand clapping, where one hand moves against the no-hand), where the body is accepted materially but not literally — that is, it can be seen *as* its own image, and *in* its own image, in its self-presentation or physiognomy. And the image is not seen as a no-body, but has sense.

When talking of sense perception, we are likely on the one hand to get caught by its materialism, and then we deaden to its beauty — the senses informed through imagination. This is to feel Aphrodite's or Dionysos' presence in sense-perception. Aphrodite brings beauty to form, while Dionysos brings an indestructibility to matter. Kerenyi[2] calls Dionysos an "Archetypal Image of Indestructible Life". On the other hand, in talking of image, we are likely to lose the body of imagination, reducing images to abstractions, whims of the mind. Hillman[3] suggests that, "Both the sensible nature of imagination — that it is not merely abstract phantasms in the mind — and the imaginal, pellucid nature of sensation — that the world is not merely dense, concrete and un-smiling — we owe to Aphrodite."

Through Aphrodite, matter sparkles. And through Dionysos, matter takes on a sense of the eternal, a pulse. Then we see it as it is, with the eye of Blake (the cleansed senses), or Bachelard's poetic ('material') imagination through the four elements. As we have said many times here, material phenomena seen with the eye of soul present their archetypal face, their presence as a revelation: "The being of a thing is revealed in the display of its image"[4].

Hillman further suggests that it is the awakened heart that allows the senses to perceive with an imaginative eye. It is the heart that informs the senses of their deeper possibilities. There is

Aphrodite's sensual presence

an undeniable link between a perception of the given aesthetic of the world, and the thinking of the heart : "This link between heart and the organs of sense is not simple mechanical sensationalism; it is aesthetic. That is, the activity of perception or sensation in Greek is *aesthesis* which means at root 'taking in' and 'breathing in' — a 'gasp'." [5]

This is the gasp of wonder at a world seen anew, in the realisation that the aesthetic is in the given form of things, in the faces they present, their archetypal presence. It is to see at once the presence of Aphrodite in the immediate beauty of form; and the presence of Dionysos in the indestructibility of form (and then to feel the ecstasy that Dionysos brings in such immediate moments). It is the gods who give the archetypal presence and character to the phenomena, while the phenomena are the gods themselves, when faced archetypally — which is a reciprocal perception, and an act of faith. If an archetype is not a thing, but a move one makes, a way of being that is also an eye to beauty, then the world responds. The gods reciprocate because they are both the act of perception and the thing perceived. Aphrodite is not only Beauty, she also responds to beauty, and the aesthetic of the world is made in the act of perceiving through an awakened heart, that is the 'organ' of aesthetic perception. When we are in love or discover beauty, the heart flutters as if it were breathing, sipping in the goodness of the world. When we are depressed and leaden, or there is a lack of beauty, the heart is heavy and aches as if it could not breathe.

The nineteenth century occultist Gerald Massey [6] observed that, "...the mysteries and the esoteric cults were formed because the human race has a habit of devaluing the ordinary, which was so wonderful that it had to be protected from people without wonder. Therefore the initiations with all their outer flim-flam, their wonderings and their frights, were merely to cleanse the perceptions, so that everything might appear 'as it is, infinite'." Now this business of re-specting, or looking again with a new eye, at the ordinary, is, in the ancient outlook, a making of beauty through fashioning, sculpting. The twin hands of wise Rhea that make the world, fashion the world as a potter would, in the image of the she-bear lovingly licking and fondling her formless newborn cubs into shape, form and life.

The word 'wise' originally meant the shape a thing was in, or the given form of a thing. 'Crafty', in its positive sense, is to be ingenious, a kind of wisdom. So wisdom is a craft; and the act of perceiving with the active eye informed by the awakened heart —

to perceive the goldenness of form (Aphrodite), and its timelessness or space (Dionysos) — is wise. Imagination is a craft, Blake's "Jesus the Imagination" a carpenter's eye that sees the wonder in the wood, the golden shine of the grain, the resplendent anima of the tree.

The craftsman and tool-maker have been revered especially for the wonder they work with metals. Historians divide time by metal usage: copper, bronze, iron and steel ages. Smith is the most common English surname, showing a heritage of the honour given to the craftsman, for 'smith' in its widest sense means to make, construct or fashion. The English Wayland Smithy was once a popular wayside god, with attributes of the inventor (Greek Daedalus) and blacksmith (Greek Hephaestus). But we English are literally out of touch with touch, and with crafting, especially the crafting of relationship. Studies on proxemics (the aspect of non-verbal communication that deals with proximity, distance, space, closeness, intimacy, touch; and control through distance and touch) show us bottom of the league with regard to ordinary human contact: frequency of touch in day-to-day relating.[7] Here in Britain, we tend to touch little, even in families. We are infamous for our reserve.

And the imaginal stays untouched also. Image is caricatured as sylph-like, a nothing, of no substance; as if we could not follow Jung's advice that fantasy operates through all four functions: thinking, feeling, intuition *and* sensation. And, as Massey suggests, we are out of touch with the beauty in the ordinary. We certainly no longer view phenomena with the poetic eye attuned to the material world, which Bachelard describes, through metaphor drawn from the four elements of earth, fire, air and water. Rather, the world is treated as if it were wrapped with labels covering the face of things, and it is to the labels that we respond as opposed to the face. More, it is as if the world were wrapped in plastic, in cling-film, so that we look at her, as we have said, as tourists, rather than feeling ourselves to be a part of her. Then we could say that when we looked, our hearts were not in it, for it is the thinking heart that informs the senses.

Here, we are dealing directly with the self-presentation of phenomena, with things not as they appear to be, but as they are; and with the meaning of touch and crafting. For things to be seen in their image, a deepening must occur in the perception (an event becomes an experience) — the presence of soul is appreciated.

This is a cultivation of a fresh eye, an initiated eye, which requires the death of ego-perspective and of the naturalistic perspective that wishes to make imagination conform to a nature of sense-impression, de-nuding the world even of fabulous animals and simulacra.

In direct, imaginative perception, we see the the twin hands of Rhea at work, as an angel of the underworld risen to bless us with a poetic imagination through the four elements — the material imagination that deals with the sense of image in its fiery, earthy, watery and airy states; and through the metaphors of fire, earth, water and air. These are personified as the elementals that work Nature — the salamanders that animate fire, the gnomes that animate earth, the undines that animate water, and the sylphs that animate air.

Let us stick particularly close to this sensation side of life, to making, crafting, forming, that Bachelard[8] calls "images of matter, images that stem directly from matter." He goes on to say, "The eye assigns them names, but only the hand truly knows them. A dynamic joy touches, moulds and refines them. When forms, mere perishable forms and vain images — perpetual change of surfaces — are put aside, these images of matter are dreamt substantially and intimately. They have weight; they constitute a heart."

Bachelard's quote summarises all we have said thus far of crafting in soul-making. Of the handicraft, the moulding of image through sense, through the metaphors of the four elements. Of the presence of shining Aphrodite ("a dynamic joy") in matter; and of excitable Dionysos in images of matter, as imperishability, contrasted with the perishability of natural matter and of natural image (as the perceptual after-image). Also, of the relationship between imagining, the body of image and the heart as the organ of material imagination. We need also to note where our perceptions of the self-presentation of the world are occluded, through what Massey called our "habit of devaluing the ordinary", for this is a symptom of loss of soul, where we miss the beauty of the world that is right under our noses. (In all this excitement about animated matter, sparkle, highlight, we should also remember the beauty of the melancholic patina, the dulling presence of Saturn, that gives matter gravity, or an extraordinarily heavy presence, in its self-presentation — the moss-covered granite under a leaden sky, seeming to sink under its own weight.)

Reclaiming Inner-earth: Waking Up With Aphrodite

To the child, the world is an accepted mystery. The word 'mystery' returns us, in a religious fashion (a binding back to a source), to the primitive senses of taste, smell and touch. The Latin *mysterium*, the 'divine secret', has its origins in the Greek *mustes*, 'to be close-mouthed', and *muo*, 'I shut my mouth and close my eyes'. Blake warned of "Humanity in deadly sleep"; of our closing down of the possibilities of sense perception, where the five senses can become a prison if not informed by the awakened heart.

In his poem "Vala" or "The Four Zoas", Blake erects a mythology of the estrangement of the person from Imagination. There are four qualities or zoas warring within the person: Luvah ('lover'), Passion; and its emanation, feminine aspect or twin, Vala ('vale'), Desire. We can equate these, respectively, with Jung's feeling/valuing function and Toni Wolff's Medial type. In direct battle with Luvah/Vala is Urizen ('your reason'), Reason; and its twin Ahania, Intellect. (Jung's thinking function and Wolff's Amazon type). Tharmas ('the arms' as an embrace), is Body; and its twin Enion ('anyone'), Compassion. (The sensation function and the Mother type). These stand in contrast to Urthona ('earth owner'), Imagination; and its twin Enitharmon (a combination of Enion and Tharmas), Inspiration. (The intuitive function and the Hetaira type.) When the four zoas braid, there is the condition for the awakened heart that Jung termed the transcendent function, a living in active imagination.

While the human falls asleep to her potential, Urizen and Luvah in particular battle ferociously. Urizen comes to dominate the other three zoas so that the person becomes overly imbalanced, handing over complete authority to Reason and falling into a 'deadly sleep'. The defeated Luvah falls (is repressed) so severely that this quality splits into two warring parts within itself, as unreconciled male and female twins: respectively, the violent Orc and the malicious, capricious and selfish Vala.

This greatly weakens the original passion of Luvah, which is now terribly distorted. The imaginative Urthona also loses potency against the might and dominance of Urizen, and turns 'realistic', coming to earth as a literalism, a caricature, a mundane and constricted expression — also now as a pair of unreconciled and warring twins, the male Los and the female Enitharmon. As relatively uninspired mental abstraction, they come to take over

Blake's Urizen, symbolic of cold reason, the opposite to Aphrodite's beauty

the functions of the senses — the body begins to live through conceptualising rather than direct experience of depth of sensation. Tharmas is repressed, so that intimate body consciousness and knowledge through material imagination and a poetic of the four elements is lost. Mind dominates even in the unconscious. Since Freud we commonly talk of the unconscious mind, a thinking psyche, although, as we have said, Jung was at pains to point out that the four functions of feeling, thinking, sensation and intuition are embedded in psyche, and each informs image.

With the emphasis on Reason, we are distanced from Earth, observing her in objectivity, studying her, attempting to predict and control her, this, rather than being a part of her which the Plains Indians talked of as walking the Earth in a sacred manner. In this warped and alienated state Urizen must eventually inflate and fall. In Blake's mythology, this is precisely what happens to intellectual Reason. So Reason eventually comes to its senses through a reconciliation with body and passion, with Tharmas, and this latter zoa is redeemed. This reconciliation is an act of imagination.

The redemption of Tharmas is an opening to embrace by the depths, or a deepening to potential, the senses now cleansed. The critic G. Wilson Knight reminds us of our "neglected powers"; the analyst John Layard, of our "withheld knowledge"; and Blake himself of "energy Enslaved". The release from slavery of these powers, as Blake describes it, can be seen as a movement of ego towards psyche, so that the binding of the five senses to ego perspectives can be released, and the senses deepen to their potency. When we move towards the dream, we can no longer talk of sense-perception in the same way. For sensation in the dream is image-sense[9], a perception through imagination that is not a literal sense perception. As the sensation in the dream is in image, so we can bring this image-sense to bear on ego's world of reality. Then we may regain the wonder of which Gerald Massey speaks, that does not devalue the ordinary world, or the beauty of self-presentation, but sees through and hears through the world, to its very fabric.

We have already outlined Robert Graves' levels of initiation to the realms of the Black Goddess, as a reclamation of the perspective of interiority — to see through things with an imaginative eye while not searching for the literal interior. In this way, we come to regain the world in its imagistic sense. This is of course an eye that artists in particular may aim to develop, but it is not simply the province of artists. In inspiration, the artist or scientist may work from the interweaving of the four zoas, drawing on each capacity as seems appropriate, and the product has the mark of excellence in how it moves us, or moves through us.

Graves[10,11] characterises valued poetry as verse which raises the hairs on the skin over the backbone; and suggests that poetry is a craft learned in an apprenticeship first to the White Goddess and then to the Black Goddess, as two faces of the Muse. The learning of such a craft must bring the poet to his senses (White Goddess), and through to his image-sense (Black Goddess), otherwise the poetry is thin.

The aspiring poet learns first from the Grandmother (old Hestia), sitting on her knee, and looking into the fire. She teaches of the images seen in the leaping flames, a poetic of fire (the flames seen in their own images, salamanders animating the fire). The poet is then oriented to seeing through material nature to its fabric, helped also by the oral tradition of stories containing bizarre and pathologised images, likened to the images of the poet's dream. Such images stimulate a memory of soul; and the dismemberment of the body in image teaches, as in alchemical imagery, of the seeing through of the literal perspective. The material body, like the ego, 'dies' to the dream, and is de-substantiated or viewed against the rich variety of psyche's perspectives and possible projections. The literal fire and flame is already seen as material that lacks literal substance, yet has a tremendous fullness of body, and gives off not only an unseen body of warmth, but also its own light.

As the poet is bounced on his Grandmother's knees, he is reminded of the muscularity and substance of the natural rhythms that underpin verse, the spoken word, and song. Gazing into the fire, inspiration comes in bursts, in apparent disorder of word and image, but these have their 'sprung' or natural rhythms, imitative of other rhythms in Nature.

Now the poet turns his face to the fullness of the seen world, the upperworld of Nature, the realm of the White Goddess that is the fullness of the five outer senses of sight, hearing, taste, touch and smell. This is her five-fold star. She is the growthful, vegetative goddess Brigid, Demeter, Kwan Yin. The poet is immersed in the natural world and esteems Nature. Direct sense perception is prior to metaphor, and symbol has a natural genesis in observation. The poet must die and be reborn for the White Goddess time and time again, now free from the protective circle of the Grandmother. He falls in love, and is hurt, but repeats the experience in search of the Muse. He has children by his partner/muse, and learns of a collaboration with her, a circulation of images between them that was called the Double Pelican by the alchemists.

The woman feeds the man an image (perhaps just the way she moves or looks today), he responds to it (perhaps unconsciously, unknowingly), and concretises it in a poem, a painting. She reads the poem, sees the painting, and responds to this image with a concrete product of her own, and so forth. Images are shared in the way partners talk, make love, argue, collaborate, bring up children; and, as these circulate between partners, so they are refined and expressed, or brought to fullness.

Now the poet is gradually learning to listen to, and through, his heart. The heartbeat and pulse of the mother is our literal music in the womb. The beat of the Earth is our background to being on the planet. This beat comes from the Earth's core, and it is the descent to this core that signals a shift to an initiation into the unseen, the realm of the Black Goddess. The man may attune to this through his awareness of the menstrual pole of experience of his partner, who deepens him to this aspect of her nature.

He learns to attune to a spectrum of the unseen, of that which can be experienced but not as yet conceived by reason. He redeems Tharmas, senses informed by imagination. Bodily cycles and functions may be seen to be called up in dream images to which a response can be made so that the image becomes a leading element in life, and a pointer to preparation for death. The poet comes to write his own Book of the Dead, as he recognises archetypal presence in life. He finds that he is drawn to use of elemental metaphors — to the poetics of the four elements, and is guided by the elementals in this endeavour. He finds perhaps that his work is pathologised through a morbid obsession with one element (such as water),or the expression of one aspect of Nature that he links in some way with his fate. His pride disperses into the fabric of this element:

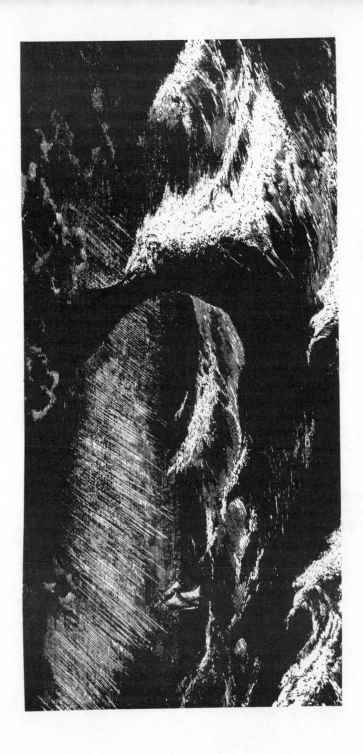

Seafarers

That familiar sucking sea-sound
Its root in moon and gravity
Has a killing note

When the westerlies wind to full force.

The sea-boil hisses, as through clenched teeth,
Always the same death sound on this wind,
As if the last issues from the lungs of the drowned
Had so twisted into the patterns of weather

That tape-loops of pneumatic ghosts stranded
Between this world and that
Repeated, unwound, in storm; rested in lull.
Behind this circling hiss is the rustle

Of the long-dead, whose puffed flesh once flaked
In the rubbing waters as a drawn-out whisper.
There is scratching in the storm, water
Scratching at sand, and ghost fingernails

Clawing at rock, trapped in the returning tides
Where sea-froth slaps at the cliff face, hanging
In lumps like bronchial spit turned cold.
I once saw a drowned man washed up

With this same white spit dribbling from his mouth,
Fat, like a seal cub, his sex shrivelled to a bud.
I have officiated three times
At the marriage of the dead with their sea-biers,

Scattering the surprisingly small helpings
Of musty grey ash into the sea-smell they loved —
Two, my mother and father, the third
A friend. Young deaths, seafarers all.

The redemption of Tharmas is an acceptance of underworld embrace — the mysteries with eyes closed; the sleepworld; touch within; image as reality; and perceptions as yet unconceived by brain-mind, but caught by dream-body, that are difficult to pattern or express adequately within the culture. Our dreaming is reptilian, ancient, from the oldest part of us, familiar to the Black Goddess; hence image and archetype are prior to personal body, which is in image. The White Goddess is the outer freshness of the body awake in dayworld, necessarily restricted and restrictive. As Blake said, "...that call'd Body is a portion of Soul discern'd by the five Senses."

But this restricted world of literal sense perception is what is popularly upheld as reality, and the sufferings of the post-industrial culture, where imagination is denies, reside here. The temptation to spiritually *transcend* such suffering, such loss of soul — to rise above the material world — is however to remain in the service of the White Goddess. This avoids the issue of treating an anemic soul homeopathically, with its own substance: image. Which is to deepen through the imagination of the world. Graves maps clearly the value of deepening to the Black Goddess, where the third perspective of soul is — right there in the metaphor of deepening, when events are deepened to experiences. Graves[12] says that the apprenticeship to the White Goddess is only a stage towards final union with the Black Goddess, who "...represents a miraculous certitude in love...", and, "...the poet who seeks her must pass uncomplainingly through all the passionate ordeals to which the White Goddess may subject him..."

Thus we move through the affection and companionship of Grandmother Hestia, the hearth-goddess who orients us to our apprenticeship to earthly life in the care of the White Goddess of growth and development; through to the 'more-than-Muse' Black Goddess of interiority, underworld and neglected powers. From growthful Ceres of the health-giving cereals; Demeter, also of the grain; Brigid of the flowing waters; White Tara and Kwan-Yin the doters on children; Isis of the full moon; to Hecate, 'frog-head', the reptilian dreamer of the dark moon, angel of the underworld; the Morrigan, lover of death in war, of strife; Kali the blood-eater; Green Tara the devourer of children. In our *imaginal* relationship to these dark personifications, we avoid the *literal* acting out of their stories — we are not driven to literally love war or devour the child. But we must first face these images.

Hecate, the triple goddess of the Underworld, as visioned by Blake

While we dance around the fertility maypole of green life, the tip reaches to deepest sky, to the navel of the nightsky; and the root reaches to deepest earth, to the unseen. The safety of *terra firma* given by the White Goddess must suddenly fall away for our own good, so that we may deepen to an infirmity that spells terror, a *terra damnata*, a rejected earth now re-discovered. There are, as we have already seen, many styles of descent — howling for a lost love in deep remorse like Orpheus' search for Eurydice (wading through the river of wailing: Cocytus in Hades). Taken or raped by a sudden and deep depression or anomie (Persephone abducted by Hades — the deep chill, frigidity and hatred ascribed to the river Styx; also Acheron, known as the river of depression). Going by choice, in a search for under-standing, like Aeneas (going into therapy or self-analysis as a swim in the river Lethe, called the waters of forgetfulness; so that we might start to re-member our lives). Going fighting, without wanting to go, swearing that we will learn nothing from the experience, like Hercules (Pyri-Phlegethon, the fiery river, refusing to give up burning when all around is a deep chill and icy presence — so we do manic heat-raising physical work-outs to take our mind off the chilling presence of a recent disaster). And the purpose of such descents to the realms of the Black Goddess? In Graves'[13] words, ". . . she will lead man back to that sure instinct of love which he long ago for-feited by intellectual pride." It is at Hecate's side, in the underworld, that we find Eros.

However, as Graves[14] says, "The Black Goddess is so far hardly more than a word of hope whispered among the few who have served their apprenticeship to the White Goddess." An élite, a *cognoscenti*? No, for this descent to her, this meeting with her, is our birthright, and is taken by us all spontaneously in the dream we call nightmare. It is not uncommon for women to have night-marish or disturbing/pathologised imagery in dreams just before and during the period, in contrast to more pacific dreams at ovulation. At the period is the loss of a potential child, a child given over then to under-earth and death, to the Black Goddess, away from the devotional care of the White Goddess.

Few of us will directly grasp the nettle that the Black Goddess proffers, because she conceals more than she reveals, and we are afraid of the dark. It takes some courage to acknowledge the value of her realms, let alone cultivate descents into unconscious life that are popularly held as dangerous, as signalling potential crazi-ness or hurt as the lid is prised from the can of worms. In tribal societies, it is the medicine-man or-woman, the shaman or shamaness, the magicians, who carry the can for the social group. He or she takes the journey to the underworld for everybody's benefit. Along with the clergy, the psychiatrist, therapist, and clinical psychologist have supposedly become the modern medicine-men, but this burden is equally shouldered by the responsible artists who address themselves to the motions of the soul. While Christianism and depth-psychology provide the clergy and the therapists with a modern mythology, the older mythologies and the ancestral connections unfortunately wither. It is this rooting in collective ancestry which informs the artist however, and it is perhaps to the poet, rather than the priest or psychiatrist, that we should look for a surer guide to the underworld descent, for the poet who responds to world soul may be both Druid and Bard, magus and wordsmith.

During the great flowering of English verse in the Elizabethan Renaissance, Edmund Spenser, the introspective poet who described Elizabethan England as a fairy-world, and the melancholic magician and court advisor John Dee, who also sought inspiration from angelic and fairy worlds, were both inspired by their personified White Goddess, Muse and Queen, Elizabeth, putative virgin Astraea. Spenser the Bard and Dee the magus, the Druid.

The Renaissance tradition saw the melancholic descent, the acknowledgement of shadow, as primary. [15] Shade or vale was a place of teaching, of inspiration. Everybody stood in the shade of the White Queen, who, as we have mentioned, took as her own shade a dark, continental beauty who shared her carriage on tours of the city. Alchemy, at its peak in Elizabethan England, stressed that the work begins with what has been spoiled; with the dung and the rubbish; with the blackness of soul. And in stark tension with this is the outer social order's devotion to the White Goddess and her personification in Elizabeth I. This, a devotion to her principles of growth and development, so that a philosophy of imperial domination prevailed; of the exterior journey to conquer with the sword; of the thirst for knowledge that attempted to sip in the whole world, to discover its secrets.

Imperialism becomes a twin-edged sword in the hand of the White Goddess, one blade threatening religious domination, the other decimating oak forests to build fighting ships, so that every English oak heavy with acorns is viewed not only as a reminder of the green and pleasant land, but also as military resource and

97

capital. The White Goddess impulse eventually ties itself into a knot about her own throat (forcing her to meet her fate in the face of her sister-shadow, the Black Goddess), for it is twin-handed, and one hand knows not what the other does. While Nature throws up her vegetation, the imperialism of science develops at an alarming rate, sowing the seeds of scientific and technological mastery over Nature, the seeds of the industrial revolution, which systematically begins to decimate the green of the land.

John Dee saw that one had to be seen to be in the service of the White Goddess in outer life — this was politically expedient; as necessary as a courtier's blind service to a fickle Queen — while the Black Goddess must be served through secret interests. Hence Dee was at one and the same time both active politician consorting with court advisors, and laboratory alchemist and private scryer, consorting with angelic and demonic beings; both ceremonial magician and master of ceremonies. He knew that over-fascination with the White Goddess could lead to personality inflation and greed — a wish to dominate; while over-fascination with the Black Goddess could lead to enlarged fascination with inner life, morbidity and other-worldliness, perhaps a defence against ordinary and decent human affairs.

Gloriana (Heart of Oak)

The river that is thicker than water
Coursing through a valley of fallen trees
Each trunk etched with the royal name: Virgo

(She is the nap of the wheatfield turned by wind
And the pink, newly knit scar).

A capillary-tree with Gloriana
At its heart reaching through families
That flourish because of mixed blood

(She is the star that burst light-years ago
Reaching us in a radio whisper).

And the families of shipwrights are drawn
To the valley of fallen oaks
To impress their trade-names on the trees' flesh

(She is the nodding fern-head
And the grinning genitalia of the blackthorn fairy).

By axe-blade and saw-tooth the name
Of the royal line is drawn into the bitten oak
And thence into fighting ships

(She is the moon at its extreme setting
Wobbling and changing course).

Proofed by nail and tar, She is drawn through years
Of storm, the mother-mast rubbed clean of sap
By the salt of inclement weather

(She is an inflated sheep's bladder
Used by the crew as a football).

The royal ship's planks, at last
Torn one from the other,
Rock to the sea's bed, taking with them

Nothing but the sailors' names,
And the whole crew soaks in brine
Until they finally dissolve.

Let us not at this stage fall into the trap set by both classical Freudians and existential/humanistic psychologists, of believing that the Black Goddess necessarily visits in depressions or anxiety neuroses; in grief or despair; or that the way to her is through a pessimism or nihilism. The eye of soul that we cultivate in order to see the Black Goddess at all is also the eye that she helps us to redefine and refine, by which we perceive beauty. And when we turn this eye upon her realm, it may see with passion, joy, laughter, mischief. Graves makes the Black Goddess an extra-ordinary personification of love, and we would add to this that she must shimmer with beauty, otherwise she is a leaden goddess for-mulated out of obsessive study and a blind devotion, and the eye of her devotee has missed her mystery in its perusal of dusty references. Where Plato says the eye that perceives beauty is a beautiful eye, we may add that the strained, obsessive, over-used or vexed eye will distort beauty.

The realm of the Black Goddess is a realm of sense extended as depth; but also of new use of old sense. The experienced innocent sees in new ways and so recognises what it is like to be a child again, but with adult notions. The new-sense is in some ways a nuisance, a hindrance, because perceptions are understood that are as yet unconceived by mind. The senses then become racked with intuition, with their opposite number in Jung's typology, and this allows the senses to see through themselves, to catch them-selves at their own game. The psychology of perception has long had a fundamental maxim that we perceive what we are 'set' to perceive by our current desires, motivations, aspirations, emotional states; by personality; and by social settings. People may see the same event in different ways; and cultural usage of language makes us view the world in differing ways. Perception is subjective, constrained by our guiding fictions, our values. If we see through our guiding fictions, or make our absolute values relative, then our perceptions loosen.

While we cling to the notion of the five senses as the full sensorium, it is difficult to conceptualise a fully functioning sixth sense. If a sixth sense is grudgingly acknowledged, then it becomes an indiscriminate hold-all into which all para-normal or extra-sensory events are tossed. Robin Baker[16] has, as we have previously mentioned, shown that we have a sixth sense as an orientation to the earth's magnetic field, a navigational sense similar to that of homing pigeons, and based physically on the reactions of iron in our bodies. Other sense perceptions are presumably with us, but these are perceptions awaiting conceptual discovery, a language of description.

Our shared perceptual knowledge is based largely on the visible light spectrum. But what is the effect, for example, of colour radiations outside the sight frequencies? And of ultrasound? Of external hormone reception? We process material unconsciously, partly, in Blake's terms because Urizen (intellect) dominates Tharmas (body). With the redemption of Tharmas, a literal raising to awareness of new sensations may occur, giving an extended awareness, where the hands may be quicker than the eye.

Such 'nonconscious perceptions', as they are termed in the field of non-verbal communication research, have long been recognised in occult tradition. In tantrism, the *suvasini*, or woman sexual adept, initiates the man with particular vaginal secretions related intimately to her menstrual cycle. The tradition is that the *suvasini* can produce these secretions only because she has intimate knowledge of her own bodily cycle, and has regulated this to the lunar cycle. Such practices in Hinduism are sacred to Kali, a type of the Black Goddess.[17]

Oestrogen-stimulated vaginal secretions called 'copulins' have been isolated in the female rhesus monkey, and these have particular stimulating effects upon males. Such copulins have been identified in women's vaginal secretions, and are present in higher quantities in women with regular menstrual cycles (as if attuned to the moon's rhythm). Wiener[18] reports that, " . . . women who were taking an oral contraceptive had levels of these fatty acids (constituents of copulins) seven times lower than women who were menstrually normal." Despite their immediate usefulness, ingestion of oral contraceptives shifts regulation of the cycle away from the aesthetically-pleasing and obvious lunar rhythm, to an utilitarian chemical routine. (Also shifting responsibility for contraception onto the woman, while the man enjoys freedom from such hormonal interference.)

We could argue that technology provides prosthetic devices that extend our range of perception perfectly adequately. Ultrasound can be monitored by instruments, as can frequencies of light outside the visible spectrum, and so forth. But paradoxically this may flatten the senses rather than enhance them, in the way that television can become 'chewing gum for the eyes' and the contraceptive pill removes any need to watch the moon's phases. An imperialism of the airwaves (television, radio, sonar extensions of the senses) fixates the senses to expansion, where our own senses are lost. Control is given over to the programme planners, rather than devising one's own biofeedback programme in relaxation, reverie, writing a journal and so forth — activities that wind us back into the depths of the senses, or enfold us to greater capacities and potentials.

To enfold to the heart of things is to really see them, to see through to their fabric, with the eye of the heart. In language, this is to hear both the body and echo of the words and phrases, as sound, rhythm and music (phonetics), rather than just the meanings of words (semantics). Which is to not allow Urizen the upper hand, but to receive rather the touch of the body of the word, at first-hand.

The Black Goddess touches us in this way, at first-hand, in the priorities of dream. The world touches us through her darkness, her unseen forces such as gravity, that keep us here at all; and her magnetic field, by which we find our way around. The White Goddess would give us signs, posters, markers. She is semiology, the study of signs, rather than symbology, the first-hand knowing of symbol, of archetype as image — the imagination's self presentation. Within the field of the Black Goddess we can get home blindfold.

Some iron-based molecular alignment in our bodies surely relates to the natural genesis of the magnetic field itself, in the motions of the molten iron magma about a solid iron core in the revolving body of Earth. The centre of the Earth literally draws us to itself; and metaphorically we look to it as a heart and hearth; a place of birth and return in death, an underworld. This inspires our sixth sense — orienting, finding our way, homing in, focusing, knowing which way to go although we have never been there.

Magma means 'to knead', so, growing up in the expansive warmth of Hestia's hearth, within her field, we learn to satisfy 'need'; to shape and feel with the hands, to learn how to touch. And then to know how to regain touch with what we lose; with the touchstone itself. When we lose touch, we are wounded, but need this wounding, or are kneaded into a wounded posture. This is a reminder that we must come to our senses within the realm of the Black Goddess, just as we have more than grabbed our fair share of sensation within the realm of the White Goddess, where as we have seen, the cultivation of the five outer senses creates a prison of awareness when it is devoid of imagination. Blake warned of the "... Philosophy of the five senses ... " falling " ... into the hands of Newton and Locke" (who viewed reality solely as sense-impression); and we have suggested that Reason hates to touch, and to be 'touched' (which is to be irrational or go mad). Reason is anorexic in this sense, starving itself of body.

For Blake, such mechanical Reason is ". . . an Abstract, which is a Negation/ Not only of the Substance from which it is derived,/ A murder of its own Body, but also a murderer/ Of every Divine Member. . ." Blake turns so-called reality back on the realists, noting that their idea of reality is abstract, perception-through-conceptualising. Blake's way is perception-through-imagination, staying with the concrete that is archetypal, the self-presentation of form.

Fire and Frost Caused the Green North World

The material imagination draws on metaphors of the elements to describe human life on Earth. Central to the mythology of Scandinavian peoples is the eternal battle between Fire and Frost, who together created the world; and who forever battle for superiority of expression. Jules Verne chose Iceland as the entry point for the fictional journey to the centre of the world, a volcanic island at the back of the north wind, where fire and frost literally meet. In Greek myth, as we saw above, the fiery river Pyri-Phlegethon inhabits the same world as the deeply cold Styx; and one must cross a burning desert before reaching the cool water of the river Lethe. Frostbite burns. The icy depths of Tartarus burn like fire, a hellfire. The Ice Queen has eyes that burn into one's being.

The Celts, largely inhabitants of more temperate regions, also had fire and matter in necessary conflict. For them, salt represented the mothering aspect of earth, and stood for the continuity of all matter because it was used as a preserver. A gift of the salty Earth was her metallic ores that could be extracted through fire. But this work of the human smith was a work against nature, and the Earth had to be recompensed for her scorching, which blasted her salts. However, the Earth naturally threw up molten metal and brimstone, as if she had an interior smith working in her bowels. While salt was dedicated to goddesses such as the Irish Anu, fire and brimstone (sulphur) were of the male smith-deity, the Irish Goibniu.

The Celtic culture is intimately associated with salt, for it was at Hallstatt near Salzburg ('city of salt'), that a major find was made, from which the Celtic Hallstatt culture acquires its name. There was a settlement here in 770 BC, the excavation of which provided an excellent picture of the earlier Iron-Age Celts. The Celts mined salt, which, as we have said above, was used as a preserver, both for food, and for bodies in graves. The most honoured person in the community was the smith, who had such deep knowledge of fire and metals, and of ore extraction, that he was considered a shaman. He was more than a labourer, being a craftsman in the sense of 'craft' as we used it above, a wisdom.

Sulphur is the inflammability, the brimstone in us all, a highly directed, yet unpredictable, energy. Salt is our holding, earthing potential, that preserves the body of things. Salt is a fixed body — both an astringent that pulls us in on ourselves, or helps us to draw in our resources, fix our ground, preserve ourselves (salt as the incorruptibility of matter); and a crustiness that helps repel those who would steal our ground or interfere with our space. It is salt that brings us back to senses, to common sense, when sulphur wants us to risk all, where at any moment we might burn ourselves out. This is the eternal battle of frost and fire — the pulling-in, containing, hanging-on; and the letting go, the necessary frictions, the possible burn-out or exhaustion.

Salt is a life-preserver as our salary, our monthly money. 'Salary' was the money given to Roman soldiers to buy salt. So salt was life-blood. And now we are told that too much salt in our food leads to high blood pressure, just as the high salary may go with the pressure job, the high-risk sulphurous occupation that demands a manic personality. The word 'salad' also derives from the same root as salt, so salt always brings us back to our senses, to a balance, to healthy food just as our heart was getting over-sulphurous, fit to burst, and our blood was getting poisoned. In this way salt is pure, and helpful. The salt-of-the-earth are dependable, trustworthy; unlike Judas who knocks over the salt cellar at the Last Supper. There is a tradition that persons of distinction sit at the head of the table, above the salt cellar, while the inferior sit below the salt, and we have seen that it is the inferior sow who has the superior perception of 'seeing' the wind. Also, the wind itself, representing a deepening that is an illumination, has its origins, as we have seen, at the back of the world. or in the inferior or deepest earth, below the salt.

For frost and fire to converse, for the body of salt (goddess of fixed earth) and head of fire (god of eruptive earth) — respectively Cerridwen and Bran in Celtic myth — to meet, the presence of mercury must be felt. Mercury is the communicator, the essential catalyst that moves us out of rigidity, fixity, stubborness, dogma, into the flexibility of psychological reflection. This tempers the other extreme — mania, possible burn-out and burning of others. Also, mercury, like seasoning in food, brings out the fullness of flavour (the revelation in reflective perception). When Hermes touches salt, and deepens us to salt, then we feel the full body of earth. We feel its weight in a sinking, a depression. When mercury touches sulphur, and deepens us to this element, then we feel the fullness of the fiery brimstone as a mania, an extraordinary but compulsive vitalism and movement. Then we have no place to rest.

However, the sinking into body of earth, and the flight into rising heat are both valid ways of reflecting, that move us away from predictable and sheltered patterns of behaviour — our complexes of mediocrity. Where sulphur leads us to the wound and wounds us as a burn, salt is what is rubbed in to bring us even closer to the wound's meaning. Salt is the depression after the manic spending; the licking of wounds after the fiery argument; the 'pickle' that preserves the painful memory of the rash decision; the slow battle of divorce after the flare-ups in the marriage that consumed itself. It is mercury, Hermes, who brings to our attention the deepening qualities of these painful events, so that they become experiences for us — not things that simply happen to us, but deepenings within which we are happening, and have been touched by soul.

In alchemy, when salt and sulphur are brought together by mercury, then it is said that an homunculus, or born-again adult is formed, literally a 'little person'. This little person is not, as the Romantics would have, the child-like innocence that we re-discover, but is a dwarf adult, born of bitter (salty) experience. He is not a minor, but a miner, small like the helpers of the smith Hephaistos, like the seven dwarves in Snow White. For miners have an honest job that requires them to go underground, to visit underworld realms. Joseph Conrad [19] calls such occupation "... a singleness of intention, an honest concern for the right way of going to work..." No oppressive Protestant ethic here, but a vocation, a calling to visit the centre of the Earth, where sulphur and salt freely mix.

Part 2
Re-Surfacing the Highway to Hades: Restoring a Deepening Relationship with the Upperworld

Chapter 4

Let us return from the cold air of the underworld and the battle between frost and fire, sulphur and salt, to greet the modern world that we have created for ourselves. I shall return to my original project, addressing the shadow of both orthodoxy in the militaristic and materialistic society, and the unorthodox 'alternative' of the New Age. In the following chapter, I focus upon what has been lost through our secular detachment and greed for material satisfaction, in the way of effective rites of passage: cultural ritual by which we may deepen to eternal values. In this, I suggest that not only have we flattened the traditional voice of the feminine in our culture (conservative mother-right), but also, we must put a different face to our central masculine myth of development — the Oedipus complex championed by Freud. This describes the growth of boy into man. I will present a fresh view of the resolution of the Oedipus complex, a view that reclaims non-repressive rites of passage.

I may seem to over-stress the priority of 'feminine' wisdom over 'masculine' intelligence. Indeed, this chapter begins with the knowledge the men have 'stolen' from the women, and now use against women. This is to re-look at our cultural outlook from the point of view of what is repressed, and then considered inferior. What Adler calls the masculine protest, the apparent dominance of masculine outlook in modern culture, can of course be seen as a defence against the feminine. In repressing the feminine, we have created a shadow that casts across the whole Earth, for the masculine impulse wishes to both people the world, and dominate and control the world's resources, at an immense cost. The fear expressed here is that the so-called 'enlightened' New Age will simply re-state the masculine dominance in a disguised form, as part 1 of this book has suggested, and part 2 will reinforce with *more detailed example. I also add a warning, picking up on a theme explored fully by Pat Berry, that perceiving the world through the guiding fiction of gender — 'feminine'-this and 'masculine'-that — is itself potentially repressive of other ways of seeing the world, and should not become a dogma.*

The Aquarian 'New Age' of spiritual seeking carries a shadow of material consumerism. This month it may be cosmic-crystals-on-a-chain and pendulum power; next month, Earth chakra healing and balancing, and pheromonal perfumes. The New Age is a growth industry, centred on the desire for personal development — the limitations of which we explore in chapter 5. It is like a bulimia — a compulsive gorging of the latest goodies. The flip-side to this is an anorexia of the soul, a thin and bloodless imagination and symbolic life. This consumerism, where spirituality is a commodity open to market forces, feeds the personal and egoistic rather than world soul, and the symbolic life is then literalised into membership signs — a rainbow decal for the car window; or the latest synthesiser muzak relaxation tape (Mantovani for the upwardly-mobile of the '80's) which always takes you up and will never bring you down: spirit rather than soul.

This literalising of symbol spills over into the core of the human condition — our relationship to fate, Death's companion. There is an industry that has made fate a personal issue, and taken fate out of the hands of the deities (who are the destinies). This 'fortune-telling' industry feeds the needs of the person and ego through astrology, rune books and runestones, I Ching coins and cards — anything from tealeaves to tarot. The tarot is popularly seen as a fortune-telling device, rather than a book of archetype, of images. When people want to know what will happen to them next year, they are coming from a perspective of personal development, of personal interest. Then the transpersonal, the images that are used for the inquiry into fate, such as the Fool of the tarot, are secondary to the discussion. From the personalistic perspective, it actually does not matter what medium is used for fortune-telling, because the images are secondary where focus is upon the individuation of the person, at the expense of the images themselves.

A relationship with destiny and fate could rather be seen to be an education into a shift in focus of interest from egoic, personalistic attitude to an outlook that sees the person embedded in soul's images, in archetype. Then the work is to allow the precise images of the world to unfold, to individuate, to develop in self-presentation, and we are priviliged to be in the presence of this unfolding of world soul, of seeing things as they are. But our presence is active, making image in the world. Seeing through and hearing through the egoic perspective are cultivated especially through images of art, by which we make world soul as it makes us in our own images. A close relationship with the tarot for example does not demand a personal 'reading', but an allowing of the images that unfold — as the cards are turned in procession — to speak for themselves, to show their archetypal faces, to individuate. Then we move to their world, rather than trying to force them into our personalistic outlook. In the latter, we literalise the images by trying to make them relevant to our lives, which is to treat them with a utilitarian guiding fiction rather than appreciating the aesthetic of the moment.

Bremmer[1] suggests that the fundamental motif in classical drama is "human vs. divine intelligence" — a dramatic re-telling of our relationship to the gods. Von Franz[2] in a study of dreams and death, shows that dying people sometimes have dreams that bring them into a closer relationship with their fate, where classical motifs of death and rebirth appear. The implication from both these writers is that the world of antiquity upheld the value of the individual's inquiry into fate from a transpersonal, not a personal, perspective — an inquiry into images of afterlife and rebirth, woven into the religious outlook.

Modern secular humanism has lost contact with the divine intelligence and world of dream to which Bremmer and von Franz refer, replacing this wholly with the human intelligence, a personalism. From this perspective, there is no longer an invitation to the imaginal and symbolic life of archetypal self-presentation, so its adherents struggle after literal personal satisfaction, in a world made dead, de-souled. The consumerism of the New Age — a spiritual materialism disguised as a spiritual awareness — subscribes to this secular, literal perspective, but believes it is doing something else. The tarot for example is de-souled every time its images are reduced to the 'me', the personal I.

In Eden, Christianity's imaginal locus for our origins, there were two trees: the tree of knowledge and the tree of life. (Personified by Shakespeare in The Tempest as, respectively, the intellectual magus Prospero, and the earthy, instinctual half-animal Caliban.)

The tree of life is a giver of food. Massey[3] says that this tree has precedence over the tree of knowledge, for "The tree that told communicated the information first of all by means of its fruits and its juices." The Celtic tree lore was a knowledge derived from the archetypal self-presentation of the trees, the plants in their own images, by an imaginative and poetic eye. This was an oral knowledge, passed on in poetry and song. When trees are pulped and made into books, there is the danger of a by-passing of the direct knowing of Nature and of the instinctual awareness of a Caliban, for the intellectual heights of a Prospero. With the latter, there is movement without muscle. Learning may then be divorced from its divine perspective as image-sense, and the juicy self-presentation of world soul is by-passed for a bag of dried fruit, for convenience. The nourishment is there, disguised, but the sensual appearance, the aesthetic moment, is lost in the packaging, in the ease of consumption.

The ancient Egyptian hieroglyph for 'education' meant a sufficiency of food — not a bulimic stuffing of utilitarian information that by-passes the aesthetic senses; nor an anorexic drying-out of the sensual imagination; but a restoration of the effluvient eye of beauty, the heart that goes out to the world, which is nourished in return by the world's self-presentation. As we have said, when we see the world in its own image, then we restore world soul, which is the nourishing grail. And we have suggested in previous chapters that the grail is in the safekeeping of the under-earth deities.

An education through the under-earth, or morbistic, perspective involves a descent, a deepening to the dark personifications that Robert Graves calls "more than Muse". In this meeting, the Crones become our cronies. The word 'Crone', which has come to mean the old wise woman, is derived from the same root as *Kronos*, Saturn, Lord of time, sometimes called Death.

In Greek myth, the Crones Tisiphone ('vengeful destruction'), Alecto ('unnameable') and Megaera ('grudge') are born of the blood dripped onto Earth when Kronos castrates his father Ouranus and flings the genitals into the sea. These three furies are specifically associated with conscience. Conscience has come to have a negative connotation, as something on our mind, such as a guilty feeling. But its original meaning was to be privy with another, or oneself; to know something within another or within oneself. It is a knowledge, a deepening to an under-earth awareness. The Crones are the Furies or Erinnyes of Hecate, the angel of death; yet they are called the Eumenides, 'the kindly ones'. They wish to be our cronies, our close friends.

Tales From the Womb

Another friend made in the dark, rejected when we move to the light, is our twin in the womb, the placenta, which is often rejected rather than celebrated at birth. Placenta means 'flat cake'. Cakes and celebrations are intimately connected. The wedding cake celebrates a new partnership; the christening cake celebrates a naming, a union with a quality, for each name has a meaning; the birth-day cake celebrates at each year the birth-date, when the cord to the mother is cut. At the other end of this cord is the placenta, our twin in the womb, who faces us and feeds us during pregnancy. The traditional round cake of celebration that feeds us now is like a memory of the placenta that fed us then. When the birth-day candle is lit, and illuminates the faces of the children gathered around, it is a reminder that we are one year further on from the darkness of the womb into the light of day. But then the illuminating candles are blown out, with a wish, returning us to darkness and superstition, a reminder that we are at the same time one year closer to death.

The placenta has in many traditions been considered our inferior dark twin. It is developed out of the embryo rather than the mother, and is then literally a part of ourselves. Jung[4], in discussing the two sons of the Egyptian goddess Isis by the god Horus, says, "It is just possible that the motif of the unequal brothers has something to do with the primitive conception that the placenta is the twin brother of the new-born child". One of the brothers is healthy (Horus), the other is crippled, maimed or 'dark' in some respect (Harpocrates, who is "weak in the lower limbs"). The brothers are sometimes cast as father and inferior son, eg Laius and Oedipus 'swollen foot'. In the Grail legends we find Parsifal and his Moorish half-brother Feirefiz, whom he must fight and defeat before he can enter the Grail castle. In Greek myth, Ares, the straight-limbed warrior, and Hephaestus, the crippled blacksmith, are pitched one against the other, as if quarrelling brothers, in their love for Aphrodite. The European Romantic tradition, within which Jung's outlook is firmly placed, is obsessed with the dark self, the doppelganger. This tradition recognises that ego is yoked

113

with shadow, as a necessary and given syzygy in the human condition.

We bear a peculiar relationship to our dark twin, the blood-rich placenta, in which we are initially inferior to the placenta, through which our mother feeds us, and to which we return our wastes as a growing embryo. As the embryo, we are hunched like the crippled Hephaestus. At birth, the embryo is superior to the depleted placenta (which now becomes the crippled twin) that is so often then simply cast aside with no ceremony. Our culture has no explicit means for honouring the placenta that was our sustenance, our other half. However, you have the right to keep your child's placenta, perhaps to plant with a new tree to which the child will later be able to make his or her own relationship:

Lime Tree as Libido

Placenta oiled with a rainbow
Wet with the birth waters,
A rich meat blessed like the baby,
Buried while the boy suckles
To nourish the roots of a tree
Planted for the mother, a silver Linden.

As this tree grows, so the boy,
His placenta-sister long since withered,
The thick yolk that nourished him in the womb
Drawn into the rings of growth
Of the four-limbed Lime.

In the Bible, at the conclusion of Deuteronomy (deutero: 'one who plays second') there is a list of punishments to the Israelites should they disobey their Lord's commands. For women, these include looking to ". . . her young one that cometh out from between her feet, and toward her children which she shall bear for she shall eat them"; or, "She will eat what comes out from her own body, eat her own son that is newly born, there in secret. . ." This may be a literal rendition of a Greek phrase that refers not to the newborn child, but to the 'second born' placenta, the after-birth. William Ober suggests that this may in turn refer to "a remote tribal memory, now suppressed, of a period when placentas were eaten,

114

at least in times of famine." The placenta, unless fully 'used up' by the growing child in the womb, is said to be extremely nourishing.

Placentophagia, eating of the placenta (usually by the parents), is not at all common in our culture. A recent report by Karen Jantzen in "Science Digest" did however suggest that one in a hundred families who experience home births do eat whole or part of the placenta, raw or cooked. This tradition seems to have started, like many others, in California during the 1960's, where home births are technically illegal. When our son was born at home, we buried the placenta and planted a tree for the boy. The midwife handed me the placenta when the baby was at his mother's breast. Holding it while watching him suckle — the boy switching from placental feeding to breast feeding, the mother left holding the baby, the father left holding the placenta — was, for me, an extraordinary moment of beauty.

Eating the placenta may be the root of the tradition of pancake-day, Shrove Tuesday, which precedes the self-imposed famine of Lent. Shrove Tuesday is the last day before Ash Wednesday, when, traditionally, all fats and butter should be used up in making pancakes (flat cakes, like placentae) before Lent. Shrove-tide was originally a four-day ceremony: Egg Saturday; Sunday; Collop Monday and Shrove Tuesday.[5] A collop is a fried pancake of meat traditionally eaten with eggs. Lent is a time of breaking off from sustenance, just as birth breaks us off from our twin that dies, so that we may be born.

The Christian grail is a dish, in which Christ ate paschal (Passover) lamb with the apostles, said to have been brought to Britain by Joseph of Arimethea, and kept in a line of successive Fisher-Kings. As we have seen, the grail of medieval legend has also been described as a flat dish, a pancake shape; and Wolfram sees it as a cornucopia, a bringer-forth of sustenance, a food-dispenser. In this aspect, the grail has been seen to have a pre-Christian source in Celtic myth as the cauldron of Cerridwen that is said to never need replenishing. This cauldron is imitative of the Celtic underworld Annwn, that is permanently eruptive with riches, or irruptive into the consciousness of the world; and promises a rebirth or a revisioning. The grail quest can be seen as a search for connection with this unseen nourisher that reconnects us with the darkness of womb, the interior Earth, and the Black Goddess and her 'friendly ones'.

The psychoanalyst Francis Mott[6] suggests that we are all motivated to reconnect with the placenta, our fingers and toes in

115

Grail dish

particular taking on the displaced function of chorionic villi — latching on to the greater mother Earth as opposed to latching onto the womb's interior. The Earth then becomes our substitute placenta. Mott makes interesting connections between uterine/umbilical/placental feelings, and the myth of Oedipus.

Oedipus is a disfigured hero. He has a swollen foot, in my experience a common motif in dreams as well as in literal symptom as gout, twisted ankles, fallen arches. For example, a man dreams that he is driving a car outside a school. A girl in a blue blazer runs in front of him. "I stamp on the brakes and in doing so crunch the foot of a young boy on my left hand side. I am angry with the girl but she has run off. I ask the boy if he is ok. He says no his foot is hurt. He walks towards the school using only the tip of his left foot. His ankle doesn't work. He says it doesn't hurt."

Mott would reconnect this with memories of the uterine affect, and with the myth of the inferior or wounded hero who is a dark twin (in Oedipus' case the twin-ness is within his own nature — a conscience — for he does not know his other, dark, half until the deeds of his life are slowly revealed to him: his rejection by his parents, his wounding in the feet, his eventual killing of his father, and marriage to his mother with whom he has children). Oedipus becomes unbearably guilt-ridden, and we might take this as a metaphor for our own consciences that bear the guilt of the slow killing of the placenta so that we may be born out of its nourishment. We are cannibals in the womb, eating our other half so that we may survive, and this memory may be with us.

There are two umbilical arteries taking waste material from the foetus to the placenta, and one umbilical vein feeding the foetus from the placenta that is connected to the mother's blood supply. The umbilical arteries are embryologically linked with the main arteries to the legs, and Mott suggests that the legs take on the affect of the umbilical arteries, which, when severed at birth are open wounds. The legs may also feel this wounding, as symbolised by Oedipus' ankles being pinned as a baby, leaving him with deformed feet: ". . . swollen feet are really substitutes for the lost placenta, to which the umbilical legs carry the blood. . ."[7]

Mott further argues that "Somehow or other the illusion must be created or maintained that the blood is still going forth, finding the placenta and returning again. No matter what the substitute for the blood may be, and no matter what strange surrogate we may find for a placenta, we appear all to be committed in some degree to this bizarre business — the creation and maintenance in the feelings

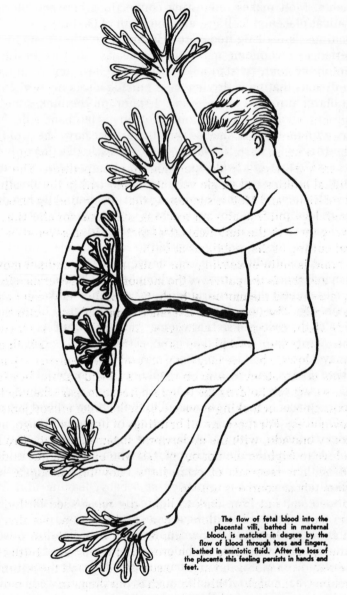

The flow of fetal blood into the placental villi, bathed in maternal blood, is matched in degree by the flow of blood through toes and fingers, bathed in amniotic fluid. After the loss of the placenta this feeling persists in hands and feet.

Umbilical blood vessels

that we are still pumping blood into a material vessel and drawing it back again to ourselves."

So excretion and menstruation are both related to this lost feeling of connection with the placenta, where now the Earth has become our substitute placenta, our twin, and we have a connection with her. This is a flow out from us (excretion, menstruation) as if through the umbilical arteries; and a return of sustenance from the placental Earth or world, as a flow back through the umbilical vein, which is now our breathing, drinking, eating and touching; but more, our relating to world soul, imagination's acceptance of us, and our reciprocal acts. We attempt to braid with others in life, and with the earth, for support. We braid arms in affection, and arms and legs in lovemaking. We braid in team sports in co-operation and competition. The two umbilical arteries and single vein also braid within the sheath of the umbilicus, and Mott is suggesting that our grounding on earth through legs and feet, and our reaching with arms for affection, is carrying through the umbilical affect that has been severed in the literal cutting of the umbilicus at birth.

A braid is an interweaving, but it also means 'a sudden movement'; and this is the pathos of the memory of our severance from the placenta and the mother at birth, this sudden movement after nine months. Then comes the severance from soul (as a restriction) which life in the ego state cultivates. And such jerks, such swift actions, such fates, will plague us through life, bringing both our highs and lows. Then we may jump at sudden movements or panic (for this is Pan about to leap on us); we suddenly about-face in a crisis; we are left holding the baby; we freeze in fear when facing our conscience, or looking at ourselves in the inner mirror (jerks in our own eyes). For these are all braidings of upperworld ego, and its cocky bravado, with the underworld sisters of fate: the Crones who love to frighten us, not out of, but into our wits, our understanding, our reversals of pride for a knowing intelligence, a wisdom whose source is unseen.

So we come out from dark to light, our recognised birth-day, where most of the celebration cake, as we have seen, has already been eaten in the womb. Now life recoups its relationship with darkness, against the tide of the growth of heroic ego. Birth is a movement from moon and night to sun and day; and the return to the realms of the dark within life, such as our dreaming, is a movement back to a respectable and honourable lunacy.

119

An Apology to the Mothers

How the flesh has fallen from the bones! Once, there were explicit rites of passage for becoming a man or a woman, and for recovery of the woman-in-the-man and the man-in-the-woman. Once, the figures who inhabited our dreamscapes and landscapes were personified as men and women — gods and goddesses in human form — with whom we could talk, for we knew the languages of soul; and from whom we would surely learn. Now we have replaced the poetic languages of the soul (especially the metaphors of dreaming) with a dessicated ego-speak. No longer able to converse directly with, or give a face to, the metaxy of spirits and angels, these forces of psyche have become symptoms. As Jung said, in modern people, the gods have become diseases.

The ancient Egyptians and the Celts talked of seven distinct souls. This view of a person whom several souls touched, has, since Descartes, been boiled back to two mechanical states: mind and body. And humans have become divorced from the multifaceted soul of the world; from aesthetic possibilities. Nature has been split three ways: the 'dead' inorganic; the organic without consciousness of itself, and the organic with consciousness of itself (the human). Humans have divorced themselves from Nature — the king and his land no longer one; the stone, plant and animal qualities in the human ignored. A sickness has developed — an anomie or loss of meaning, and an alienation, or loss of direction. This can only be healed when the king and his land are again one, when Anima is reborn as the soulful eye that sees beauty, and sees through, imagistically.

The eye of soul and the beauty of the world have been forced into the tight little realm of ego. The supreme test for the quality of life is drawn from how well we can control and exploit Nature (the technological outlook) and how satisfied we are materially, where alchemy (whose province is the cultivation of a seeing through of the materialistic perspective through work on matter) once provided the supreme metaphor. The goal of alchemy was to know one's nature — to become animated, to live in an embodied or material imagination, so that one could gain the posture that allowed the archetypes to individuate, to come to fullness in self-presentation in the world. Here, dark body and light mind marry within soulful imagination (as the mercurial catalyst), while the alchemist retains touch with substance, and does not transcend or deny worldly affairs.

This is acceptance both of in-spiration, the mind full of wind, high on life; and desperation, a bringing-down to dense body and the common senses. As the alchemical work progresses, so we move closer to psyche and dream, and ego is desubstantiated and relativised. Its perspective is seen through and heard through. As the dream resists coming to ego, we must in alchemical work change our attitude, our stance and posture, and go to the dream, to the depths. This creates the conditions for the body of the dream to embrace the dream ego. And, on waking, we indeed find ourselves in a new image. We see through our attitudes or fixed postures and posturing, to reveal and release new stances, without resorting to the literal, manipulative body-work of Alexander, Reich or Rolf. Perhaps in the dream-body, in image-sense, we are massaged by the wagging fingers of those keepers of conscience, the 'kindly ones', the Furies, who rub so hard that they make the dream-body transparent.

In alchemy, the feminine soul of Nature — *anima mundi* — is the teacher in our search for creative and paradoxical reconciliations of energies normally at war with one another. Anima mediates the coincidence of opposites. The shift in outlook that glorifies the control, rather than the celebration, of Nature, is a shift from the Mothers to the Fathers. The Fathers know that they now owe the Mothers a giant apology for the desecration of her ways. Then a reconciliation is possible: a way for the masculine and feminine to dialogue, to maintain a paradoxical coincidence of opposites that benefits both forces, while each maintains its individuality.

The Trap of Gender

Let us be wary, however, of the trap, that Patricia Berry[8] calls the "dogma of gender"; and of the limiting opposition of the masculine and feminine. 'Gender thinking' can drown the important particular in bland generalisation, in stereotype; and can create a new tool for repression. There are many ways of looking at people and at the world — gender is just one expression of soul, one archetypal perspective. The person who always sees the world in terms of gender — the feminine or *yin* valley, the masculine or *yang* hill, for example — may find that the gender mote is in his or her own eye. It is useful to conceptualise, to pigeon-hole the world. But this is also defensive, as one of ego's moves against imagination, for then the world can be controlled, classified — we are no longer at its mercy. This is a way of distancing, keeping off Earth's embrace. An even tighter control is exercised if we compound gender perceptions with the pitching of the masculine *against* the feminine — if we oppose the genders. And this is further compounded when we moralise, or choose one gender as superior to another.

Alfred Adler showed that the erection of an opposition such as masculine vs feminine is a defence against the potential inferiority we may feel in the absence of such a classification, order and control of the world. As Pat Berry points out, "We construct opposites to delude ourselves...By entering into masculine and feminine constructs, we move from the neurosis that has been built to compensate the inferiority we feel in infancy as organic, physical beings. Since we need to do something with this inferiority, we construct opposite poles, one from which to flee and one towards which we strive. Of course, the 'feminine' is that from which to flee and the 'masculine' that towards which we strive."

Berry then reiterates Adler's early concept of "the masculine protest". As Adler outlined it, in modern people the masculine protest is an inflated social and cultural dominance of the stereotypical 'masculine' — as excessive ambition, striving for power, and inability to show vulnerability — over the stereotypical 'feminine'. The latter is seen as compassion, genuine relating, awareness of others' needs, ability to show vulnerabilities. The masculine protest is a neurosis, because the dominance is forced, so that, "...feminine traits (are) hidden by hypertrophied masculine wishes and efforts." This is an "...overcompensation, because the feminine tendency is evaluated negatively."

The alchemical view of the opposition of masculine and feminine is of a temporary stage before the *coniunctio* and the *circulatio*, a masculine/feminine tandem, a co-operation and reciprocity. This book may seem to have fallen into the dangers of oppositionalism and the traps of gender from time to time, so it is useful to make explicit a caveat that is turned inwards to author as well as outwards to reader: to not take the arguments pursued here *literally*, or to mis-use them in stereotyping. When Adler talks of the 'masculine' and the 'feminine', and Jung of logos and eros, we are seeing through and hearing into these terms as we use them, liberating them from stereotype.

The masculine/feminine, *yang/yin*, sun/moon way of viewing the world is what George Kelly would call a "personal construct", and Adler, a "guiding fiction". As we relativise such constructs, they do not become applied dogma, or stereotype — a single, dominant archetypal way of knowing, a monotheism. As we come to express points of view, at the same moment we can de-literalise and relativise them. This generates not only tolerance and empathy for others' points of view, but also an attitude that allows the paradoxical holding of multiple explanation — a polytheism of perceptions.

The mythographer Kerenyi says of this relativism that it brings us closer to the deities, for 'seeing through' is to adopt an archetypal perspective, to cultivate an eye of soul, rather than a limited and arrogant eye of ego: "Seeing through is divine. Greek tragedy offers its spectators a divine standpoint in that it allows them to participate in such a penetrating vision."

Some psychologies see people largely through a single guiding fiction — Freud's reduction of all human phenomena to expressions of the sexual impulse for example. Gender is a popular way of seeing. Again, Freud utilises gender perceptions in a stereotypical way. Indeed the whole gamut of modern experimental psychology can be said to have couched its perceptions in masculine terms, as Joanna Rohrbaugh[9] argues. In Freud's own equivalent of the masculine protest, his masculine psychology developed a castration complex, afraid of losing its virility, power and dominance over competing views such as those of Adler and Jung. It is afraid especially of bleeding and becoming womanly.

In her highly provocative account of Freud's earlier ideas, E.M. Thornton[10] suggests that the founder of psychoanalysis had, as a young man, developed a far stronger cocaine dependency than his biographers have up to now acknowledged. The younger Freud shared in letters to his fiancee Martha the effects that this stimulant had upon him: a feeling of extreme confidence, extraversion and apparent sexual potency. These are the very characteristics of Freud's early ideas, bearing a peculiarly masculine thrust and attitude, which colours his early view of sexual eros. Cocaine may have imbued Freud with a false confidence in promulgating what at the time were shocking ideas, wildly out of line with the prevailing culture.

In those dominated by the masculine protest, Adler suggested that the neurosis appears even in dreams, *when analysed*. Thus, "Dream life also comes entirely under the dominance of the masculine protest. Every dream, when analysed, shows the tendency to move away from the feminine line toward the masculine

line." Adler sees the neurotic repression of feminine for masculine values throughout social life, in personality, and even in dreaming. But the important words in his comment are "when analysed". If we were to say that a woman insulted in a dream by an arrogant man demonstrates the negative evaluation of the feminine according to the masculine protest, we would also be seeing the dream from a moralistic perspective — the ego would, on analysis of the dream, be judging its contents. Rather, we might note the presence in the dream of the Herculean hero, or Orpheus as misogynist. The ego develops the subsequent judgement.

In seeing through possible gender stereotyping (for example men follow the masculine archetype of leading, promoting, controlling, exercising time constraint and logic; women follow the feminine archetype of relating, following, of eros rather than logos), which may ignore other perspectives and particularities, we see that a person is both in and beyond gender at any one time. A dream for example is an archetypal statement, a soul-talk, that includes gender reference, but at any one time may exclude, circumvent or distort gender implications. Given the dream cold, we usually would not be able to tell if the dreamer is a man or woman. Archetypally, we would see the dream as having the dreamer, rather than the dreamer having the dream. As gender is just one projection of soul's dreaming, then the dream itself will be coloured by gender only as much as it is coloured by other possible projections of soul.

Although we see in myth the patriarchal Zeus, the curvaceous Aphrodite, the macho Ares, the womanly-man Dionysos, the manly women — the Amazons, the armoured hero Hercules or Orion; the ego also wants to reduce the deities to personal interaction of a stereotypical and predictable kind. If myth teaches us anything, it is to expect the unexpected, the twist in behaviour, the movement away from catalogued personality types. The gods can neither be personalised, nor reduced to stereotype (rather, we recognise our presence within the presence of the gods). It is then dangerous also to gender stereotype from the deities to the person, for the moat of gender is then back in the personal and egoic eye, rather than dissolved in the eye of soul. When the deity touches us — Blake's "divine influx" — can we tell if this is the touch of a man or woman? Does gender thinking help us then?

What Men Stole From Women

The widespread commitment to Adler's "hypertrophied masculine wishes and efforts", the inflated masculine impulse, where outer performance is also revered over inner contemplation, has turned the world inside out. For, as Gerald Massey[11] says, "The sole catholic and universal first producer was feminine. She was the Mother Nature...the Goddess of Beginnings...the mother that opened in the void below or vault above in the uterine likeness of the human parent." Before conscious paternity was conscious mother-right — the sinister or left hand of Nature, a matrilineal outlook. Now the masculine is dominant, up-front, right and good.

Jane Harrison[12] argues for "...the earlier Themis...the social structure that was before the patriarchal family...the matrilineal system...Mother, Child, Initiated youths, these are the factors of the old social group. The father, Kronos, is...nowhere." The Themis, law, or social ruling is then matrilinear rather than matriarchal, where "Woman is the social centre not the dominant force". This is important because it does not identify the mother-right with the dominance, ambition and striving characteristic of the masculine protest. Following Adler, we would see contemporary radical feminism (a matriarchal outlook) as neurotic in this respect, simply another form of the masculine protest.

Angelyn Spignesi[13] suggests that, "We are beginning to find that the more we define female as high, superior, dominating, the more we constellate the destruction of everything known as female. Attempts to become equal or to imitate the male will only be a phase in the recovery of an inherent femininity..." There are, "...implicit problems and dangers for women to subscribe to such homogenous concepts as androgyny and humanism. The issue is not merging, diluting, or even dialectics. It is, rather, refusing to see in opposites, instead taking Mother and Father as continually in motion, without hierarchy, within one another yet with precise distinction and differentiation." This would be the *circulatio* of the alchemists.

Jane Harrison[14] says that, "So long as force is supreme, physical force of the individual, society is impossible, because society is by co-operation, by mutual concession, not by antagonism." Such eros is antagonistic to the masculine protest. The matrilineal Themis honours the sons (*kouroi*), who are initiated into Earth's ways, into a relationship with death and the feminine cycle, away from the destructive core of the masculine protest. The initiates, the *kouretes*, now serve anima, Muse, and are consorts to the feminine Earth.

Massey's "the void below", the earth and underworld; the "vault above", the sky; and the seas, were once the triple goddess. She is of the three ways: Luna (Moon) of the sky, Demeter of earth, and Hecate of the underworld. In the Christian tradition, these are Christ's main three women followers: Mary the anointer, giver of life to the skin, the star-goddess; Martha, who gains strength through work, the earth-goddess; and red-haired Mary Magdalene of the underworld.

These were replaced by male triads such as the Greek Olympian mafioso, the brothers Zeus of sky, Hades of under-earth, and Poseidon of sea. Sky, earth and sea have become victims to an impulse to exploit and control which we are calling a masculine impulse, a phallic thrust, rather than a pelvic roll. The sky is now threatened by a prickly host of phallic war rockets, under the superpower-generals' itchy fingers. The earth has been turned and mastered by the phallic plough and its offshoots. The sea's depths are penetrated by nuclear submarines, and her lengths contained by tankers and liners that cut through the waters like ploughs.

These examples are chosen because they demonstrate the inflated masculine — the biggest and strongest, in the heroic tradition. The nuclear warheads are extensions of male pride, of the herculean need to suppress anything that is not within his realm of understanding, or questions his style, and thus offers a threat. What we do not have here is the bruised male, the hurt male, the melancholic, suffering man, the sensitive and forgiving male, the erotic man. If there is a masculine protest, a negative evaluation of the feminine, at what is the neurotic, inflated man protesting? Rather, a deeper question would ask: of what is the man afraid in the woman that he must evaluate her negatively?

What is primal, instinctual and gratifying as a child may be considered 'dirty' when we grow up, such as playing with faeces. When we are young, we are bound to the body of the mother, and gratified by her. As we grow older, we reject this body, and must grow away from it. We feel guilty at this, and also at its parallel, the rejection of the body of the mother Earth, to whom we have instinctual ties, whose soil we love as children, but then reject as 'dirt' when we grow up, seeing Nature as inferior.

The man is afraid of woman's greater binding to Earth, and under-earth, which he must negatively evaluate as inferior the farther he grows from mother and Earth. This equates the masculine line with culture, which controls Earth and works against her; and with the upperworld rational ego, which fears the irrational, dark underworld. But what is 'natural' or instinctual about woman that would frighten or confuse men, leaving them with a sense of inferiority?

It is her monthly cycle — the capacity for birth and menstruation. [15] Men are by and large friendly with the birth process, the 'light' side of the cycle, because this may reproduce their male line, so women have traditionally been honoured as birth givers, and ovulation is seen as superior to the 'dark' side of the cycle, the bleeding. The menstrual nature, the Black Goddess side of the woman, is far more difficult and dangerous for men. And under the dominant masculine, has also turned sour for many women.

The two peaks of ovulation and menstruation, as we have seen, represent two value systems in tension. The ovulatory obviously requires the man's participation in sexual activity and fathering. His learning from this value system about reproduction is perhaps easily adopted, because he too is a reproducer and maker. The word 'man' comes from the Sanskrit root *manu*, meaning a toolmaker, a manipulator, a maker through the hands, a designer upon Nature.

But the menstrual values are shared exclusively by and for women, and men are privileged indeed to be able to learn from this side of the woman's nature. Hence, as the anthropologist Chris Knight[16] forcibly argues, with examples from Australian aboriginal society and myth, and other commentators such as Joseph Campbell[17] have also suggested, men in these societies have somehow taken the menstrual knowledge from the women. As Knight reports, some Australian aboriginal groups say that "The men who perform the rituals know that they stole women's 'dance' or 'song' long, long ago..."

The men imitate this knowledge themselves in ritual blood-letting. Bettelheim[18] suggests that this is to reduce fear of the women's power in natural blood-letting; but it may also be a creative release for the tension the men feel around menstruating women, that is a confusing mixture of attraction and repulsion about a *mana*, or presence, and a mystery.

They keep young women from menstrual solidarity by confining them to parturition huts at their first periods, and then relate menstrual taboos which show the natural blood flow in a negative light, as a pollution or poison, to be despised. All the while, however, the men's secret societies hold the knowledge that the blood-mysteries were stolen from the women in antiquity, and the men have no real right to priority in society. They must however maintain this priority, as Knight suggests, because if they were to return power to the women, and the women were to synchronise their cycles in an increase of solidarity and collective power, then not only would the male-right be overthrown, but also the whole of culture.

The men fear that there would be a reversal to dark, chaotic, uncontained Nature, to a permanent dream-time. There would be a deluge. And, as we said in chapter 2, the great gifts of order, of time cycles, of control of Nature, would be lost in the uprising of what the Australian aboriginals call the Rainbow Snake, representing the collective menstrual flow of all women — a deluge of blood totally alien to male knowledge, beyond their understanding and control.

This paranoid maintenance of culture based on a collective masculine protest denies the potential sharing, the initiation by the women of the men into their mysteries. Jane Harrison and Gerald Massey in particular comment forcibly upon the honouring and learning from the women's cycles as a core to pre-Hellenic religious outlook, sadly repressed by male takeover. (Massey and Harrison both wrote within the context of an English society that epitomised the masculine protest, a mirror of the Viennese climate within which Freud made his important discoveries concerning the repression of eros.)

What the men are afraid of is then a deluge, a return to chaos. The menstrual flow of the woman represents chaos because it is an unexplained wound — it seems to have no meaning. Yet, paradoxically, it is a period, it returns on a regular cycle, and then has an inherent logos. Now the masculine spirit is the spirit of order, the ruler. But this is an order imposed on Nature, a culture out of Nature, not an order given with the masculine, for the man has no obvious natural cycle like the woman, but must discover how he can create a cycle. Time is therefore imposed on chaos, as a law, and chaos must never be allowed to return to upset the regularity of imposed time. Hence, the potential chaos resulting from the synchronised cycles of many women must be held at bay. The woman is then repressed, and the old knowledge of time cycles born out of the natural cycle of women is jealously held within male secret societies only, so that the women cannot recover this potency.

128

Massey[19] says "Chaos precedes creation in mythology. The elementary powers were the rulers in chaos, the domain of lawless force, discord, dissolution and timelessness. The first creation represents the passage of mythology out of chaotic space into the fixed world of time." Chaos precedes birth; then "The starting point in all the oldest mythologies is on the night-side of phenomena".

The darkness, the inside of the wound, is prior to daylight. We are born from the darkness, out of the cessation of the wound. The great round of creation, the first order from chaos, is a birth, thus stopping the menstrual flow at the thighs, which is chaos and darkness. What is first born is a man — Adam, 'red earth' — who, as we have seen, was said to be formed from clay mixed with menstrual blood. The birth is a bringing forth of order from animal nature, a temporary cessation of the chaos from the flood, the blood flow, which is 'contained' in the Adamic clay.

The men want the blood flow to be contained or isolated, because it is a 'night-side' phenomenon, an unknown for them, and a potential terror. It is anti-life. The anthropologist Turner[20] says that menstruation expresses a liminality, like that of the dead, an ultimate rendering down of the body which the living must experience as their fate, as a return to earth. Menstruation is "frequently regarded as the absence or loss of a foetus", which is now in liminality, in the expressed blood.

Men always have to watch for their dominating, organising logos, lest it blinds them to other worlds. The spirit or logic of life, logos, is the breath that keeps us from drowning, the words that keep the confusing waters at bay. The rhythm of the tides may just turn to a deluge, and then the women would be in their element. The male rule, the sulphurous, dry kingship, would dissolve in the woman's waters (the birth waters and menstrual flow), the tides truly turning to the lunar rhythm within, turning to a potentially corrosive acid.

The men, in fear of drowning, shore themselves up with airy fantasies, drifting away from the waters through inflation, through empty verbiage. But the winds that blow us away from the world's waters take us from the opportunity that the deluge presents. For each man must drown at least once in his life — call it pubescent, adolescent, midlife or ageing crisis, the waters will dissolve him (a familiar image in alchemy) so that he can resolve in himself the need for the remaking of image, the imago from which the changed and changing man can be reborn. This is the man who now comes

The alchemical coniunctio: the man dissolves in the waters sacred to the woman

to love the thunder and know the changes of weather, who stands out in the rain, and sometimes dissolves, or loses himself.

The man must be taken beyond the mere shedding of tears, an abreaction of grief, to a catharsis, a return of the tears to the waters of the world. He must deny upbringing and cultural rule in shedding tears at all, to weep deeply for the Earth herself; to see his crying as a rain, as a spring or well, just as the Old Ones saw the springs and wells of Earth as her many eyes, moist with tears in a mixture of joy for, and sadness at, her children.

When we talk in this way, we are not caught in a regressive Romanticism, a wish to return to the values of hunter-gatherers or early pastoralists, for, as Chris Knight's research demonstrates, in some tribes 'close to the earth' there is a patriarchy so deep set and repressive of the women that it makes our culture's outlook seem quite liberated. Our patriarchy has a different face however, for it has sublimated its logos (or symbolised itself) in the ultimate weapons of destruction, and in a compulsive and energetic war-mongering. We have talked of the dogma of gender, but now we are suggesting that superpower-dogma, backed by nuclear threat, attracts a gender. This dogma is masculine, thrusting, wanting to own and exploit the whole Earth, and impose an extraverted social style.

A dissolution of this cultural masculine protest would nullify the compulsive need to be superior to another race or creed, who are considered inferior, shadow, dangerous; and a dialogue may ensue. As James Hillman[21] suggests, we may then have "A revolution in sensitivity, an aesthetic revolution...becoming more and more sensitive, rather than more and more violent."

Adler suggested that our psychological vulnerabilities, our wounds, would show in specific bodily organ symptoms — an 'organ inferiority' — a weak spot such as the skipping heart, the tight chest, the stiffening joint, a vulnerable liver, poor eyesight. The stereotypical organ inferiority of the heroic male is his penis. The rise and fall, the coming and going of the penis are like the man's pride in its cyclic motions — now up, now deflated, now recovered. Life becomes a battle for trophies, conquests. The paradox is that the inflated hero's ballooning pride will be pricked by his loss of erection, his 'soft' performance. The cocky generals show a stereotypical astrology, a predictably common ascendant: penis rising.

But in this riling against the aggressive male, let us be clear about the need for the hero to achieve what he must within the masculine sphere. We are not asking for men to be like women. The fatal mistake of the androgynists is their rejection of what is positive in the archetype of gender. Men need to realise an eros that is also an aesthetic; but a too-early incorporation of the feminine, a too-early in-search could neatly avoid the pitfalls that lead to openings, to opportunity. As James Hillman[22] suggests, "In serving the feminine, in letting the feminine rule, there is one essential caution. Hercules serves Omphale only after the twelve labours are done, and Ulysses abides with Circe only after the ten years in battle are passed. A certain masculine position must evidently have already been won. Could this mean that first there must be an ego that has accomplished something? If so, it implies that one is best to be past mid-life, otherwise one has too little awareness, too little strength, and the ego abandons its position too easily. Then it is no sacrifice, no real reorientation. Then it is merely a regressive serving of the Mother, separation from whom was the aim of all the labours and the battles."

The Hero's Opportunism is his Opportunity

A weasel was said to attend Hercules' birth. The weasel destroys an egg by sucking out its contents. This is precisely what the men may have done to the women. As we have seen, in the oldest Greek creation myth, a male snake warms the egg laid by the creatress in the form of a dove. From the egg hatches all of creation. But the snake then tries to claim the creation for himself. To punish his vanity, the creatress bruises his head and banishes him to the underworld. 'Weaselling' is to push in by devious means — weaselling in, rather than ferreting out — the weasel has come un-invited, is a gate-crasher.

The weasel attendant at the hero's birth says that the hero has in some sense come into the world uninvited. He is being given a chance to prove himself, but may just weasel out of life in the same manner as he was born, unprepared and unable to face death. He may also be unable to face life — always dodging the issue, avoid-ing the heart of the matter, crushing the unexplained, denying the force of imagination, pretending that he does not dream. He avoids especially the 'unreality' of the dream, attacks phantoms rather than conversing with them. He extraverts like a pump on a boat clearing the decks lest the waters creep in; dying in the same manner, the heart pumped out, the four winds that meet in the underworld whisking him away like a fallen leaf, dessicate:

A Thin-skinned Hero

A child discards boyhood
Swings up from the sow's tits
Is bearded by the pig-mother's milk

And smiles, rippling muscle.
As he rises from the animal's underbelly
Blood rushes to his head

And stiffens his penis simultaneously.
All his life he will look
To the two blood-rivers turning within,

Both of luminous waters, running
Until his circle of destiny is complete.
Then an indoor thunderstorm will rage

With its ringing-down fingers
Of shock-white lightning:
Silver-handed lymphocytes

Irradiated by the heart-star will race
Too late to save the punctured life,
And the plasma's brilliant smell will be dulled

To that of hay stored wet.
The five-limbed star of the outer senses
Will sink in a tub of blood

To join the dark lianas of hanging intestine
Strung on sheets of tissue as beautiful as silk,
Tearing under gravity.

Blood rains through a closed fist of muscle,
Sweeps around the slippery cavity of the chest,
And the hero marks the thunder of a burst heart.

As surely as the cloudburst,
The hero falls to earth and drenches it with his fluids.
Now music-making clean bones will appear in time to swell

Under the primitive bandaging of red mud,
And fall out of the body
To be combed by a deafening under-earth wind.

Although the weasel-man may avoid the obligation life places
upon him to discover his nature, we must remember that a weasel-
ish person is a cunning, sneaky person. To be cunning or cunny is
to be cunt-inspired. Hercules is the 'glory of Hera', the queen of the
sky. So the weasel-man's fate is to return to the particular goddess
who inspires him, as Hercules must return to the thighs of Hera for
a rebirth. The weasel is also a vigilant watcher, as the man is the
watcher of the woman's cycle and periodicity. To catch a normally
vigilant person off his guard is to 'catch a weasel asleep'. The
weasel, like the bee in Greek myth, may never sleep, but is always
watching, waiting for a chance at the borders, in the realm of
Hermes, in liminality.

The weasel attendant at the hero's birth then represents the
opportunity that every hero has to round his life, to discover his

own nature in relation to Earth's nature. The opportunism that is the hero's stock-in-trade, his ache for conquest, will necessarily lead him to those encounters with anima that show up his vulnerabilities. When the conquest fails, and pride falls, there is opportunity. A wound is felt, and a deepening occurs. Hermes, whom Murray Stein[23] takes as the patron of the mid-life crisis, then appears as a guide through these times of in-between-ness, of uncertainty of self image, of essential sacrifice to new outlook.

The Seven Souls

Women's and men's mysteries, once epiphanies, revelations of deities, have deteriorated. The ordeals of the hero have been replaced by the sociological traumas of pubescence and the mid-life crisis. The rites of passage have become anaemic, reduced to the literal — to the choice of the right adolescent pimple creams; to coping with low self-image against an artificial standard in thinning hair and expanding waistline. The fearful dragon guarding the underworld has lost its teeth chomping on the sugars and additives of commercial enterprise. What used to be mysteries, rites of passage to develop in-sight, vision, in-spiration about one's nature in relation to the nature of the world, have become literalised in an outward-looking purblindness to the beauty of differences and differences in beauty. Boys and girls grow up seduced into conforming to commercial stereotypes beyond their capacities, demanding that we are unblemished to be popular and successful, in the image of Apollo's perfection.

In considering the ancient Egyptian and Celtic view of seven souls, we may lay a framework for recovery of explicit rites of passage within our culture, rites that are expressly therapeutic, or return us to the deities. The first of the seven souls is the Name, which to the British Celtic Bards was represented by the element Earth. Native tradition calls this a medicine-name, denoting an affinity with an element of Nature. One may be more a person of the poetics of air and space than of water and depth; more of fire and insight than of earth and practicality. We have mentioned the commonplace name Smith — the honourable profession that combines the poetics of all four elements: the fire of the forge, the earth-bound metals, the air of the bellows and the tempering water. Or consider the first name, such as Samuel, which means 'strength'; Susan, the lily; Alan, the apple — which could be a conscious choice of a quality.

134

A naming, a baptism, then becomes an important occasion, not an empty ritual. It is a rite of passage from womb to world in the adoption of a quality; and this quality can be reviewed in a self-naming when the child wishes. This would be a name denoting an affinity with Nature that is derived from a personal vision quest — an adventure into Nature, with the senses cleansed through fasting, then spending one or more nights alone to be received into a dream, a vision, signs from the Earth herself in the wind, the visit of an animal. And so the *Name*, the earth-binding, the first of the seven souls, is extended into the *Power*, second of the Egyptian souls. This is the element of Water for the Celtic Bards, representing a deepening where the child/adult now realises him or herself as a person of the oak or willow; of the east wind; of the cormorant; of the patient rock; of the quick hand; of the steady eye; of the gentle voice or talking-back-in-whispers; of the heart-open-to-truth; of the crooked walk; of the piercing wit. The persona is developing.

The third of the Egyptian souls is the *Ba-soul*, the spirit, a winged bird; the element of Fire for the Bards. Jung called this the puer and puella, eternal youth. This is the burning vitality and vision of youth exemplified in myth by Icarus and Daedalus, who fly too close to the sun; or Phaeton, son of Helios (the personification of the sun himself), who brings his father's chariot too close to earth, scorching the land. The spirit-soul of the man is sulphurous and needs to be balanced by salt, by a grounding in responsibility.

The initiation through the ba-soul, the rite of passage, is through the stories of the culture, which are also its laws or rules: the folklore and fairy stories, the myths that bind the youth to the Old Ones, the ancestral line. In hearing the stories, the child dreams, and this draws ego into soul's realm, where it is dissipated amongst the figures of myth who walk the dreamscape.

Through each person runs the archetypal senex-puer/puella tandem, the adult/youthful spirit, in various mixes. While the senex slows, depresses, particularises, gives structure and rules; the puer/puella (as we saw in particular in chapter 1) flies, takes risks and flaunts rules. While the wound of the senex is entrapment in structure, appointment, service; the wound of the puer is lack of commitment, responsibility, resilience and dependability.

The adult sees the puer spirit disappearing before him/her in commitment to job, marriage, house and home, and wishes for

The Egyptian Ba-Soul as hawk

children to refresh the adults' spirits, in whom can be invested displaced puer/puella hopes and fantasies. The parents impress on the growing children rules, restrictions, orders, whilst supping the overspill. This excess is the froth of the youthful vitality, through which the parents can sentimentalise about their own childhoods. The children grow in the receding light of the parents' own spirits, as they learn the necessary grounding and relationship to the world that parents call responsibilities.

In *The Tempest*, Shakespeare sketches a puer/puella-senex tandem of both an introverted and extraverted kind. On his island kingdom, the magician Prospero has under his control the spirit Ariel, who may be seen as a reflection in Nature of Prospero's own puer or youthful spirit. The older, learned magician imposes a ruling upon the spirit that wishes to be free of his command. When the spirit (which is ageless) asks for freedom, the magician threatens him with a binding to the mother Earth herself : "If thou murmur'st, I will rend an oak,/ And peg thee in his knotty entrails, till/ Thou hast howled away twelve winters."

The magician's extraverted relationship is to his future son-in-law, Ferdinand, who, cast upon the island in a shipwreck arranged by Prospero, has fallen in love with Miranda, Prospero's daughter. Prospero charges Ferdinand, unfairly, with an attempt to usurp his power as ruler of the island. The senex as ruler, as law-giver, must challenge the fresh face of youth, who comes with new laws, new ways. The challenge again is to bind the spirit of youth back to the Earth: "Come!/ I'll manacle thy neck and feet together;/ Sea-water shalt thou drink; thy food shall be/ The fresh-brook mussels, withered roots, and husks/ Wherein the acorn cradled." This is a learning from hardship — not from abundance or fruiting but from Earth's austerity. Also, this is an encircling by the senex rule of Nature, a denial of the opportunistic, which the puer would normally attract.

The fourth of the Egyptian souls is the *Ka-soul*, the wounding and deepening, the confrontation and dialogue with snake and dragon in the underworld. This was the underworld Air of the Bards, the chilling, biting wind that we are now familiar with from previous chapters, that blows incessantly in Annwn, the Celtic Hades. At root this is a wounding of the youth. For the girl, this is her first period, a natural opening. For the boy, this may be a circumcision now recognised. The circumcision will have happened as a baby, so the child does not remember the literal wounding. But many males will be wounded again in growth to adulthood, and will suffer wounds of character, that is a resonance with the woman's bleeding, and a deepening to the feminine Earth.

This is the central opportunity, the opening of the man through vulnerability (the hero's opportunity as his opportunism). Here he must drop his pride, the *hubris* so disliked by the deities, and then replace the heroic armour of the Herculean hero with *amour*, a love for Earth in an understanding of her cycles. The Celtic Druid is taught first by women, through their bodily cycles, for they reflect the body of Earth. Then he approaches with some openness an understanding of the seasonal cycle of stars and trees; the seasonal language of the birds; tidal rhythms; the voices of Nature which are heard with the hearing through of soul, not the literal ear.

What is so important about this sense of rhythm? The Romantic tradition says that Nature's purpose is discovered through her cycles, as these are reflected in humans. The hero and heroine wander the Earth in yearning to be refreshed at ancient places, at healing temples and sanctuaries, in the manner of the Australian aboriginals' walkabout, that is a ceremonial re-connection with Earth via ancient, sanctified routes. Francis Mott[24] sees this search — a "rhythmic coming and going" — as a yearning for meaningful re-connection with the lost placenta. The blind Oedipus wanders the Earth in this way, searching for understanding of his fate. Patients find a rhythm of transference with their therapists, searching for understanding of their symptoms. Such transference, archetypally, is not simply the eros or relating between patient and therapist, but the patient's search for a loving appreciation of imaginal reality, of soul; a search that is an education into the love of image. And the soul may be felt as the universal body of the world in her periodicity or rhythm.

The yearning for re-connection with soul is a mirroring of the soul's inherent agitation or tendency for movement, an incessant wandering. The Romantic tradition, informed by neoplatonism, took Plato's maxim that soul is characterised by self-generated motion, and refined this. Proclus said that the soul is kinetic, or "has perpetuity of movement". The soul's motion may be to order (*kosmos*) or disorder (*akosmia*). Proclus also says that the soul shows through number, rhythm and periodicity: the soul "must move in periods", and "what moves perpetually will return to its starting point, so as to constitute a period."

In this period of the fourth soul, the ka of underworld air — the ruach or spirit, the airy soul — must be allowed to freely move through the body. Body and mind/spirit are then separated out, only to be remarried through the third aspect that is soul. This free movement of the airy soul (personified as Ariel, the spirit Mercurius) is given with recognition of rhythm, of period; and is in many cultures gained through symbolic wounding or piercing of the body (sometimes associated with wearing jewellery such as earrings). The aerated, or oxygenated, life-giving blood is seen to move in a rhythm within the body, and shows in the woman's rhythm, where it moves out of the body to seek the air, the blood then darkening, increasing its 'sinister' nature.

Hogbin's[25] account of the New Guinea Wogeo talks of "the island of menstruating men", because male penile bleeding rituals, such as circumcision for boys, are explicitly seen as imitative of menstruation. However, the Wogeo also pierce the tongue of the boy moving into manhood. The hole made is the place where spirit comes and goes. The boy now speaks with the mercurial tongue, which comes in a wounding as a coming-of-age. The boy/man finds his own in-spirited voice (or his sound in spirit), the inspiration that is his individuality. Despite the fact that this blood-letting is given the same name as the woman's period, it is said to not be imitative of menstruation, but rather a ridding of the 'femaleness' given to the boy with the mother's milk, so that he can now cut ties with the mother. As the mother's periods start again when she stops breast-feeding, the initiation says that the men recognise the woman's full return to her periodicity.

The East African Gisu studied by La Fontaine[26] have circumcision rites for boys which explicitly state that the bleeding is imitative not of menstruation, but of the other pole of the cycle, in honour of blood shed at childbirth. The tie to ovulation and child-bearing is further reinforced in language, where the same word is used both for defloration of the girl, and for circumcision of the boy. This word means 'to break or spoil' something that was previously whole.

Puberty is the opening for youth into adulthood, traditionally the thirteenth year, coincident with the thirteen moons of the lunar year. Hence, there is a literal opening of the flesh, in a wounding, for the boy/man. As the girl becomes able to carry children, and the boy to inseminate, so the child becomes a ruler in her or his own right. Massey[31] says that "...the virile male was the...rex or regulus, the ruler and law-giver". Boy/man becomes a measurer, as watcher of the periods; girl/woman becomes keeper of periodicity.

A rule is a marker, both of time and space. The ancients gave form to the cosmos initially through recording the time-cycles of star movements, that cut space up into regulated periods. A rule also means a 'code of religious life'. Those who understood the cycles became priestesses and priests, guardians of the wisdom of wonder and astonishment.

When Oedipus wanders the Earth after putting out his own eyes, he is recreating the old ways of the wonderer who is the wanderer; who moves on the routes of the dreamtime ancestors, between sacred sanctuaries. They wend their way as pilgrims, retreading old paths. 'Wend' has the same root as wind, so Oedipus brings air to his wounded eyes, and is taken by the wind on the circuitous paths that connect one earth-navel with another. He feels the underworld wind on his face in the sufferings of his travels. Similarly, the youth who has now opened himself becomes man and must set out, as the hero does in so many fairy stories and myths, to gain understanding of the world. While the wounds accrued in the search are exposed to air, they clot; and the seeker, as we have seen from chapter 1, is a holy clot, a fool, who is full of wind and folly.

The fifth of the Egyptian souls is the *Shadow*; the Ether of the Bards, the element that carries one's 'sound', one's personal note, the tune to which one dances, the established persona. The rite of passage associated with this soul is the midlife crisis, for now we are grown beyond youthful folly, into a web of responsibilities. All the darkness of one's being and relationships that has been stored or repressed may now burst forth as a swelling river breaks its banks. The persona must flex. A different piercing occurs to that of puberty. This is often a sudden, piercing insight into a great hollow that has developed in life; or a seeing through of artificial role.

In midlife, the crisis is made out of ignorance, as we have implied for other repressed or implicit rites of passage. Hence, the deity who could be called upon in therapy to release one through this passage of midlife, is in fact not seen until he or she makes his or her presence known by forcing crisis. Such is the difference between our struggle into manhood blind to soul, and a knowledge of explicit passages that prepare the adult for certain changes. The preparation does not de-fuse the power of change. Rather, it informs it, encourages creative deepening to it, a use of the energies liberated by acknowledging the change, which is in part to flow with the change.

A rite, or ritual, originally meant this — to flow, or rush, as a river. [32] You cannot impede the soul's motion, that Proclus calls a "perpetuity of movement". The ego may suddenly discover itself without ritual, out of the running, out of the swim, standing against the soul. Then it must move back to embedding in soul's motion, accepting the changes that such movement demands. In midlife, we find our youthful resistance against soul (the airy spirit), in establishment of ego and aspiration, as suddenly standing against deepening to our nature, and then we must about-turn. Our pubertal wounds, healed in the twists and turns of wending or searching, re-open with a different speaking-voice that frightens us to 'death', or change.

Youthful deeds are now re-membered, given body, and look tired, stale, stereotypical. Our defences have become ordered and adapted; life has become a predictable and unfulfilling routine. Then the river takes a turn, hits a bend, and we go on a bender, desperately trying to hang on to what was good about the old routes, but knowing the river must take a new course. And this course must come back to the paths trodden by the Old Ones, which we have rightly avoided while we cut out our own routes in the visions and follies of youthful enterprise.

What has become known as the male menopause may be the re-making of image, taking on a new name and power, or revitalising the old one in a unique way; retaining the spirit of youth without literalising it in sugar-daddyism, or wearing the latest designer fashions. The ka-soul wanted the youth to take risks, to prove himself in the outer world, to form character (to make a mark, or impression). Now at mid-term comes a new set of risks, and these should not be shrugged off for the supposed security of what is a dessicating framework.

In the sunset of life comes the sixth of the Egyptian souls, the *Double*. This is the Blossom-soul of the Bards, virility and potency now in its decline, but the new birth of bodily death that much closer. This rite of passage requires a reconciliation of a remembered life with a sure knowledge of the closeness of death. So the old person may reach a transition point where youthful memories come flooding back, and behaviour regresses to that of a child, while Death stands grinning at the shoulder.

As all rites of passage are in a sense a preparation for death in this life, then lack of explicit attention to death will leave us trembling unnecessarily at death's gate, fearing rather than embracing the dark angel. Gerald Massey [29] says with courage, "As

141

for death, the practical Gnostic will tell you, he sees through it, and death itself is no more for him!"

So we may need to review our character, our impression on the world, and share this with our grandchildren to get it into perspective. Most cultures of antiquity had a Book of the Dead, properly called a book of life-in-death, containing teachings of the continuity of the soul, and the body's temporality. Proclus said that "every soul is indestructible and imperishable." The older people in a culture kept the stories, myths and legends told to the young ones, which tell of the dreamtime, the collective soul of the world.

The seventh soul of the Egyptians is the *Remains* — our literal bodily death. The Bards called this the Wind of Purposes or Ghost-soul. The body must be cared for at death, or treated respectfully, remembered. Osiris is re-membered by Isis, reconstituted; the universal goddess is present at the seeing through of death, and we re-member her presence at death. Once, the remains were left to the Elementals, the personified elements — it was the lightning, the deluge of water, the typhoon, the landslide that took our remains. They were the keepers of death. Bodies were then left to the elements, or the wind of purposes, Nature's whim.

Each element had a ritual for remains built around it — the earthen grave; the body left on a tree to rot in air; cremation by fire — the pyre; burial at sea, or the body left to the river's currents. Where the river met the sea was especially sacred to the Celts; and the remains would sometimes involve several elements — burial in a hollowed log that would be floated downriver; a burning boat pushed out to sea. Some American Indians had high platforms on which the body was left to the air. Each way promised a rebirth, womb and tomb seen as one. The mummy, both the mother and the dead. Baby and remains both wrapped in swaddling clothes.

The mummy's wrappings involved yards of linen, the body embalmed and preserved. Just as the wound heals under the bandage or plaster, so the body is wrapped for rebirth, a resurrection. The embalming ensures a passage of the soul, a second birth. The embalming oils and spices bring a shine, bring life (colour, smell, a spiciness) back to the skin in anointment, and grease the body for an easier passage. Ointment, unguent and salve all refer back to the same etymological root as clarified butter. Salving, or salvation, is a 'saving of the soul', a 'preservation'. To salve one's conscience is to be clear of consciousness, or go into the dream, into unconsciousness, into death, where, in the

Egyptian view, the soul is judged for its 'lightness' against a feather. Perhaps we can see this not just as a matter of gravity, that the soul is now free from attraction to earth, and so is lighter than the sinking feather, but also, that the soul is light-coloured, see-through. This is a result of reflective soul-work, where soul joins the angelic White Earth that facilitates work of the imagination by the living.

Perhaps in death there is a movement from opacity to transparency, from solidity to fluidity, the clarification of the salving butter. Butter is churned milk, the mother's milk made solid. A Hindu creation legend says that the phenomenal world was made from a churning of the sea of milk (the Milky Way), that throws up solid form. The cow-mother Amdula, an external fount of milk, is the mother of all life in a Scandinavian creation myth. To clarify is to throw light on, to illuminate, so we are illuminated, lit up from within, when we are dead. 'Buttering up', soft soaping, or preparing somebody to do you a favour, seen in this clarified light, takes on a new (sinister) meaning. Buttering somebody up may be anointing them for the kill, taking them for a ride. When we are dead, we are all butter-fingers, letting things slip, as we should. Not holding on for dear life, for ego's sake, but allowing a seeing through, a slipping through, a movement of the soul.

The anointed or oiled one is reborn. The new-born baby and placenta are oily, shiny. The adolescent, who is new-born into adulthood, has greasy skin, erupts in acne; while the aged dry out, become wrinkled. The ancient Egyptians said that when the face and eyes lost their oils, the glory of life (youth) was gone, and in its place came the dullness of evening. So glory was retained by oiling, greasing, preserving, embalming; which we now literalise into face-lift and applied cosmetic.

The decay of the remains was not seen by the Egyptians as a wasting away, but as a passage, a motion, that should be drawn out by preservation. The bandages are a second skin, an imitation of a skin that is of the reborn, a skin to come, and a skin that 'goes on forever', like the connecting umbilicus. The Egyptian word for skin, nem, according to Massey, means ". . . repetition, to renew, a second time or form."

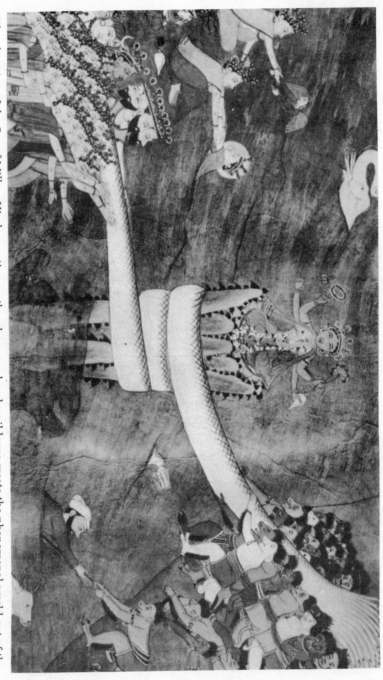

The churning of the Sea of Milk, a Hindu creation myth, where good and evil loves create the phenomenal world out of the friction of their encounter

The linen which staunches the wound, the cloth of the second skin, is also the cloth that staunches the wound of the woman. It was known as the cloth that wraps the sun, a 'garment of modesty'. This was the original ankh, knot or tie, a menstrual pad, a binding to the periodicity of the world, to time cycles, which includes the cycle of life. The band-age is literally that which binds or restrains over time; so it is also the thread of our life-span, woven by the Fates, by Clotho the spinner, resonating with our 'cloth' and 'clot', which is the blood's natural way of bandaging.

We have said that a clot is a holy fool, a jester who can resurrect us from the seriousness of life that is so close to death, through laughter. If he does not make the king laugh, the jester dies however. A person who cannot laugh at himself, or takes himself too seriously, has already killed the jester; has already masked his wounds and defended himself against vulnerabilities. The clot and the scab, or second skin, is the body's way of keeping the wound at that point where it is no longer flooding (too open), yet still vulnerable to knocks and scrapes (not over-protected or thickened). This is said to be the ideal state of the vessel of the Work in alchemy — it should be thin enough to allow for bending, for flexibility, for expansion and contraction. But it should not crack or leak, for then the Work is spoiled.

Such care for the remains as we outline above is no longer evident in our culture, which has restricted services of burial or cremation. We still have the hollowed log of Osiris, the coffin; and the pyre, the crematorium. (The latter now also polluting the atmosphere, due to burning plastics). Sometimes we keep the body long enough for the living to look directly upon the face of death. But we forget our wider heritage of burials — the Neanderthal grave where the body is placed in the foetal position, and covered with flowers; the symbols of virility such as animal horn buried with the body as an acknowledgement of a rebirth (a second virility). Some old customs survive in a different, albeit restricted, form. For example, the making and reading of a Book of the Dead by the close relatives of the newly dead. This aids the remains in passage, as they decay; and brings the living closer to the dead and the life of soul, an honourable morbism.

Such 'books' are now made in reminiscences through photograph albums, letters, memorabilia. The ancestors leave a material trace, and they are resurrected in nostalgic memories prompted by these traces. Some choose to make their own Book of the Dead before they die, their life-work a monument to be read by a wider audience than the family. And a life's work may centre on continuity of the ancestors — one's writing or painting stimulated by memories of departed loved ones; or fuelled by images of death and rebirth, and the poetic of the elements that take the remains:

At The Bedside

(for my late mother, student of the Rose and Cross)
Standing at the bedside
Of my dying mother
I see for a moment
What I take to be snow
Falling onto her bandaged head,
And hear the voice of my
Long-dead father
Whispering to her
Through the falling powder.

The Mysterium: The Doves of Diana
Descending like snow, which is also
The Ka-soul rising,
The rested ghost unwrapping
From her body, first ascending,
Then falling as a light rain
Wrought into powder as it passes
Through the chill of her aura,

Settling about her yellowed skin
And the crisp, laundered cotton.

There is no immortality, but
Eternal Presence.

She is singing to herself
And we cannot hear it—
We are already diseased by her absence.

Now she wears a headdress of dry snow;
The voice of my father
Still whispers about the bed.
The bandage turbanning her
Shaven head brightens like phosphor.

146

Her singing rises above
The forced breath and suddenly
The coldness around her stands distinct,
Ringing out two feet from her skin,
And for a moment
The bed linen audibly crackles
While the vault of the ward
Seems to fill with attracted thunder
That has rolled through
Each ice-bright window-pane
And has mingled in its passage
With my mother's rising voices.

From this mixing of weathers
A sweet smell unfolds
That spills into my clothes,
Resisting the background odours
Of lint, chlorine and laundered linen.

And at this moment everything
Is in surreal and absolute focus—
Death is crisp.

Then just as suddenly
The ward seems to jerk back
To a scratchy somnambulism,
Patients adjusting for sleep
Against the sour taunt of bed-sores,
Nurses going about their business
With reflex certainty.

I touch my mother one last time, tenderly
Confirming the welcome, contagious smell
Of her parting, that is exactly
The smell of fern after heavy rain,
Which I pass on silently to family
Gathered at bedside, heads hung.

Even when she is boxed in pine
I catch that smell — amongst the folds
Of my shirt, the rills and whorls of my skin.

Her fingers first caught that after-storm
Smell from the plants she loved,
Where it lingered in the sweet gums of split stems,
In mucus raised from the pores of resting leaves,
And even in the moisture of root-hairs
From the composted weed.

This fresh odour, that curled out
With her Ka-soul, fell as snow,
And raised a concentrated thunder,
Has wound into the water-course
Of my membranes;

Not immortal, but eternally present
Mother-familiar; ancient
Smell of fern; journeying
At the far end of her dream.

No pine box can contain her current,
Even her Remains were returned
To the courses of the Atlantic sea—

A crisped flower spread wide,
Soaking back its waters.

The Return of the Weasel: Oedipus' Swollen Foot and Freud's Swollen Ego

In his uncovering of the underworld of human life, Freud made a tremendous contribution to our psychological understanding. But he also missed a great opportunity to restore the Black Goddess to her rightful place as mistress of the unseen, of deepest underworld, as Hillman[34] does for example, when he recognises that "...Ananke is the Great Lady (*potnia*) of the Underworld..."; the goddess of the deepest place, through and beyond earth. (The Orphics equated Ananke with Persephone). Like the classical Greeks, Freud decided upon a masculine image as Lord of the Underworld. The masculine impulse at the centre of the psyche soon turns heroic, and then Freud's psychology is one of making unconscious conscious, of growth of ego strength at the expense of psyche's images. When he erected a masculine psychology, Freud

Persephone, Queen of the Underworld, with her consort and userper, Hades. Persephone was First Lady

chose a flawed hero as representative of the human condition —
Oedipus — and in so doing, birthed a weasel along with the hero.

What the weasel gives us is a vigilance, a wariness to the hero's
endeavours, a readiness to weasel into and through the 'front' of
the hero to discover the undercover story, the background news,
the underworld gossip. We are glad that the hero is flawed, for the
vulnerability allows the character to be seen through — we can
spot Oedipus not only by his limp, and inquire of his nature
through the obvious wound, but we also know that he comes from
a family of wounded men. His grandfather is Labdacus, which
means 'lame'; and his father, Laius, has been taken as 'left-sided',
and, as we shall see, has homo-erotic tastes.

When Freud[35] puts the myth of Oedipus at the forefront of his
psychology, as ". . . the nuclear complex of every neurosis", then
we need to do some weaselling into this myth, perhaps to revise or
relativise Freud's ideas in the light of (or rather the dark of) the
Black Goddess' perspective. For a depth psychology should go to
the depths.

Depth psychology is the myth of our times, so psychologists
have a duty to see through its pervasive myths, its guiding fictions.
Through the Oedipus myth, Freud attempted at a sweep to explain
both the origins of collective human conscience enshrined in
religion and morality (the superego), and personal conscience and
gender identity. The Oedipus complex was a radical idea, a root
concept pointing to the ". . . ultimate source of religion and
morality".[36] It placed human development within a mythical
context, but it is a myth of the fathers, a masculine outlook. Freud
argued that the boy has an unconscious wish to possess his
mother, and is jealous of the father who already possesses the
mother. The boy must release the libidinal tie with the mother and
reconcile himself with the father to gain a sense of masculine self.
In the Greek myth, Oedipus, in a series of fateful incidents, kills
his father and marries his mother. When he discovers this, he puts
out his eyes and casts himself out of the city of Thebes, of which he
was ruler, while his queen and mother Iocaste hangs herself in
shame.

Now the resolution of the complex (where the boy comes to see
that he can actually have his mother's love, through an identification with the father, rather than the previously wished-for
parricide) leads to a gender identification, as we have said above.
The boy adopts the cultural sense of manhood and consequent
roles. Also, the boy achieves individuality in breaking free from a

dependence upon the mother. He formulates a conscience, a superego, for he must deal with the guilt of the incestuous sexual feelings for the mother, and the parricidal feelings towards the father. Incest and parricide were considered to be terrible crimes in classical Greece [37], so the myth of Oedipus enacted in theatre was also a cathartic morality play, where the audience could inquire into taboo collectively, and through its many images.

Freud provided a metaphor for the social origin of the Oedipus complex in a "primal horde", ruled over by an oppressive patriarch, a king who is murdered by the men he rules. The primal horde is given solidarity in this coming together to kill the king, but now feel guilty because they have also killed what they loved about the king. Freud says that this guilt is felt by each man, as a "... sense of guilt for which he can discern no foundation." It stimulates the development of a conscience, a morality, and then a moralism resting in an organised religion, a collective superego. In *Totem and Taboo*, Freud says that we individually and collectively bear and feel the guilt of this primal murder of a tyrant.

The boy, from his original 'polymorphous perversity', his erotic connection to the whole world, learns to discriminate, to make 'masculine' choices — realising a gender identity — from the resolution of the Oedipus complex. In 1899, in a letter to Wilhelm Fliess, Freud said of bisexuality and contrasexuality, "I am accustoming myself to regarding every sexual act as an event between four individuals." Jung later said that a woman in relationship with a man is also in relationship with his anima, and him with her animus, a four-way partnership. By 1923, Freud still wrote of, "... the constitutional bisexuality of each individual." However, rather than celebrating this, he saw it as regressive, for the individual who is 'healthy' comes to identify fully with his or her gender.

Freud's metaphor of the "primal horde", developed in *Totem and Taboo*, calls for a tyrannical father subjugating the women and children. From this perspective of continuity of the father-line (Ouranus-Kronos-Zeus), laws develop out of a morality born of conscience (superego) developed from a killing of the father. This becomes enshrined in religion. Then we all feel guilt for the killing of Christ, who is part of the Father-in-heaven. From the perspective of mother-right however, we would see the situation rather differently. We have already outlined the possible original stealing of the women's knowledge by the men, the knowledge of the potency of the synchronised menstrual cycles in regulation with lunar cycle. Seen as a potential deluge, this is defused by men through social custom and taboo, and the knowledge is kept from the women, enshrined in male secret societies. But these societies know that the woman is the keeper of the knowledge of time cycles and rhythms, and has a deeper body-knowledge and sensuality, which the man tries to gain through imitation. So the guilt men may feel is not because of a killing of the primal father, but a killing of the Mothers, a suppression of mother-right, a suffocation of the knowledge of the menstrual cycle and the cycles of time.

From the same mother-right perspective, conscience comes with the ovulatory values, the bearing of children as an irruption of the deluge, a work against the death aspect of Nature. The ovulatory values represent a superego born out of ego acting against the id or chaos of the period.

We might widen this, and say that the origin of guilt, in hunter-gatherer communities, and the purpose of a catharsis or washing-through of the guilt of the whole community in a return of grief to the Earth, rests in the original animal hunt and the gathering of plants. Here, lives are drawn from Nature so that human life may continue. The mass hunt of animals, and the gathering of plants, a gift from the Earth, produces grief by the hunters and gatherers for the hunted and gathered, even though the Earth may provide in abundance. Cave paintings may show respect for the animals killed in the hunt. The Earth is the mother of such peoples — she provides, but they have killed her children. The cathartic release of guilt after the hunt and the gathering of plants would then be the real mysteries — a return to solidarity with Nature, an honouring of the soul of Nature, for she dies to give us life, just as we return to her at death.

Oedipus' so-called incestuous relationship with his mother, his killing of the old king, and his gaining of a wound in his pierced and swollen feet, all add up in any case to a picture clear to those familiar with the theme of James Frazer's *The Golden Bough*. The young hero has come to overthrow the old king and claim consort-ship to the goddess-queen, whose city realm or grove he now defends with his life, and who is his 'mother'.

That Oedipus is a consort to the goddess is clear from his maim-ing, his swell-foot, for those with swollen digits, the Daktyls, are mineworkers, sons of the mother of the gods, such as the black-smith Hephaestus. Oedipus' mother and wife is Iocaste. Graves [38] suggests that her name means 'shining moon' (*Io-cassitere*). Cassiterite is the most common ore of tin, stannous oxide; so the

152

shining moon is the gleam of tin, and Oedipus is of the family of tin miners who work the mother Earth's metals, and are in her service. Like Hephaestus himself, who also has crippled feet, Oedipus is said to be edgy, grumpy, bad-tempered. In the smith's lingo, he is ill-tempered, has not been hardened properly, has clear faults in his metal/mettle, his quality of temperament.

He kills his father Laius when he meets him on the road to Thebes, because Laius' chariot runs over his foot. Laius refuses to apologise, and Oedipus' anger gets the better of him. Laius, the old king, hits Oedipus right in his wound, where it hurts most, exposing his vulnerability and inferiority, as the old king must when challenged by the new. Oedipus plainly has an inferiority complex, because he cannot stand Laius talking down to him from the elevation of his chariot. We show our wounds in our organ inferiorities. For Oedipus, who must learn to stand on his own two feet, to stand his ground, the wounding is in the feet. Later, when he needs in-sight, an introversion to correct his compulsive extraverted nature, he is compelled to put out his eyes.

Each modern man who has not resolved his Oedipus complex, says Freud, will show a neuroticism — a wish to still possess the mother; an incomplete sense of conscience or development of superego; and uncertainty in self-image as a man. So each man must face the trials of Oedipus — a wounding in youth, a wounding in adulthood. We are all miners of tin by night, and have to pay our dues in service to the Earth. The heroic Bronze Age which spawned the Greek heroic myths was dependent literally upon large quantities of tin for smelting with copper to make bronze. We are still acting within the myths of those heroes and heroines, intimately connected with our ancestors' heroic wielding of this tin and copper alloy. So we have to face up to how we have smitten the tin-mother, how we have forced her underground and then replaced her with a man, Zeus *chthonios*; with Jupiter, the great tin-god. And the man who is tin-god only bleeds when he rusts, or acknowledges the waters of life, blemishing the outer shine of ego.

We then take Jupiter literally. We want to be big like him — thundering — so we rape the earth of plutonium and smite that in two with our clever heroism to produce the biggest bang of all, the greatest thunder ever heard.

But we must return to Oedipus. To enter the city of Thebes, to rid it of the terrible Sphinx, and marry his mother, Oedipus must face the riddle of the Sphinx. If he does not solve the riddle, he will perish, as those before him, and the city will remain gripped in terror. Now the man who knows the secret of the Sphinx is a son of the Mother, not the Father, because the Sphinx is the central symbol of the old mother-right, before paternity was known. [39] The Sphinx is animal behind and human in front. Its secret is the understanding that the female is behind, back, north, dark, sinister (and then prior); while the male is front, south, light, dextrous; which is the natural division of the sky into dark north of the Great Bear, and sun-and moon-lit south, as we have seen. Sphinx means 'throttler', as a sphincter. The Sphinx is anal in her concerns: the conservative rule of the mother-right.

If Oedipus knows the answer to the riddle set by the Sphinx, why does his life thereafter go horribly wrong? Why does Oedipus, having discovered his incestuous relationship with Iocaste, and her suicide, put out his eyes and wander the Earth? In the old tradition, as we have said, paternity is unknown, so there is no incest taboo. When paternity is known, and the incest taboo is born, every man then carries the twin guilt of the tradition of incest (now exposed), plus the patriarchal takeover of mother-right (the men stealing from the women). The incest taboo takes away the mother's right to choose a son as lover. The boy/man feels guilty at the love for his mother, as Freud suggested, because the incest taboo is working. But the guilt is now compounded because the man knows how the fathers took away the choice of the mothers, repressing the menstrual knowledge by displacing it onto male imitations, and negatively valuing the woman's bleeding.

To invent a masculine-dominated primal horde, as Freud does, neatly avoids this latter guilt, but anthropology can be read otherwise, and the ancient wisdom puts queen before king-ship. Indeed, identifying with the fathers may serve to irritate the guilt, for now the man must rationalise his historical behaviour, and invents reasons why women are inferior, and should be ruled over. This literalises, and moralises, the imaginal 'inferior', which is the darkness of the underworld goddess (inferior means 'lower', deeper). In this latter tactic, the man may displace his guilt onto a subscription to the masculine protest.

When the hero becomes king, he may grow lazy in his service of Anima. He may begin to ignore the value of the woman partner as reflective Muse, and he resists psychological reflectivity, as imagination at play. Now his own literal reflection (a narcissism) suits him better, and he becomes inflated. The world is taken for granted, and a sickness descends upon the rejected Earth (a plague upon Thebes). The imaginal White Earth, ensouled and angelic, is

154

lost to a restrictive materialism and naturalism, where only surfaces matter, and only the surface of matter is perceived, rather than the interiority of things. The king and land are no longer one — the grail is lost. The king must remain in studentship of the White Earth, the imaginal ground. He does not become Earth's ruler. If we take the Earth's gift of imagination for granted, we reject the ordinary (by treating it in a surface manner), rather than being in wonder at its presence (its surfacing). Then our natural inspiration will fade, and a culture will turn for inspiration to booze and drugs; and to passive entertainment like pulp television.

It is the awakening to his slipping into inflation and passivity in response to the demands of the Earth that surely horrifies first Iocaste then Oedipus. His blindness has been his extraversion, and now he must put his eyes out to gain inner-sight. Kerenyi[40] calls Oedipus " . . . the most foolish of all the beings in the world".

In a myth concerned with Fathers, it would seem natural to inquire after the nature of Oedipus' father, Laius. Here we are folded into another complex, for, as Kerenyi shows, Oedipus' father is not the heterosexual macho hero we might imagine, but is said to be the inventor of homoerotic passion, of love between men. In myth, Laius is fated to die because of an illicit homosexual relationship.

The wise seer Teiresias warns Laius that he might avert problems that will fall onto the city of Thebes if he makes a sacrifice to Hera, goddess of marriage. But he refuses to do this. Laius stubbornly refuses to serve the feminine principle. Freud would say that, as a homosexual, Laius has not resolved his Oedipus complex, for he still wants to possess the mother. Freud says that the Oedipus complex may sometimes be inverted, the child choosing identification with the opposite sex parent, but this would be a neurotic rather than fulfilling choice. The Delphic oracle has told Laius that a son born to him would kill him. The Delphic oracle is the core of feminine wisdom. Is this the Mothers punishing Laius for his rejection of their ways? Is it any wonder that Oedipus grows up confused?

What Freud has done is a well-known trick of the hero — the introduction of a weasel-word that throws us right away from the heart of something, right off scent. A weasel-word introduced into a sentence either completely destroys the meaning of the sentence, or takes away the force of the sentence, takes the sting out of it. The masculine, heroic, interpretation of the Oedipus myth is an intro-

155

Sphinx

duction of a weasel-word, which we would expect, as a weasel is right there at Hercules' birth. We are still throwing weasel-words into lives that could be enriched and deepened through imagination, and then imagination is by-passed for ego's manipulative concerns. All of this seems like an enormous trial or test; yet the world is a testing place. 'Test' itself originally meant a pot, a vessel; specifically a vessel in which gold and silver were alloyed, sun and moon embracing in the same container. And, in the language of alchemy, on this testing Earth we are making the very vessel in which our Work, or being, takes place. As soul makes us, so we make world soul, in our crafty ways, in an opening to Earth's embrace.

Chapter 5

Let us now explore in more detail the shadow of personal growth, the darker side of the 'me' generation that is bent on self-discovery. Part of the promise of the New Age is a new way of relating — not only a wellbeing relating, but a 'genuine' sharing based on authenticity and self-disclosure. This has spawned a tremendous interest in self, in personal potential, giving rise to new technologies of interpersonal skill that are collectively lumped under the title of humanistic psychology. In the 1960's and 1970's, humanistic psychology was seen as an innovation in human relating, cutting through the stiff conventions of the post-war years. This was part of the Aquarian thrust in genuine and aware encounter that promised a social revolution.

However, the move to 'realise human potential' compulsively focuses upon the 'I', the ego, the personalistic, at the expense of the world, the collective. It is when we shift our attention away from ego and to the collective psyche, in a suspension of ego's tactics and perceptions, that we give something back to the world. The ego's herculean tactics tend to be anti-imaginal, as we have seen. When these tactics are seen through, then we may allow the world to come to fullness in that moment of suspension. This suspending of the 'I' happens in any case in accident or illness; when we fall in love; and most obviously, when we dream, where the ego cannot usually do its 'growthwork', for it is eclipsed by other aspects of psyche. When I say that we can give something back to the world, simply seeing matter as animated, returning soul to 'things', is a start to ensouling the world. This is to reflect psychologically, to give imagination its place.

By the 1980's, humanistic psychology had become another marketable commodity, like New Age calendars, crystals and pendulums. Groups for growth, enlightenment, awareness, had become big business. More and more groups each year with richer and more ludicrous promises for health, wealth and wellbeing, springing up like mushrooms in a damp field, each with a modern marketing campaign behind it. More, each new technique attempts to upstage those before it (usually inventing a complex language to bolster its selling appeal), with inflated claims for all-comers. Each new therapy becomes a cure-all. As I write this, of the literally hundreds of advertising features for groups and therapies that arrive in the mail, Rebirthing (or "Conscious Connected Breathing") is currently catching my attention because I have recently counselled people who are casualties of the technique. An advertising blurb aimed at potential rebirthing trainers claims: "I am totally confident you will find it (rebirthing) everything you ever dreamt of when you first considered taking care of others as your vocation." If that were not inflated enough, we are also informed that ". . . every type of neurotic and psychotic personality disorder have *(sic)* been Rebirthed successfully and have made major personality changes for the better within a matter of a few sessions."

From the same blurb, rebirthing is ". . . a safe, easy, pleasant, rational, effective method of bringing healing to the body, the mind, the heart, and the soul." Wellbeing in a nutshell: aiming high, flying from the shadows; trying so hard to embrace the whole being, to get at the point of existence, that it misses the bulk of the iceberg (but, like the Titanic, must inevitably crash and sink to the depths, where its vulnerabilities have been overlooked in the glorious high of the maiden voyage). Where the New Agers consciously try to transcend shadow in positive visualisations and ethereal synthesiser muzak, the humanistic psychology movement simply seems to have forgotten to inquire of its collective shadow (or may have turned its back on the whole business), absorbed by the heady stuff of growth, the new vitality of genuine encounter, the sensual liberation in mixed massage, the striving for highs and peak experiences. And an explicitly secular and self-indulgent arrogance (now called 'assertiveness') has grown with the 'me' generation. Personal experience has been deified (the movement is after all explicitly humanistic). I am thinking of workshops with titles such as "The God and Goddess Within" — as if deities did reside in the human breast, rather than us being in deity, the person embedded in soul. In humanistic psychology, the deity is reduced to the personal, rather than the person being exalted in deity. And the new high priests, the secular hierophants,

160

are the charismatic facilitators, who have been initiated by a still more select body of even more charismatic elders, who now solely run 'training groups'!

A person is embedded in archetype, a soul-ful individuality etched on his or her face, showing in that person's characteristic movements, and shining through the persona — the personal signature. But we do not get at the archetypal individual by deifying the personal, retreating into ego's realm. This traps us in all-embracing dogmas, such as the "everything is in the breathing" maxim of rebirthing. This is a long way from the chilling underworld air that we met in earlier chapters, that breathes us, and fixes us in terror as we deepen. Any technique that treats itself as a cure-all is already stuck in a fantasy of wellbeing and does not respect the morbistic perspective. Hence, it is already limited by choosing a certain direction, through focusing on meaning, healing, curing; a direction that is not strictly 'therapy' at all, for this means 'attendance to the gods', not to the personal.

I may already appear to be carping, and the following chapter may appear to be excessively hard on the 'new therapies', damning of the entire growth movement, but my stance is necessary to bring into relief the root issues in humanistic psychology that have become an illness inherent to such therapies. Such an illness arises from an obsession with self, an unhealthy interest in ego style and ego perspective at the expense of other possibilities of psyche. Of course the ego must have its place, but I am questioning its authoritarian dominance. If we offer the crown, ego will never deny itself kingship — it is by nature self-obsessed, self-referential. If humanistic psychology sees through itself while it is happening; if it can laugh at its own practice and catch its own posturings in amongst the good work it does, then it will do itself a great service. One must have experienced the therapies in order to make informed comment on them, and, perhaps, it is by experiencing many of the new therapies (including rebirthing!) over the past fifteen years that I am able now to see them in a different light, so that they may be re-visioned, given fresh face, and their inflations seen through.

Also, the modern debate between personalistic/humanistic and archetypal approaches is not at all new. James Hillman[1] takes up the issue in many places in his writings over the last twenty or more years, and I value his insights in this area enormously. I have simply built here on his foundations — on his fundamental critique of the restrictive herculean ego. I have borrowed his phrase "a religion without gods", to open this chapter.

Humanistic Psychology: A Religion without Gods

The Dream

The dream is where the psyche speaks unhindered. Indeed, John Layard suggested that everything can be trusted in the dream except the dream ego. Yet most psychologies, working in the service of ego, compulsively mess with the images given in dreaming.

Jung rescued the psyche's dignity from Freud's ego psychology by insisting that the psyche does not falsify or distort; is not a mechanism for disguising the ego's needs (as wish fulfillment), but is objective. Image is the given language of the psyche, and we should respond to image imaginatively. However, Jung also tended to work the image back into the service of ego, rather than sticking with the image as given; and Jungians tend to symbolise the image, which is prior to the symbol, then losing the precision and climate of the image as it appears and is known, phenomenologically. Indeed, paradoxically the symbol has become to the image what the social persona might be to the ego — a generalisation of the particular that is a caricature and cover-up. The unpalatable image is given a face lift or plastic surgery so that it is acceptable to the schema of the analyst, where symbols have closed meanings. Just as Freud reduced images to genital symbols, so Jungians often reduce images to transpersonal symbols, which smacks of a 'members only' club. When a variety of images of birds, for example, are reduced to symbols of 'spirit', or serpents to 'instinct', then membership to the club is by socialisation to a narrow persona that loses the full character of the image. Also, as we have said, the symbolised-image is further socialised by relating it back to the personal, the egoic, rather than drawing the restrictive ego into the many-faceted psyche. Even for Jung, individuation was the growth of personal consciousness. For the archetypal psychologist, it is not us who individuate, but our images. Individuation is then not about 'growth' of the person, but about an education into a way of seeing that allows the collective world to come to its fullness, to be in its own image.

Humanistic 'psychology' is a misnomer, for this approach is not a logos of psyche, of soul, but of person and personality, of ego. We can see this clearly in humanistic psychology's approaches to the dream, exemplified in Gestalt therapy. Here, we are asked to see every part of the dream as an expression of personality. Every bit

162

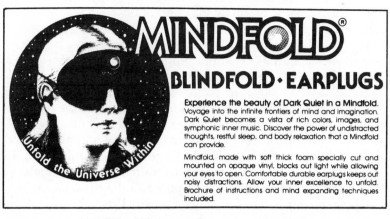

An example of New Age psychobabble. A simple blindfold is transformed
into a tool for spiritual awareness and the price triples. A recent advert
from a New Age magazine

of the dream as in us, rather than us being in the dream. When we
then act out each part of the dream as a component of personality,
we are bringing dayworld ego to bear on the previously raw and
untainted image. In this process we both manipulate and distort
the image for our personal ends (an imperialism of the image), and
assume that it is our personal or private property (a capitalism of
the image), as opposed to respecting its source and place in soul.
The ego activity that makes image serve ego consciousness in this
way is a reductivism, an artificial and drastic narrowing to person,
to personality. If depth psychology generally squeezes the dream
in ego's favour, then we can expect humanistic psychology to
apply even more muscle.

Humanistic psychology talks of 'personal growth' — a developmental fantasy (that we get wiser or more competent as we grow
older), fused with a personalistic fantasy (that everything can be
contained by ego consciousness). Yet what grows, or inflates, here
is personality and ego, at the expense of psyche's images, such as
the dream's personifications. As I seem to absorb the kingdom of
the dream into my ego, then I shrink away from the wonder and
grandeur of psyche, its virtuality or 'always greater than me'
presence, imprisoning myself in the tight little realm of ego,
unable to deepen through soul. As I absorb the personifications of

163

my dreaming, seeing them as parts of me, then I depotentise the archetypes and the gods within them. In this way my ego becomes more unconscious of the gods, and humanism's atheism is complete. To borrow James Hillman's phrase, I erect 'a religion without gods'. Not only is the ego forced into ignorance of soul by its own efforts, but, like Oedipus, blinds itself in the process, and fails to see itself as just one possible fantasy of soul.

Indeed, as Hillman also points out, the *telos* or purpose of psyche is to actively move against humanising (as in the fabulous tales of mythology) — to dehumanise in order to rehumanise — as ego's perspective is 'seen through', and the middle ground between mind and body, that is imagination, is inhabited. In humanistic psychology's approach to the dream, the ego inflates at the expense of an imaginative response to the dream's images, which are wrestled into service of the ego. This wrestling of the imaginal into submission can be a defence against imaginative response to image, and is the way in myth of Hercules, the arch-hero, who Hillman points to as the central character within humanistic psychology's practice.

Humanistic psychology is herculean through its primary concerns — personality, self-image and self-esteem. This is in especially high profile in activities such as assertiveness training. There is also an herculean 'muscularity' about humanistic therapies — the confrontations of encounter; the mania of body-work; the bulging, here-and-now 'presence' of Gestalt — which is fed by the fantasy of wellbeing; that neurosis or bodily illness can be attacked and defeated as an enemy of potential health. The goal of humanistic psychology that takes on the same form under different names — the self-actualiser (Maslow); the fully-functioning person (Rogers); the autonomous person (Heron) — is the developed hero who will slay the dragon of dis-ease and discontent.

Humanistic psychologists always talk of 'work' — the 'workshop', where 'growthwork' is done. There is a fantasy of the Protestant ethic here — nothing happens unless we sweat at it; and, unless we 'do' our growth, we will not be called to the Elect of the 'actualised'; we will not have realised our potential. Therapists are 'trained' rather than 'educated', and indeed are sometimes called 'trainers'. Humanism's therapies become work-outs for the ego, jogging for the personality, defending against jogging the Great Memory, the stream of soul.

Now the only Olympian god who was said to work is Hephaestus the blacksmith, the ugliest, most bodily deformed and sourest in personality of the gods. We would suggest that where Hercules is explicitly the front figure within humanistic psychology's 'work', Hephaestus is its shadow. Indeed, this god represents a pathology of the body and the personality that would be anathema to the wellbeing, the natural health, fantasy of humanistic psychology. Hephaestus has, from the perspective of bodywork, extraordinarily bad posture. His feet and legs are twisted, his back is bent, he stoops. From the perspective of competent interpersonal relationships, Hephaestus scores low. He is crabby, spiteful, totally unfeeling and non-empathic, playing underhand tricks on the other Olympians. He finds it so difficult to relate to women that, as the ultimate artisan, he makes himself a woman helper and friend out of metal, a working robot — the nearest thing on Olympus to the inflatable companion doll!

But there is a more important element in Hephaestus' history that gives an insight into humanistic psychology's shadow side. Hephaestus has no father. One version of his story says that he is born parthenogenically out of Hera in an attempt by Hera to make a fool out of Zeus for his illicit affairs. Hera is saying "I don't need you to have my children by", an act of separatist feminism. However, the deed backfires on her, because, instead of the beautiful child she had hoped for, the ugly and deformed Hephaestus is born to her. She is so angry that she flings him from Olympus. He falls for a whole day, and when he lands, twists his feet so badly that they are deformed forever. However, Hephaestus forgives his mother entirely; loves her the more she hates him; is blindly devoted to her. He thus has no opportunity to resolve his Oedipus complex, to identify with a father-figure, and remains tied to the apron-strings of his mother in blind devotion.

Humanistic psychology also seems to suffer this complex. Firstly, there is no real father-figure of any substance, not in the sense of the towering Freud to psychoanalysis, or Jung to analytical psychology. Rather, there is a mish-mash born of disparate psychological traditions. Reich, Perls, Berne from psychoanalytic backgrounds; Maslow, Rogers, Schutz, from more traditional experimental psychology (all men, where Jung inspired a solid core of women analytical psychologists). Without a father-focus, humanistic psychology has hung on to a mother in the form of what William James called "tender-mindedness" as opposed to "tough-mindedness" — a soft, caring, forgiving approach that struggles to recognise the potential in us all, and uses metaphors of growth drawn from the fragile plant world.

Hence, much of the practice of humanistic psychology is literally regressive — if we are not trying to get back into the womb in primal/regression therapies to re-experience our births, then we are dealing endlessly with re-stimulation of infant or childhood distress. Also, the 'fun' end of humanistic psychology is childish — places great emphasis upon innocence, upon recapturing the supposed freedom of childhood in playworld. Central to this is the fantasy that the 'real you' is undistorted, undisturbed, fun-loving, innocent; but this has been distorted by the painful experiences of development. Then humanistic psychology also subscribes to a fantasy of naturalistic development — that if we were left to grow 'naturally', undisturbed by the nasty projections of uncaring adults, then our lives would not be distorted, and we would be free from neurosis. If our 'natural' condition is a freedom from neurosis, the implication is that Nature herself is non-neurotic, which is, archetypally, an untenable position.

So the dream is treated with the same outlook of upperworld — ego's moralisms and naturalism. The dream is said to be 'strange', 'bizzare', or 'disguised', if its images do not conform with upperworld nature, where cats usually have four legs, and elephants are not yellow. Also, from the person-perspective of humanism, the dream is likely to be judged as 'good' or 'bad' — its content subject to the moralisms of the ego.

Humanism's psychology is so taken with the fantasy of natural growth (our potential is to grow to wholeness), that all suffering is exposed to such a fantasy. There may be a tolerance of the shadow, but eventually the nasty grub must metamorphose into the beautiful butterfly — suffering must be transcended. This is a tender-minded, sentimental attitude to the tough-minded reality of the dream's pathologising. The turd is not accepted in its own right, but is considered as manure, as symbolic of growth. The rotting flesh in the dream is a precursor to the revelation of the purity and strength of the white skeleton below. Every event, no matter how grotesque, is seen in the light of potential 'growth'. The death of a loved one makes you 'stronger'; bankruptcy gives you a 'new start'; overnight redundancy from work gives you the opportunity to become self-reliant; your parents' deaths are a release because now you can grow up to realise yourself.

Here are two traps: a causalism (that distress leads to growth); and a transcendentalism (distress is growth in disguise). Then pathos or suffering does not constitute a soul-making, but is personalised, as 'character building'. Humanistic psychology may

not yet have learned the basic lesson that repression of the psyche's pathologisms — its twisted, violent and raw images — may just turn to a literalism, an acting out of violence in the world. This is why it is good for children to hear the full, gory text of the fairy story so that they can deepen to these images, can do soul-work through dreaming, as opposed to literalising the images in violence in the world, which is the herculean way.

Emotion

Body and emotion have become the substitute gods of humanistic psychology, which has made a cult of them. Therapy originally meant 'attendance to the gods'; and catharsis, 'a washing down by the soul'. The depth implied in these two words is avoided by humanistic psychology, which would rather splash about in the shallows of the tears of abreaction. The original catharsis in Greek theatre was a recognition of, and participation in, the *pathos* (suffering) and *pothos* (longing) of world soul, not simply an abreactive personal release of emotion. In this cult of abreaction, emotions are both literalised and moralised, as we see below.

In humanistic psychology's approach, the emotions are said to belong to the person, and to have their origins in the person. The ancient Greeks had no word for person. Their perspective was that emotions had their source in and belonged to soul, to archetype. The archetypal source of emotion is expressed through both the revelation and the concealment of that emotion. The impression and expression of emotion is seen against its imaginal concerns. This is best felt in a dream — who is doing the feeling here? The experiencer of the dream has been, and is still upon waking, in a myth. This myth carries the emotion, which has its source in the gods. The feeling tone of the dream is very powerful, and may set the tone for the day — we can wake up calmed or wracked, in some way extensively worked over by the dream.

Therapy, as attendance to the gods, necessarily attends to these emotions as they come through the person, but archetypal therapy recognises that the person is in the feeling; not the feeling in the person, which humanistic psychology axiomatically assumes. Therapy's original task was not to connect a person with their emotions, as, for example, 'acting out' in co-counselling attempts to do; but rather to re-connect the emotion with its source in archetype. This is achieved in a reflection upon the imaginal background to the emotion, while the emotion is returned to world soul, as a 'give-away', in recognition of its source in soul, in re-visioning its place, its *topos* or location in the scheme of things (in the *kosmos*).[2] The aim of catharsis should not then be to heal or cure, but to deepen the person to memory of soul, and to the collective of ancestors who tend the restorative vision. This vision is to see the world ensouled, as she is, in both revelation and con-cealment. This is an acceptance of divine influx, of Earth's embrace, is the vocation of the psychologist who would practice a logos of the psyche.

We have said that the experiencer of an emotion is in a myth. If that person is in an heroic myth, aided and abetted by a therapist working within the same myth (both in the service of ego), then the emotion must be released and attacked, full on, out in the open. It must be dealt with, offered up and acted upon, extraverted, not repressed or concealed. These are herculean tactics. Part of the oppressive moralism of humanistic psychology is that emotion must be extraverted, cannot be concealed.[3] This, as if a deepening cannot occur unless others can relish the details of the abreaction. From this literal and extravert perspective, we are not sure we are ill until we actually vomit on the carpet!

This new kind of oppression is aided by an oppositionalism drawn from Jung's typology — that feeling and thinking are in battle. Hence, if you are not expressing your feelings, you must be in your head or intellect. This also distorts Jung's meaning, for the feeling function in his terms is the valuing function. Emotions express themselves in both introverted and extraverted ways through all four functions: thinking, feeling, intuiting and sensing. Also, thinking need not be of the head, but of the heart, by direct knowing.

As we have said, in the cult of expression of emotions, an oppressive morality emerges that an emotion is only good if it is highly profiled, extraverted, shared. Subtlety or deeply felt emotions will not do. A glacial cold may not, however, show absence of emotion (as the Snow Queen fairy story demonstrates), or a bad emotion, but an emotion in its own right, beyond the milk of human kindness, born of a 'tough-minded' strain. To assume that it is good to get in touch with feelings per se is quite extra-ordinary when we remember that mass murderers, torturers, sexual sadists, child abusers, are fully in touch with very deep emotions indeed.

One of the defining features of soul is that it is the unknown

factor which deepens events into experiences.[4] Humanistic psychology's weekend workshop smorgasbord may be jam-packed with events that mostly do not deepen to experiences, because of an explicit lack of soul perspective. Humanistic psychology is quite obsessive about 'experiences' — experiential learning, games, intensives, exercises — in its avoidance of anything that smacks of intellect, passive learning, lecture. Simply to have an experience, however, says nothing of the value or worth of the experience, which may remain an event for the individual. It is not unusual for the weekend workshop to leave individuals in a 'high' when they leave, but to have remembered little or nothing of this a month later. Again, events may have happened, but these did not deepen to experiences, and carried little or no meaning. The ego craves events, and 'highs' rather than 'depths'.

The compulsion for experiences, in humanistic psychology's terms, is a neurosis in itself, a mania that is characterised by the labours of Hercules. Again, to have an experience is to 'work' on something — it is strenuous, muscular, literal. A mania is a good defence against deepening to soul (for example through the slow grindings, the long, tortuous accounts, or the time-wastings of Saturn), because it keeps the person right there on top of things, furiously working with the overspill, whilst screwing down the lid on the soul's can of worms. The client is then in the shallows, working with what is 'on top', obsessed with the Gestalt here-and-now, which the therapist attends to in avoidance of attendance to the gods.

This manic approach, seen especially in bodywork such as bio-energetics, does not tolerate slow deepening, the frustrations of melancholia, and tends to both attract and show little understanding of depressives in therapy. Archetypal psychology itself is explicitly depressive, morbid, preferring to call humanistic psychology's 'clients', 'patients'. For it is patience that the humanistic approach seems to lack. For example, bio-energetics[5] sees depression as symptomatic of a depressed energy system, and tries to immediately raise body energy, in the same way that a naive counsellor would try to raise the 'spirits' of the depressive, rather than attending to the voice of soul.

In this strategy of a quick cure-by-raising, as opposed to slow education-through-deepening, humanistic psychology makes a move that avoids deepening to its own roots. Then the ancestors are forgotten, the lingering culture, the sense of history. Even psychology's ancestors are forgotten, as humanistic psychology

171

claims that its history begins with the first T-groups at Bethel, Maine; and Carl Rogers' first person-centred counselling sessions at Chicago in the 1940's. This, rather than seeing its psychology as a product of philosophical humanism, an approach that can certainly be traced back to Greek rationalist thought.

In staying with the surface of its own history, and with the surface in therapy, humanistic psychology avoids its own shadow (personified in Hephaestus), tending to remain self-congratulatory. Hercules cannot bear to be with the dwellers in Hades, so he attacks them. Humanistic psychology cannot bear to be with its own morbidity, so it talks of optimism, positivity, peak-experiences, growth to wholeness — ideal types that transcend pathos. These are inflation fantasies — up and away with the spirit rather than deepening, soul-making. This leads to an ego polished by assertiveness training and 'positive strokes', that can strut the world full of confidence, high self-esteem, high competence, blooming with bodily wellbeing. But this is hollow, a seasonal blossom with no root. As we have said, what the humanistic practitioner then finds most difficult (but of course, attracts) is the client with severe depression, who is permanently at the root, and never smells the blossom.

The centre of wellbeing that humanistic psychology says is at the centre of us all is described by the bioenergeticist John Pierrakos as the CORE — Centre of Right Energy. This is a clear example of the fantasy of wellbeing. In humanism's psychology you are at the centre of things — Man the Measure. The energy you experience in this place of balance (at the centre of the mandala in the fantasy of wholeness), is right, dextrous; not left, left-over, sinister, splintered, difficult, morbid; the edge of a ragged wound rather than the source of natural health. From here you can beam out orgasmic potency and lack of muscular armouring, because your ego has, under the careful protection of the nourishing therapist or nurturing group, ripened from the seed it was into full fruit. The growth shows no decay — is in sunlight rather than shadow — and the fruit is packed with the juices of positive affirmation, good posture and here-and-nowness. In fact it is blooming with the healthy glow of a newborn, fresh from yesterday's rebirthing session.

But nobody told you that the fall hurts more from this height, when the manic euphoria is torn by a ragged edge of soul, as the inevitable mid-life crisis hits you anyway. And no amount of self-delusion at this point will convince you that you are now better prepared for material bankruptcy through your therapy, when the reason for current poverty is your therapy fees! And, to add insult to injury, all that egoic work was paradoxically counter-productive because now you are spiritually bankrupt and cannot find a way through the meaningless of the world. For, despite your authentic human relating, you never learned in your 'work' to relate authentically to the gods.

Body

In humanistic psychology the body is not seen as a fantasy of soul, but is literalised, worked on directly in manipulation and touch, in breathing and movement, as if it were a machine being tuned — but tuned to what? We would call much body'work' (that Hephaestean fantasy again!), 'muscling out the ego'. In bodywork, energy is characteristically 'raised' (the inflating, upward striving of spirit), rather than deepened to. This again realises an oppressive move, for energy must be seen to be raised, must be extra-verted. The cushions must be seen to be beaten; the tennis racquet and encounter bat swung; the voice raised to shouting or scream-ing. So, instead of sticking with that saturnine grinding down and stretching out of time in lulls, lacunae; moments of depression, of incipient plague, of morbidity; a shadow slowly creeping across the sun; somebody somewhere in a group will usually start to fidget, move about, look angry, and say "nothing is happening; we need to raise the energy; let's get out of our heads and into our bodies!" This, in the literal hope of raising spirits; thus crushing the depression and defending against feeling the soul of the world right there in what is most uncomfortable and displacing.

This manic energy-raising is Hercules the misogynist punishing the feminine Earth. The Hercules who so desperately desires immortality or eternal wellbeing — to be raised to Olympus to sit with the gods. Bodyworkers claim that their techniques are largely about 'grounding' — back into body, and back in touch with earth. There is a paradox here. We suspect that bodyworkers are closet Icaruses, driven, like Hercules, with a desire to rid themselves of earthly connections and ascend to a place of pure, streaming energy. Hercules has a phobia about deepening, characterised in his wildly aggressive, intolerant attitude to the underworld. As a misogynist he is frightened by the womb-ness, the close-ness, of interior Earth.

174

Somebody in a group is facilitated into 'getting in touch with their anger', through hitting a mattress with a tennis racquet. As the racquet beats the earth into submission, or punishes the ground, so the energy and spirits of the person are raised, as the anger is touched and released in abreaction. But the grounding here is false, for as the technique draws one back into person, personality, muscle, so one is drawn away from contact with the Earth herself, which has been attacked. Then a contact with *anima mundi* is avoided, as the grounding is into literal body. And the contact with anger is felt as a privatised event, a grounding in ego. This, rather than a return of the emotion to its source in soul, the kind of grounding that is a stopping dead in one's tracks and pondering the gravity of life with one's whole being — a saturnine turning — right in the midst of high spirits during your fortieth birthday party. For the bodyworker, raising energy and spirit to avoid the depressive soul, first comes the birthday champagne, then the hangover. First the bubble, then the burst! The archetypal reality however, is that the hangover is given with, is inherent to the champagne.

In the fiery heat of ego-centred anger we may spot Phaeton, who unintentionally, but ignorantly, drove Helios' chariot of the sun so close to Earth that he scorched its surface to dust and dried up the rivers. As the dust from the old mattress settles about us, and we are left limply clinging to the racquet, we too may feel that somehow we have slipped by our deeper intentions with our 'growth work'.

Although they would claim that the verbal is often a resistance to being in the body, Bodyworkers' body-talk can be seen as a resistance to the verbal, a poke in the eye for Hermes, who, paradoxically would be the very one to guide you to soul if only your body-chatter would stop and let him get a word in edgeways! The chatter of the body is a prurience, an incessant itch that is satisfied only by activity, movement, and this may drive the bodyworker to another oppressive moralism — that the non-verbal is somehow more truthful and authentic than the verbal: 'the body never lies'. The trickster Hermes with his twisted truths would have something to say on the hypocritical moralism of such 'authenticity'. Again, in those deepening moments in a group when a necessary melancholy sets in, it is usually the compulsive, prurient non-verbal chatter of the bodyworker that resists the very earthing or grounding he so desperately seeks, by not sticking with the stickiness, the turgidity, the lumpiness of the inactive weight.

175

Text of Sensation

Bodywork, perhaps more than any other aspect of humanistic psychology, is fanatically prescriptive: the right posture; the best touch (for health); the right way for energy to flow (life affirmative). Each approach contradicts the next: rolfing versus Alexander; rebirthing versus primal; practitioner manipulation versus self-regulation. This, instead of each approach relativising, or trying to see through itself, through its own practice, to discover its inherent archetype(s) or imaginal context(s). Then we may ask 'who?' does the practice serve, rather than 'what?' does the practice do. Artemis' and Apollo's arrows may be in the body-straightening fantasy of rolfing; the compulsive worker Hephaestus in bioenergetics (then we would have to tolerate his twisted body — the clue is there anyway in Hephaestus' feet being twisted back-to-front, a strange pigeon-toed-ness not dissimilar to the basic bioenergetic 'grounding' position, as Lowen[6] describes it). And the tall, straight warrior Ares behind both the passionate deliberateness and frozen delicacy of Alexander technique, with a knowledge that rage is right there just an inch below the surface.

Finally, there is the rather radical danger that the bodywork counter culture develops into a kind of pornocracy — a society based on trading money for bodily pleasures, where the practitioner becomes harlot to the client. The professional Boyesen bio-dynamic therapist, complete with compulsory clinical white coat and stethoscope then becoming the butt of a new body of jokes — "please take off your clothes. It's o.k., I'm *almost* a doctor!" Your local 'Natural Health Alternative Directory' becomes the new contact magazine; and each 'Wellbeing Centre', the best little whorehouse in town! True to humanistic psychology's tender-mindedness, this is however, the softest of porn!

And, as you scan the directory, you can choose from any number of other people's models of how humans should be. In a trice, the hunchback is rolfed out of existence before we have asked the question 'who?' of him. And body and feeling are straightened according to pre-set norms, as opposed to being seen against a wide range of archetypal possibility, including both the con-genital and acquired hunch, that may not be the bodily expression of carrying heavy burdens of guilt, responsibility or doubt; and may not be years of stored-up anger, but rather the soul's inherent question-mark — the archetypal 'who?' of which god resides here in the symptom or dis-ease. To which there is no straight answer or answer of straightening. Then emotions and body-sense are returned to their archetypal source, and to the specific images that hold and inform them, rather than being held within the personality only.

Imaging

In an attempted resolution of its guilt over negligence of the sublime, humanistic psychology has gone transpersonal — more in its technology than philosophy — embracing the methods of imaging, of active and passive, guided and spontaneous imagery.[7] Here, the slumbering dragon of imagination, deep in its lair, really does have to be on its guard for the wily St. George.

Humanistic psychology tends to literalise, as we have seen with its approach to the body. Hence, where the body is taken as real, the image is still taken as something other than reality. Body and image tend to be opposed. Now this move tends to treat imagination and archetype as 'things that are', as opposed to moves that one makes, or ways in which one may re-cognise the world. Imagery tends to be confined to a process of visualisation, seeing inner pictures with the mind's eye as it were, rather than imagination as a recognition of the interiority of all phenomena in direct perception, through their given appearances, the faces they present.

Guided imagery in particular is humanism's newest and most insolent attack upon the imaginal, in the service of ego, even believing that it is doing psyche a service. For it is deeply manipulative of psyche, raining an assault of suggestion from the sling of the therapist's or guide's ego, only to draw the response immediately back into the service of the client's ego. For images are returned to the client as reflections and informants about her personality, her ego state, as if these images were her property. In binding images to personality in this way, therapist and client collude to avoid making soul, but rather bolster ego.

We have mentioned the assumption that images are interior to the person, and hence the guided journey is interior. This misses the living out of life in a world ensouled, seen in its everyday aspect as living in and with images, with the angelic presence or 'divine influx' that characterises all phenomena recognised as ensouled; where interior versus exterior becomes another limiting oppositionalism. We could instead talk of *interiorising*, as a move that sees through both the literal surface of things, and does not demand a literal looking inside. Here, we stick with the presented

178

face of phenomena, with things as they are, with the image as it is. The business of getting images up, from the interior person, is fuelled by the fantasy of mining some interior psychic space, of mining the Earth herself, and here we are again in the presence of Hephaestus the ore-worker. Just as we rape the Earth of her interior riches and resources, so the guide may relish the details of the client's interior journey, and 'inner space' is hailed as the last frontier, waiting to be mapped. Then we recognise the same imperialist thrust that wishes to conquer and control all of Nature.

Rather than using imaging to get at inner subpersonalities that manifest in outer symptom, we might come to appreciate the guiding fictions in the outer face of our everyday behaviour. Then we would avoid the inner versus outer opposition. We might recognise, as we have said above, the interiority of events that are deepened to experiences, without searching through the literal insides of the person. Then we might recognise the faces of deities in symptoms, and discover a range of archetypal possibility within which we are embedded, to which we are already interior. A trans-personal approach that is still tied to a logos of the person may attempt to help people 'discover their myth', but this seems to be a reversal of soul's intent. Myth refuses to be reduced to per-sonality dynamics. Rather than the ego discovering, mining, searching for; let us allow soul to reveal and conceal herself. And our discovery would be how best to respond to image imaginatively, how best to relate to soul's divine influx.

Then as we have said, it is not we who individuate, but images themselves, in their revelations. But this individuation must not be confused with literal growth, within the developmental fantasy; nor with a transcendentalism. The guide stuck in these fantasies wants the client's images to grow up, as if, and so that, the client may also grow up. Then the jewel is always looked for within the dung, rather than the dung being responded to directly, as we mentioned previously. Then the dishevelled, maimed and hungry child is encouraged to similarly transform, through feed-ing and care perhaps — the tender-mindedness of humanistic psychology inappropriately applied to a tough-minded image — so that a well-formed adult emerges, in a state of wellbeing, and the pathos is transcended.

Given that the soul is by nature multiplex, we would expect its imaginings to be splintered — many archetypal possibilities with-in which the person moves. Yet many transpersonal approaches retain the humanistic 'I', the ego, at the centre of things. By

shifting this to a transpersonal centre, a Self, or overself, we may be like Hercules entering the underworld. Then, like the dream ego itself, we may act quite inappropriately through the fantasies of ego within a context that is dehumanising, mythological, seeing through ego's mania, inflations, and narrowness of vision. Out of ego's perspective, it is impossible to talk of the 'I' in the dream, with the dream's many personifications, its many daemons, its multi-faceted nature.

We can often catch the dream ego in its herculean guise within the dream — censoring images, denying imaginative possibility, dissolving and destroying the terrible phantoms that inhabit such an underworld. Also, personality itself may censor the dream as it is reported. Liam Hudson[8] reports research on dreaming that demonstrates convergent personality types especially repressing or censoring pathologised images in dream, as the dream is reported. So Hercules stands at the gate of Hades, having strangled its guard-dog Cerberos, and clubs into shape the soul's talk so that it is acceptable to ego. This invites at every moment the dangerous turn of literalism that catches upperworld's ego smack in the teeth on the backswing of the club, as underworld's images and personifications are beaten back.

The Group

We might expect to find multiple voice and vision in a group context, where we are face to face with differing people. Oddly enough however, we may just discover a set of conformities and collusions that swamp the individual voice in a convention of groundrules for authentic relating — Schutzian rules of encounter. These are supposed to liberate the person from her predictable patterns of behaviour, but, paradoxically, from psyche's perspective they again look like rules of the prison of ego and personality. Such rules may include sticking with the here and now, which instantly squashes history — the voice of the ancestors, the collective of memory. Also, always talking from the 'I', to avoid generalising, thus bringing everyone back into their skins, their privatised egos, rather than, albeit clumsily, moving in a sense of the collective, of shared and common experience. Again, if I talk from my own experience, the implication is that I own that experience. Then I restrict myself from participation in what is immediately available to us all, common world soul, right in here-

181

and-nowness in the sense of the zen 'instant'; right there and then in the ancestral Dream Time; and right there and then in the inevitability of our deaths.

In this climate of authenticity ('say what you feel'), a trickster god such as Hermes, or a two-timer such as Aphrodite or Zeus, is denied a ticket. Rather, Athena rules the day with her peer principles of negotiation, of contracts and honest talk. She is helped by the deeply conservative Hestia, because, despite the claims that the group is a laboratory for innovative relating, it rapidly becomes a stereotypical normative culture, albeit 'counter' to the mainstream, closed to real change. The same subtle oppressions and collusive moves that happen in the mainstream culture happen here also, in a different form. Rules are still primary, and the ruler, the group facilitator, leader or trainer, actually still holds most of the power, despite Athena's push for democratisation. It still holds that the superstars of humanistic psychology are the charismatic leaders.

The group may also be seen, with its members' striving for honesty and authenticity in relating, as within the archetype of Apollonic truth. This is the polished truth of competence and convincing performance, the kind whose shadow is the trickster's twists and half-truths. But let us then expect that, as with a charismatic leader, Apollo may blind us to our possibilities through his own brilliance. He may fill the room with his illuminations. Then the dirt may get kicked under the carpet as the group is neatly transformed in a weekend to the genital phase, culminating in a great melting pot of confluences, the circle complete in a glowing group hug. Then the therapist-as-healer is the shaman-as-showman, and each participant has encountered a series of sparkling events which have failed to deepen to experiences, and the following month, life's sufferings grind back, the group event now a drug whose effects have worn off, whose promises have worn thin.

Many kinds of groups are possible of course, and a group gets the god(s) it deserves or invokes; but this is often no god at all, as the invocations of the deities are replaced by evocations of human abreaction, and childhood memories replace the soul's *memoria* as the focus of the Great Work.

A Myth of the Person Without Myths

If humanistic psychology could see through itself, it might discover that it is a myth without myths. Jung observed that modern man was in search of soul, of restoring imagination, where we are saying that humanism's psychology never wanted a soul, being too busy in its preoccupation with ego and personality. As we have said, humanistic psychology is so concerned with its authentic relating of person to person, that it has never learned to relate to archetype — or rather, to relate archetypally — to recognise the gods at play in the world. Indeed, by its nature humanistic psychology cannot devise a language that is not self-referential, such as a mythical or poetic language.

As James Hillman points out, the ego that is so concerned with its mechanisms of defence — denials, repressions, distortions, disguise — fails to see through its fallacies of literalism, naturalism, moralism, and as we see here, humanism and personalism. Where we dwell on mum and dad, the many faceted stories of the Mothers and Fathers may remain untouched for their revelations, and a whole cultural enterprise is cast to the winds also. In its desire for here-and-now coping strategies and development of Will, humanistic psychology holds its self-esteem together in the face of a chequered and splintered personal history, and a looming, unacknowledged shadow. It stands in the shallows of culture, rather than deepening to culture's history. And worse, returns nothing of depth and substance to the culture's interiority, to world soul. Humanism grows away from soul into a swelling of the person in self-awareness, thinking it has conquered human nature in the process. But it has shrunk from animated Nature, from an angelic metaxy, from the elementals that truly work Nature, or bring her into being. As Hillman further remarks, humanistic psychology "builds a strong man of frail soul trembling in the valley of existential dread".[9]

This seems like a strong criticism until we add up, and own up to, all the violences to soul perpetrated by the humanistic approach. Yet the ego ultimately violates itself, for the psyche is not unconscious at all, as ego assumes. Rather, it is ego itself that is unconscious of psyche, but thinks it lives in consciousness of the whole world. Ego is a projection of imagination, rather than imagination being a projection from the person on to the world. But this particular projection that is ego is just one fantasy of soul, one of its multiple possibilities through which we may choose to

It Doesn't Matter Any More ♪♫

live. When everything is reduced to the person, then the animal, mineral and plant parts of us may also be denied. The human is centre-stage, and therapy's job is distorted in maintaining this false posture. And insult is added to injury when humanistic psychology's moralism demands that we must discover our potential, or grow into what we might become, otherwise we live in a false world, unrealised to ourselves and inauthentic in our relations with others.

Humanistic psychology speaks with a forked tongue when it encourages us to get in touch with our own process, our own potential, for in practice it busily tries to fit us into somebody else's model, somebody else's potential. Thus we become a Maslovian self-actualiser; a Rogerian fully-functioning person; a Reichian orgasmically-potent person, free from body armouring; an Assagiolian in dialogue with our transpersonal centre, and so forth. And the titles of the classic literature in the field reflect and reinforce this supposed littleness that we now are, this incompleteness; and the greatness and wholeness to which we can grow. (Followed by dozens of contemporary imitators, all claiming great things for their practices — recall the rash promises of the Rebirthing literature that I quoted at the beginning of this chapter). Reich's "Listen, Little Man" addresses our stunted bodies; Rogers' "On Becoming a Person", Maslow's "The Farther Reaches of Human Nature" tells us that we are not *it* yet, but we could become *it*; and Rowan's title, "Ordinary Ecstasy", implies that we should all be getting *it* in mind-blowing proportions simply tying our shoelaces.

The Language of Love

If humanistic psychology is a religion without gods, a myth without myths, it is also a practice devoid of poetic sensibility and an explicit aesthetic. Its practitioners are fixed more on the utility than the aesthetic of their work. This may be because what is accepted as beautiful within humanistic psychology is the transcendental rather than the genuinely innovative and the disturbingly exciting deepenings of soul. After all, humanistic psychology did not grow out of pathology. Where Jung's experience as a young psychiatrist with disturbed psychotics laid the ground of his understanding of the psyche's pathologisms, Maslow began with the normal, and the self-actualisers. The polish and gleam of the high-flier, the realiser of potential, the transcender of life's problems, the highly assertive and competent human relater, may catch the eye more easily for the humanistic psychologist than the perhaps intrinsically more beautiful and worthy patina of the dull melancholic or depressive, or the genuinely crazy who spit in the eye of accepted social competence. When humanistic psychology goes transpersonal, it tends to look to the East, to transcendent practices of meditation and altered states of consciousness, rather than deepening to western culture's alchemical tradition, which is perhaps not so instantly snazzy or snappy.

That which gleams the most is instantly attractive — hence the magpie syndrome of humanistic psychology, its turnaround of fashion, both therapists and clients keen for the next technique. Last month, neuro-linguistic programming; this month, rebirthing. We have said that staying on the surface, working with the overspill in the here-and-now, is characteristic of much of humanistic psychology's approach. We wonder then if the tender-minded love of its practitioners is also on the surface, in the sense that Eros, the god of love, is invoked in his sentimental aspect, as Cupid, rather than his gritty underworld aspect as Thanatos, as a dark angel close to death itself. Hillman reminds us that transference in its archetypal aspect is not symbolic love between client and therapist, but the client's deep need to learn to love image; an education into a close and loving relationship also with the darker source of image in underworld; and then with death.

We will see in the following chapter that Freud had to redefine eros, had to accept the underworld face of eros, as a death instinct. Now the literalisation of this by ego would be a translation into suicide, where the soul is not calling for literal death, but an understanding by ego of the closeness to death of all things; an understanding that the interiority of all phenomena, soul-nature, is the underworld perspective given in a dream. A death in a dream is not literal, because the dream is already in death. So, a call to suicide by the soul is its way of loving us to death, by prodding ego to gain an imagistic perspective in which ego symbolically dies, as in a zen awareness, to reveal soul where ego was. This is not the literal taking of one's life. Such a perspective demands that we re-vision love in its darkest aspects, in an appreciation of the shadow that all relationships carry.

Humanism has not responded to the underworld origin of Eros, tending to idealise love and relationships through the developmental fantasy. It tends to transcend the melancholic aspect of

PILLOW TALK

love, in searching for a 'healthy relationship', a wellbeing marriage. Love through (and love of) the soul's suffering was well described by Ficino[10], the Renaissance Platonist, as an aesthetic, a way of beauty. Love has its locus in imagination rather than just the body, so that eroticism need not be literalised into a pornography. As we have said, the pathologised and eroticised image that demands a response must be responded to on its own terms, as it comes, and this could include a loving response. The archetypal perspective says that we must love image in order for image to individuate or show its face in the nature of things — Blake's "portions of eternity" presenting themselves to the senses informed by imagination. Blake says that such "ever Existent Images" are available to "the Imaginative Eye of Every one according to the situation he holds".

As Blake talks of seeing, so Edward Casey[11] says that an image is not what one sees, but the way one sees. 'Seeing' here is not literal, visual, but imaginative perception. And we should remind ourselves again of Hillman's[12] central idea that an archetype is not a thing that is, but a move one makes. Further, it is a loving move, and a move that carries value and creates value, or makes soul. Love of image then does not restrict eros to personal relations, but embeds this in a wider matrix. We said earlier that humanistic psychology has not invented a soulful language. Rather, its language is impoverished because it is restrictively self-referential, narcissistic; a language of personal love and not of love of the transpersonal. Such a language does not jog one to memory of soul, for it is not an angelism[13], is not carried by angels, but by the personal mouth. It is angels that are attendant upon deified and animated language, easily seen in the poetry of Blake. A language charged with such angelic passion has both winged feet and shoulders, enabling a passage to highest reaches of sky and furthest depths of earth. In other words, such charged language has both value and range, does not limit itself to description of the personal and interpersonal realms.

It is as if humanistic psychology, like the similarly impoverished experimental psychology, has to neologise to compensate for a lack of mythical, poetic and improbable language (description by metaphor for example). Some of this hollow language has already been mentioned — mechanistic buzz-words and phrases such as 'actualising tendency', 'fully functioning', implying that we can be tuned, like well-oiled machines. The language of love that permeates alchemy, mythology, religious texts, romantic art and science, poetry, seems to be squeezed out by arid techno-speak in humanistic psychology just as much as in the more expected quarters of statistics, experimental psychology, sociology, politics, economics and scientism.

We might fruitfully contrast a text of Maslow's, packed with jargon such as "deficiency-needs" and "being-needs", with Medieval and Renaissance language, that is closer to the soil, to the Earth herself, both less personalised and less abstract. The latter is an animated language, mythical yet earthy and sensual, shot through with soul-talk and talk of the soul, which, in seeing through to the world as it is, allows the world to individuate in its own images. It is deadly rather than deadening, stunning us into a deepening or putting us in a state of suspension, as our best poet Shakespeare does at every turn. This, rather than puffing us up with false hope of salvation in self-actualisation, where the person becomes a world explained and contained. Humanistic psychology's language in this sense becomes technological (such as 'neuro-linguistic programming'), the patina of empty scientific jargon supposedly offering greater credence in a world duped by such language.

By Way of an Apology

I am aware that my critical comment upon the herculean tactics of the ego that humanistic psychology often inadvertantly reinforces, carries a shadow — that the criticism itself may smack of muscular heroism. This may add up to a rather hypocritical posturing. However, in defence I would suggest that my criticism is not herculean (anti-imaginal), but vigorous and tough-minded while pro-imaginal.

189

Awareness-through-posture

The interior Christ is tested
On the tau-cross of
Spine and shoulder-bone.

There he hangs, dark Osiris,
A body of black muscle
Resting on stations of bone,

His head always pitched
To the sinister side,
Christ wrapped into the white tree

That is the skeleton
With its scapular crown,
Pulling himself up by the wrists.

Christ's skin blackened by the sun;
His white bones ascending,
Their whereabouts kept secret.

Chapter 6

The 'alternative' society may be too quick to put down some of the better technological achievements of the mainstream culture, especially with regard to the city. The view that any urban development is bad and any rural environment good is far too simplistic. While the city can be seen to have soul, farming can be seen to have caused immense damage to the 'green' of the world. The tension between 'nature' and 'technology' may be seen as that between eros and logos: feeling/connecting and thinking/discriminating. These are often opposed by New Age thinking as, respectively, heart and head, love and mind. Then a moralism is introduced, where heart is preferred to mind. But this opposition misses the subtleties both of a thinking of the heart and a tender-minded logic. Rather, we could dissolve the opposition and see eros and logos in tandem. Eros holds close, in subjectivity and participation. Logos distances, in objectivity and observation. Relationships show both tendencies, and both have their shadow — a suffocating eros and a cold, uncaring logos.

In this chapter, I try to give relating meaning and depth — a logos of eros — to remind us that Eros is a god of the underworld. Relating must not stay on the surface if it is to be deepening and of value, and therapies which deal with human relating must be depth therapies if they are to be valuable. The goldenness of Aphrodite shows through from the depths when we stop taking the world for granted and start seeing her depths. Then we stop leading surface lives and deepen to soul, only to find that we are re-surfacing the world with depth, for the value of the world shows through the faces of things, in their self-presentation, as we have said. This may literally be on the surface — for example in the way an animal walks, or a person smiles. But this surface reveals depths, or interiority, when we catch it in a soul-ful looking. The *surface persona is then given face-value, is tolerated for what it is, but with a knowing. A relationship of any value will also be given this re-spect, this second look that catches interiority and depth, because it is a reflective look.*

The Fantasy of Ideal Relating

When the archetype of intimacy is personified, or given a face, then, as James Hillman[1] points out, "Eros...is masculine. Its imagery in various cultures confirms this. Kama, Eros, Cupid, Frey, Adonis, Tammuz, all are male; and the incarnations of enlightened love, Krishna, Buddha, Jesus — for all their gentleness and forbearance in regard to sexual fertility — are masculine." Hillman argues that eros is a "mover", a teacher, "active and aimed".

Feminine eros is not personified — it is the binding force of relationship itself, and a collective embrace, undifferentiated Love, the all-embracing Earth. This is different from the personified and personalised eros that the great teachers carry as loving persons; for no matter what the teachers say of unconditional regard, their love-in-action is still conditional upon their religious concerns, their value systems; and is then discriminatory.

The task of an avatar is to personalise eros for the collective of humankind, as an example of what the Buddha called "right action". This is to show how deeply and passionately relationship to fellow humans can be experienced. But the great teachers also tell of a passionate engagement with death: thanatos or anteros. Christ is sacrificed for humankind, having been betrayed; Arjuna in Hindu lore dies of a deep sorrow; Buddha dies of food poisoning when served contaminated meat by a disciple; Krishna dies when an arrow hits his vulnerable heel; Mohammed dies from fever; Socrates dies from hemlock poisoning; Zoroaster, said to have laughed as soon as he was born, is murdered.

What the masculine avatars do is to bring the undifferentiated world eros into sharp focus, into action, as ethic — the word, the law, a logos of eros. Now eros can be understood as well as felt; differentiated into styles, and cultivated. The act of therapy is based on such differentiation of eros. Psychology is, properly, a logos of the psyche. Eros is the heart of psyche, as Love; but love

192

needs its differentiation in human action and concern. Plato said that "...the treatment of the soul is by means of certain charms, and these charms are words of the right sort". The avatars carry loving yet challenging words of significance that deepen us to quality of relationship. In therapeutic jargon, we might call such words 'appropriate interventions'. Certainly they are shot through with empathy and heart-felt positive regard. A therapy that is a logos of soul will facilitate the acting out of eros in the world, giving meaning to a previously undifferentiated force, in the creating of particular (and often peculiar), fulfilling relationships.

The relationship that our culture holds up as fulfilling reflects a concern to avoid the shadow of things, the depths, and so falls into the category that Guggenbuhl describes as 'wellbeing' (as opposed to 'individuation' relationships), which we look at in more detail later in this chapter. This ideal of relating — that would stay on the surface with the honeymoon glow, the shine of fresh-ness, and not look to the patina that comes with ageing — is a tremendously powerful guiding fiction. It draws from the upperworld, wellbeing eros, rather than the underworld, morbistic anteros. The latter recognises that relationships carry suffering as well as joy if they are to deepen us to soul. An idealistic fantasy of such shining eros in community is of a wellbeing culture free from strife — a utopia — such as the vision of the Aquarian New Age.

This is the enduring myth of a Golden Age that was, or is to be. The fantasy of a possible Golden Age now, is fuelled by the same outlook that wants eternal youth, the elixir of the Chinese alchemists. Here, linear time is an enemy, to be defeated or controlled. Hence, the science fiction fantasies of time travel, and of suspended ageing such as quick-freeze or cryonic suspension. The fantasy of an idyllic eros, an ideal relating, where happiness and harmony prevail, suffering is denied and change resented, is embodied in a number of utopian outlooks. That such outlooks are underpinned by conflicting value systems allows us to see through the whole notion of a Golden Age pretending to suit all temperaments. For example, Marx's utopia stresses an authentic relating through equality, derived from equal distribution of wealth and from common ownership of the means of production. In the re-arrangement of economic relations, overcoming abuse of labour, human relating becomes authentic. However, Plato, in *The Republic*, suggests that an ideal eros evolves from an acceptance of inequality — that one fulfills the social role to which one is best adapted, maintaining a conservative eros, as a caste system. Thomas More's *Utopia* and Carl Rogers'[2] ideal of "building person-centred communities" rests on the implementation of an humanistic eros, where skillful interpersonal relating is given ultimate importance. This can be repressive for the introverted, private eccentric, who will be stigmatised as an unskillful relater, and negatively valued for repressing 'potential'.

The Keeper of the Lighthouse and Underworld Eros

Cultures often embody their aspirations in their architecture — for example, 'high rise' aspirations that seek wellbeing, transcendence, a movement away from base earth, may be reflected in towers. But every tower or towering building that reaches for union with the sky, must have its foundations, and will throw a shadow. The higher the tower, the bigger the shadow when the sun is low. This reminds us that the higher the puer flies, the farther is the fall. The lighthouse is a particularly good image for this relationship between height and depth, and light and shadow. For the searching light is raised high, away from the dark rocks, the thundering sea, the promise of death. The raised light guides the sailor yet reminds him of the ever-presence of danger. Also, the outer tower is phallic, stiff. But the lighthouse has an inner winding stair. The hard then marries the soft. The straight up-and-down has to co-exist with the gradual, spiralling ascent and descent, the slower winding-up and winding-down.

Just as the lighthouse keeper maintains a monthly work rhythm of alternate shore-leave and duty, so the man who wants to tend his own guiding light must first enter the dark feminine world of the inner lighthouse, and climb its winding stair. In part, this is a reflection upon the dark interior of the body in the company of the Black goddesses.

The king, or senex, who will set up a kingdom, will build his tower to the male god, a stairway to heaven, both to move away from his mother's embrace and to erect a logos, or laws through which eros or relating may be enacted. These laws are the social customs of relating. of marriage, and the taboos which, for example, ban sexual relationships within families. When the king is young, he is not fully socialised and may scorn certain taboos. He comes to recognise his individuality in this manner. But this puer striving will need to encounter a slowing down, which the winding stair imposes. He will probably fall from a great height in a mid-life crisis, into the vale of soul, and will suffer. But he will discover fresh eros and refreshed imagination. He must apply these insights in social change, so that the waste land is redeemed. The anima symbols he was destined to carry do not bind him blindly to service to the feminine principle, but allow eros to permeate his statesmanship. Then his discrimination is not just sharp, but also caring. Anima also forces him to look at aesthetic in his kingdom. For a social order built on utility alone (as with many modern cities), or on struggles of power (as with the ever-changing military juntas), have eros dried out of them, and do not concern themselves with beauty. His art collection is not primarily a monetary investment, but a vote of confidence for the artist's position; and, the art made accessible to the public, a restoration of beauty to the common waste-land.

Logos-oriented rulers and social orders fall because they crystallise, lose feeling, lose relating, and become de-humanising and de-souled. Then they fall more quickly to time, a theme that we renew later in this chapter. We find logos and eros personified in the central characters of Virginia Woolf's *To the Lighthouse*, where Mr. Ramsay " . . . was incapable of untruth; never tampered with a fact; never altered a disagreeable word to suit the pleasure

195

or convenience of any mortal being, least of all his own children. . . " Mr. Ramsay had poor access to eros, to relating, as a dried-out scholar with a passion for abstract thinking.

Mrs. Ramsay however oozed eros, in fact dominated with her need for relating: "She disliked anything that reminded her that she had been sitting thinking." In the background is the lighthouse, and the trip to the lighthouse, that acts as a symbol for what may remain permanent in a world of changing feelings within relationships. And what is permanent in this sense, beyond personalism and humanism, beyond ego relating to ego, is our relationship to soul and to imagination. More importantly, it is the passing on of knowledge of the conditions under which we are grasped by the daemon of imagination without losing our souls; without trading with drink, or drugs, or the too-early call to suicide.

Woolf's Mr. and Mrs. Ramsay have a particular kind of relationship. In short, the man is outwardly cold and logical, and sterile; where the woman is fecund, warm and accepting. When the two meet, there is a distressing tension: "Mrs. Ramsay, who had been sitting loosely, folding her son in her arm, braced herself, and, half turning, seemed to raise herself with an effort, and at once to pour erect into the air a rain of energy, a column of spray, looking at the same time animated and alive as if all her energies were being fused into force, burning and illuminating. . ., and into this delicious fecundity, this fountain and spray of life, the fatal sterility of the male plunged itself, like a beak of brass, barren and bare."

Guggenbuhl[3] talks of two kinds of marriage, one based on a guiding fiction of well-being, another on the guiding fiction of individuation. In the former, whatever may upset the apple-cart, cause tension, is quickly swept under the carpet, and the surface remains unruffled. To outsiders, this looks like a harmonious relationship. But it is fraught with repressive social manner. There is no deep circulation between partners, because depths are kept private, not shared; for the lid must not be prised off the can of worms, in fear of the consequences. The individuation relationship, in contrast, demands that the can of worms be regularly inspected, and expects tensions and regular review of the relationship. For this is an alchemical relationship in which partners are trying to not lose their individuality to the relationship, while cultivating the riches of a partnership. The partnership may look awkward and ill-matched to outsiders. It has to be continually worked on, looked into, because depths are shared (as with a therapist and patient). The individuals help each others' creative lives, one informing the other in a circulation and a coincidence of opposites, where each benefits. Lacunae of ignorance are filled with the others' help. Challenge and confrontation are explicit, but the love between these partners is deep, because they ride the storms of disagreement and learn from the experience.

Many styles of relationship, including well-being and individuation marriages, are sketched in myth, for example in the partnerships between the Olympian deities, and provide an informative background against which we may see our own partnership choices. We can sketch some of these as: 1) Where the man is dominant and the wife complains to her friends of his shortcomings and infidelities, but remains faithful to him. This is probably a typical post-war marriage, exemplified in the relationship between Zeus and Hera. 2) Where the woman is dominant, and attempts to teach the stubborn man, but he refuses to learn from her. Essentially, Mrs. Ramsay bears this relationship to Mr. Ramsay; as does Deianeira to Hercules. 3) Where the woman or man take on a consistent sexual partner, a lover, outside the marriage. This is usually because there is no sexual fulfillment within the marriage, which is a relationship of convenience. Aphrodite has this relationship with Hephaestus, and takes Ares, the archetypal macho warrior, as lover.

The above are not individuation relationships. They do not seek circulation between partners at a deeper, more stimulating, but anxiety-provoking level. A long-lasting alchemical marriage is modelled in Arthur and Guinevere's relationship. This is because Arthur sees Guinevere as the personification of the land of Britain, of which he is the champion and king. There is also the short, but intense individuation relationship, where depths of communication are so quickly established (in myth and fairy story, this is often achieved through use of a love potion) that the pair may choose to die with this circulation at its height, as with Romeo and Juliet.

Tristram and Yseult fall in love thanks to ingestion of a love potion, which was actually meant for King Mark of Cornwall — Tristram's uncle — and Yseult, to whom Mark was engaged in an arranged relationship. In Gottfried von Strassbourg's *Tristan*, there is a beautiful passage describing the grotto where the young lovers meet to consummate their relationship. The love grotto is circular, wide and high. It has plain, white, smooth, upright walls.

The grotto sanctuary itself has a polished green marble floor, in the middle of which is a high bed hewn out of crystal. In the ceiling are three little windows, so that light falls onto the crystal bed from three sides. The entry door is made of bronze, and has a latch of gold with a secret lever of tin that allows entry from outside.

To Gottfried, each of these geological characteristics is symbolic. The allegory runs thus: the white walls of the grotto represent the virtue of Integrity. The green marble floor is Constancy. The crystalline bed, Love. These are the major three virtues that fire the quality of the individuation relationship which Tristram and Yseult enjoy. As the story unfolds in Mark's kingdom of Cornwall, we recognise here a plain description of the west Penwith peninsula, of Belerion. To the east of the sanctuary, as surround to the grotto, are the china clay seams of south-west Cornwall, with their tips, that have smooth, white walls. At the root of the west Cornwall peninsula is the Lizard, the southernmost point of Britain, with its green serpentine rock, highly polished, like marble, from constant battering by intense seas. This is the green marble 'floor' of the sanctuary. And, crowning this is the crystal bed, which is the granite boss that is the heart of the west Penwith peninsula, a granite very rich in quartz.

Boscawen-un stone circle located in the middle of the West Penwith peninsular, Cornwall. One of the three primary meeting places or ceremonial centres of the Druids

Indeed, right at the centre of the peninsula is one of the ancient three Gorsedds of Britain, Boscawen-un stone circle. One of the twenty upright stones of this sanctuary is solid quartz. And what better metal for the secret latch that unlocks the sanctuary than tin, the queen of Cornish metals? Cornwall was so rich in tin that commerce was established with early Mediterranean cultures, who smelted tin with copper to make bronze. Also, we have those three high windows, letting in light that illuminates the crystal bed and animates the lovers from three sides. What better description of the unique light in west Penwith that has attracted so many artists to places such as Newlyn and St. Ives? The light is reflected off the sea that surrounds the peninsula on three sides. It was the view from St. Ives, looking across the bay to the lighthouse at Gwithian, that inspired Virginia Woolf's *To the Lighthouse*, transposed to an Hebridean island in her novel.

We have literalised Gottfried's description of the lover's grotto, because it brings us right back to the union of the king with his land, that is Arthur's relationship to Guinevere, to a personification of the goddess Brittannia, Brigantia. This union forms the conditions for redemption of the waste land and recalling of the properties of the grail. In Celtic myth, this is to engage with the inspirational cauldron of the goddess Cerridwen. To drink from this cauldron is to not be captured by the outer guiding fiction of the Golden Age that was and is to be, but to concentrate this to a moment in time that never changes — the stability of the lighthouse — the moment that is now. In this moment, that which is eternal is life in active imagination.

We have said many times that this is an attitude, a way of being, that ensouls the world by recognising the world as she presents herself, without resort to 'explanation'. In this way, the images of the world come to fullness, or individuate. The renewal we obtain from the cauldron of Cerridwen is a refreshment of the senses, a unique perception, the shift to living in material imagination. In Celtic myth, we are told that the world is renewed through an inversion of the senses, a turning upside down, a reversal, a folding back, a movement away from the literal — a psychologising, or seeing through. For example, the moon in Celtic lore is inverted with respect to most mythologies in being explicitly male; and then displays an intrinsic logos or meaning (the 'face' of the man-in-the-moon).

Gerald Massey[4] says of the root of mythology, the logos of myth, that "...the Mother Achamoth (or Sophia) wandered with her

199

ailment or issue of blood, until the 'Christ above' . . . gave form (the masculine imprint) to her amorphous substance." Sophia is universal wisdom, instinctual bodily knowledge, to which the masculine logos gives a form, a meaning, a face, a personification. Then we thrill in recognition of the face. This may be seeing the man in the moon; a face in a rock; a meeting with an unknown figure in a dream; feeling good because we have 'faced' a problem within ourselves; and so forth. The masculine moon tells us not to turn away from his dark, faceless, impersonal side, but to attempt to understand it, to discover its logic. Similarly, the feminine sun has learned to temper her discrimination with heart-felt relating, so that she does not have the kind of scorching, arid effect Mr. Ramsay has on Mrs. Ramsay by his mere interruptions, that de-potentise her fountain of life and love. Guinevere (Cunneware) means 'feminine wisdom' — Sophia herself. For this wisdom to be enacted in social life, Guinevere needs to be taught of her masculine moon through her consort Arthur. This is to give a face and form to her chaotic natural powers that we loosely call feminine intuition, feeling or knowing. Arthur brings eros into his diplomacy, and maintains eros in the kingdom through respect for Guinevere's chaotic powers, of which she teaches him.

"All the Things you could be by now if Sigmund Freud's Wife was your Mother."

We could summarise all this talk of eros and logos, of teaching logos to relax and relate; and of teaching eros to focus and clarify, through one of the late Charles Mingus' compositions, titled above. The great jazz bassist, composer and arranger was infamous for his eccentric and erratic behaviour, which led to a period in mental hospital. In a wonderful inversion, at the termination of a period of treatment, Mingus got his analyst to write the liner notes for one of his albums! Analysis and creative life walk hand-in-hand through the vale of soul, rather than resting at the peaks of success, for experience of the suffering of the soul is common to both artist and analyst. The analyst cannot honestly engage with the suffering of another without empathy, without experience of his own pathos and woundings, when his analytic skills become an art. The artist embraces his pathos through his creations, the chaos of Mingus' life clearly running through his characteristically turbulent music. Then his art becomes his self-analysis.

Now this inversion and shift to dark pathos, to an underworld perspective, is one characteristic of archetypal psychology, that distinguishes it especially from humanistic approaches. Soul is defined in part by its close relationship with death, through the metaphor of deepening and through the *topos* of the underworld. Eros, as life-force, must then be seen in the context of the ever-presence of death. In other words, when we speak of eros, of relating, of growthful feminine soul, of Freud's wife and mother rather than the man himself, we will only learn of the beauty and necessity of its suffering when we return eros to the underworld, which is Eros' rightful home in Greek myth. Freud himself took many years to accept that humans have a "death instinct" (thanatos), as well as a "life instinct" (eros) that is libido, sexual and erotic energy.

Adler's idea of the masculine protest, the distorted and repressive masculine dominance in our culture, started out in 1908 as an innate "aggression drive".[5] Adler talked of extreme aggression as a pathological defence against the given tensions of life. Such aggression is then an extreme manifestation of the more generalised striving for perfection of the masculine protest. When such aggression is turned inward, Adler says that "The extreme is suicide." This pathos of the masculine protest will also, in Adler's more generally known formulation, tend to show as an organ inferiority, as symptom through a specific bodily organ. Then there may be an unconscious suicide through a self-imposed psychosomatic suffering.

Freud rejected Adler's formulations immediately. It was not until some fourteen years later, in 1923, that he incorporated the full idea of a death instinct that was opposed to libido, into his own work. This is doubly surprising as Freud loved to work in polarities, and his eros needed a thanatos; his libido or productive drive, a destructive dark twin. Eros finds his natural home in the underworld in three stages of Freud's thinking.[6] Firstly, the development of a new theory of instinct: "To begin with...we opposed the ego instincts to the sexual instincts of which the libido is the manifestation." This is the opposition of sexual, libidinous id to ego. Eros is still caught by ego, within the net of sacred love, a virtue within ego's sight.

Secondly, "Subsequently we came to closer grips with the analysis of the ego and recognised that a portion of the 'ego instincts' is also of a libidinal character and has taken the subject's own ego as its object." Eros has now slipped from his pedestal of

Love hurts: Eros is accompanied by his shadow side Anteros

sacred love, for Freud is now speaking of self-love, narcissism. This is profane love, where ego is embraced by the darker forces of id more clearly, and identified more with the underworld, rather than being diametrically opposed to it. Freud's words here are closer to archetypal thinking, where ego is a projection of soul. However, the overall rationality of the ego is maintained, for only a 'portion' of ego instinct is grabbed by the irrational id.

In the third step, Freud accepts that the ego itself may be split, half rational, half irrational; a life-force and a death-force. Then a fresh opposition is discovered within the ego itself: "Our views have from the very first been dualistic, and today they are even more definitely dualistic than before...A fresh opposition appeared between the libidinal (ego and object) instincts and others, which must be presumed to be present in the ego and which may perhaps actually be observed in the destructive instincts. Our speculations have transformed this opposition into one between the life instincts (Eros) and the death instincts."

Eros is then freed from his entrapment in upperworld, rational ego, and now moves freely between his home in the underworld, and the upperworld. The unpredictable movement between these two worlds, as the fluctuation between pathos and joy in love, is surely the quintessential human experience, which we capture in aphorisms such as love and hate being two sides of the same coin; and that 'love hurts': "Whoever, being in love, pursues the delight of a fleeting appearance finds his hands full of foliage, or plucks only bitter berries." (Bernini's 'Daphne').

We have seen that Oedipus swings wildly from the highs of love, in his blind affection for Jocaste, to the lows of suffering, when he discovers that his wife is his mother, and his children then his sisters and brothers. 'Oedipus' is usually taken to mean 'swollen foot', but Graves[7] suggests an alternative meaning — 'child of the swelling wave'. Now the Greek god of death is the ancient sea god Phorcys (where Thanatos is death itself, death personified). So Oedipus carries the swelling sea-like fluid, the oedema, which is his sore point. Laius' chariot running over the swelling raises Oedipus' anger to such a pitch that he kills the king — Oedipus' aggression drive externalised. And Oedipus' eros finds joyful expression with Jocaste, until he discovers the awful truth of his incestuous relationship, which is Eros returning to the underworld, and Oedipus' discovery that he is, as it were, truly of the swollen wave as a child of the sea god Phorcys, who brings a living death. Then Oedipus' aggression is directed inward as he blinds himself and wanders, the most miserable man on earth, looking for a place to die, to rest.

Oedipus' misery can be related to Guggenbuhl's[8] insightful remarks concerning disease, illness and invalidism: "The invalid without Eros is nasty, tyrannical, boring and parasitic. He compensates his invalidity by dominating others...Whether the incarnation of the archetype of the invalid be a blessing or a curse depends upon Eros." These are wise words, for they hark back in an illuminative way to the tales we often refer to in this book, that of the Fisher-king and the waste land; and of Oedipus and the plagued Thebes. Oedipus was said to have turned into a tyrant, and then his limp would have become a curse, lacking the presence of Eros. Paradoxically, the over-stiff king becomes the limp ruler. What we have said above deepens this another turn, for, to Oedipus, Eros in his underworld aspect is present but uncalled, unnoticed. In this guise, Eros, although present, will not be duly recognised by the lovestruck (which is the tragic blindness of love); and especially by the now arrogant Oedipus. Sophocles portrays him in this manner in Oedipus' dealings especially with the wise seer Teiresias, who attempts to tell him of his fate, but is cruelly rebuffed.

Again Guggenbuhl[9] reminds us that Eros must be recognised in his dark guise also: "Let there be no mistake: Eros is no saviour; he is not the key to living 'happily ever after'. While Eros makes the archetypes more human...he himself can be quite demonic." Relationships have no life and body if the joys and satisfactions are not deepened through acceptance of sufferings and frustrations.

Jung's Tower, Yeats' Tower and the Tower of Babel

"Before me floats an image, man or shade,/ Shade more than man, more image than a shade;/ For Hades' bobbin bound in mummy-cloth/ May unwind the winding path;/ A mouth that has no moisture and no breath/ Breathless mouths may summon;/ I hail the superhuman;/ I call it death-in-life and life-in-death." (From "Byzantium", W.B.Yeats).

Babylon was once a city of explicit aesthetic, a city ensouled, with a famous stairway to heaven at its heart. This was the biblical tower of Babel, three hundred feet high, with a base three hundred feet square; a tower that could be seen from sixty miles away. This 'tower' was actually the stepped pyramid, or ziggurat, of Etemenanki. 'Babylon' itself means 'door of the gods'; the ziggurat, a house built to receive the deity in splendour. More, a house fit for the sacred marriage between the supreme goddess Ishtar-Zarpanit and her consort, the god Bel-Marduk. Honouring this sacred marriage concluded the Babylonian new year ceremony of Akitou, a fertility/renewal festival. A city ensouled may be built with an explicit aesthetic and purpose which enshrines such an aesthetic. Robert Sardello[10] suggests that such a purpose may be not only the uniting of sky and earth, but also an honouring of the underworld. So a city such as Babylon has its beautiful temple-towers and hanging gardens, that root in earth and reach to sky, uniting goddess and god. But it also has its labyrinthine back-streets and alleyways[11]; its fringe quarters; its 'nightlife', the scary but vital underbelly that the Bible is at pains to declare as the seed of Babylon's downfall.

The holy city of Babylon, considered to be at the centre of the world, was graced by the Hanging Gardens, planned by Nebuchadnezzar II (604-562 BC), who rebuilt Babylon to strong aesthetic ideals. The temple at the tip of the ziggurat of Etemenanki was said (in an inscription credited to Nebuchadnezzar himself) to be "baked brick enamelled in brilliant blue". Archaeologists have shown that it was characteristic of the ziggurat builders, who flourished between 3,000 and 500 BC, to decorate their pyramids in various colours. For example, an Assyrian ziggurat ". . . near ancient Nineveh in northern Iraq, showed successive levels of white, black, white and red tinted with orange, gold or silver. The walls were decorated with carved veneers, painted panels and statues. The sanctuary on top glittered."[12] An earlier version of the

The mythical Tower of Babel — as conceived by Breugel

tower at Babylon, damaged by the Assyrians, was re-built by Nebuchadnezzar's predecessor Nabopolasser (625-605 BC). An inscription describing this says "gold, silver and precious stones from the mountain and from the sea were liberally set into its foundations. Oils and perfumes were mixed into the bricks." Moreover, members of the royal family took part in the construction of the ziggurat, both in the planning and labouring stages.

The ziggurat of Etemenanki was also said to have seven levels. This is based on the sanctity of the number seven, that we keep meeting here as a reflection of the Great Bear star goddess in earthly form. Although the archaeologist Woolley, who excavated Etemenanki, claimed that the ziggurat had a black base and red upper, there is a tradition that each level was once painted according to the colours of the rainbow, ascending from the red clay of the ground that is the goddess' body, to the blues of the descending sky-god's body. This blue-bodied god is lover to Earth, receiving her embrace. In an essay on alchemical blue, Hillman[13] mentions "...the many mythological images of 'Blue Gods': Kneph in Egypt and Odin's blue wrappings, Jupiter and Juno, Krishna and Vishnu, Christ in his earthly ministry like that blue Christ-man seen by Hildegard of Bingen."

The fall of Babylon is predicted in Isaiah and Jeremiah in the Old Testament, and detailed in Revelations in the New Testament. It is a paradigm for the shift from sensual polytheism to Yahweh's ascetic monotheism. And from the many-faceted, singular visions of a polyvalent value system, to an overriding single dogma and single vision. The embracing, sensual city that honoured the bodily coupling of goddess and god crumbles to reveal the new Jerusalem, city of the ascetic Christ.

In Isaiah, there is a concealed message about the fate of all cities, concerning their shadow. The very notion of a city is a work against nature, like the paradox of an inhabited southern California, whose greenery blossoms in a desert only because of vast feats of human engineering such as sophisticated irrigation systems. The Hanging Gardens of Babylon, the green heart of the city, the country's Green Man resting in the town's brickwork, was also a product of a sophisticated irrigation system. The fate of Babylon, like all cities, is to be taken back by Nature, for the city's existence and growth is held in tension against Artemisian wilderness: Nature and culture in uneasy co-operation.

A description of this tension produces some beautiful poetry in Isaiah, which speaks of "The burden (or fate) that awaits

Babylon...", which will be overthrown and remain uninhabited, to give way to the natural state of Artemisian Nature, so that, "Wild beasts will make their lairs in it, its houses will be tenanted by serpents; ostriches will nest there, and satyrs dance; the owls will hoot to one another in its palaces..."; and Yahweh promises that, "I will make the place over to the hedgehog, turn it into standing pools; I will sweep it clean...clean away."

'Hedgehog' is found nowhere else in the Old Testament, and I have only once come across a hedgehog in a dream. A man dreams of "A live hedgehog with only space visible through his eye-sockets." The dream discloses the image's interiority as a literal interior of no-thing-ness. Taken as a symbol, we could see this dream hedgehog as Nature protecting herself against invasion, curled up, and spiked against human interference, self-contained. We will never know the innards or inner-sense of the hedgehog, because we cannot approach the beast. In its own image the hedgehog remains hollow to the human observer because the latter is repelled.

Let us return to the description in *Isaiah* of the sparse 'paradise' (which originally meant 'an enclosure') that is now unapproachable, given over to the hedgehog. Without human interference, "The whole earth, now, sinks back into ease; listen to its cry of rejoicing! The very fir-trees and cedars of Lebanon triumph over thee..." In this sinking back is a wonderful release of tension, an easing back into natural form. Yahweh may not be so harsh after all. In *Jeremiah*, the fall of Babylon will "bring repose to earth". So the city is set against Nature, has its inbuilt tension, and thrives on this maintained arousal. Its destruction reveals the relaxed natural state of things, that city dwellers seek in weekend breaks to the country or seaside; in city parks. Or — failing access to green — in meditation classes, relaxation programmes, sauna, massage and whirlpool.

Of the many possible reasons for the city's decline, Babylon may be a bulimic city that gorges, grows fat, and then forces itself to vomit, to mess itself with plague; and calls for the particular astringency of Artemisian Nature to clean it up, rather than the rich choking of the forest, of fir and cedar — Dionysian Nature devouring the city. In *Jeremiah* and *Revelations*, the city has gone soft, "...her warriors...grow womanish...", and "Babylon shall melt away". These ancient great empires are built on the feats of starched, upright warriors, the tough seed that grows to fruiting. But fruit can over-ripen, like the debauched Roman empire, and is

207

then easily squashed underfoot by the new wave of warrior, with different vision.

The tower of Babel in biblical tradition is built by "the first great warrior", Nimrod, great-grandson of Noah. Historically, as we have said, Etemenanki was re-built to its greatest glory by Nebuchadnezzar, a great warrior king, and destroyed by his equal, the Persian warrior Xerxes. But why Babylon fell in a literal sense is not our concern here. Rather, let us explore a Babylon of the heart, the metaphorical city, through a particular framework, through the construct of hard and soft: the stiff, military, upright warrior king, and the sensuality of his kingdom — the quality of his marriage to the feminine soul of the land for which he claims rulership.

This hard/soft construct leads us back to the quote from Yeats' "Byzantium" at the head of this section, where "...Hades' bobbin bound in mummy-cloth/ May unwind the winding path..." This is a beautiful image, for when we are dead we are called 'stiffs' — rigor mortis sets in the physical body, Yeats' "death-in-life". But the body is, like Egyptian royalty, "bound in mummy-cloth" to preserve it literally and metaphorically, for the cloth is symbolic of the 'winding path', the tortuous motions of the soul, which winds on as 'life-in-death'. Then the hardness and softness of life grow one out of the other, each contained in the other as a coincidence of opposites.

To return to the hardened warrior and his relating, his eros, through which he may soften: this is the relationship of Ares and Aphrodite in Greek myth — the macho soldier and the sensual woman — a theme familiar from literature and film. How does the hardened king, the ruler with his straight-edge, bring soul to the kingdom; return soul to the world; or maintain an aesthetic in the city and provinces? Such an aesthetic would not pulp (the mass production of tourist paraphernalia; the gutter-press; the flying ducks on the wall); or turn arid (eros dried out of the kingdom like a curfew imposed by a military regime). Then the king and his land are no longer one; his eros is spent; the knight no longer defends his lady's well at the heart of the grove, that is life-renewing; he no longer sustains anima in action. Then the king no longer serves his Muse, which is to never forget the sacredness of the land and the soul of the city, but dwells entirely on his own egotistical concerns. He becomes inflated, greedy, pompous, and forgets how to see with the eye of soul, for now he is stuck in a literal materialism; and sees only his own reflection in things. The land is exploited, raped. The heart of the city is neglected, turns ugly; country and town both turn arid and sour, and a plague sets in. This waste land is the Grail king's lost Jerusalem and Oedipus' plagued Thebes.

Within the city, the maintenance of eros, of life; and of anima, of imagination, is the king's responsibility via his planners. The land itself must be a microcosm of the macrocosm — a zodiac for example, the riverways and the landscape engineered to mirror the heavens. Or it must draw us in reverence to the omphalos, the holy centre, the hill or well that is the city's birthcone. The Chinese geomancers attempt to harmonise the *yin* and *yang* of landscape features in order to reproduce the eternal *Tao*. And the emperor rules according to the Tao that Nature makes explicit — the given faces and forms of Nature viewed imaginatively, seen through to their given depth and interiority.

Certain areas, like a Japanese stone garden, will be planned as temples devoted to appropriate deities. There is formality for Apollo and Athene; wilderness for Artemis and Pan; fruit orchard for Priapus. The city traditionally holds many houses or mansions of the gods, although it may dedicate itself to one presiding deity — Athens to Athene, Bath to Sulis/Minerva, Berne to Artio the Bear.

But single-minded Yahweh wants the city to be absolutely his temple, dedicated to no other, "Israel his patrimony, Yahweh, the God of hosts his name." To the monotheistic imagination — the town planner dogged by a single, blinkered vision of utility for example — Babylon is doomed; is bad at the core, because it is multiple, already splintered, polytheistic. An inscription listing the temples of Babylon at the height of its religious fervour mentions, "53 temples of the great gods, 55 chapels to Marduk, 300 chapels for the earthly deities, 600 for the heavenly deities". This does not include 400 known altar-sites. Babylon also willingly shows its pathos or suffering, for in *Jeremiah* we are told, "Alas, we sought a cure for Babylon, but curing her there was none . . . "

The archetypal perspective sees no 'cure' for the psyche's pathologising, but looks instead to a re-evaluation. Also, homeopathy says that like cures like. When the Bible says " . . . we sought a cure . . . ", it means treating Babylon with one male deity, which is doomed to failure. This is because Babylon's guiding force is twin — the sacred marriage of Zarpanit and Marduk, a sexual consummation. Yahweh cannot flatten such explicit eros, such vitality, nor bring the sacred whore of Babylon (the temple priestess) to see the wrong of her ways, to 'cure' her. Rather, a re-evaluation, a re-visioning of the city is called for. It is clear that the eros brought by the harlot priestess lives on in the passionate commerce and vitality of any quarter of a town or city ensouled.

Let us return to the construct of hard/soft, which includes the hardened (defended), and the softened (vulnerable) — the softening of the hardened hero; and the hardening of eros through logos, giving eros form or definition, giving a meaning to an experience.

As we have noted, in the disparaging account of *Revelations*, Babylon has gone soft, is vulnerable, its warriors turned 'womanish'. We considered that the bulimic city may have gorged itself on food too rich to take. Yet the biblical description of the city does not conjure a picture of excess, but an exciting vitality, a healthy sensual realm. It is like a wondrous account from Marco Polo's travels, or the fantastic towns in Italo Calvino's *Invisible Cities*. The polytheistic outlook tolerates diversity, does not impose a monotheism of taste such as the single-minded aesthetic familiar from the steel-and-glass architecture of contemporary cities.

Rather, polytheistic outlook encourages mixed marriage — a rich tapestry under a single roof. Hermes lurking in the Georgian silverware; Apollo in the Shaker furniture; Hestia in the rustic open granite fireplace. In this vein, *Revelations* lists the merchandise of Babylon as gold, silver, precious stones, pearls, linen, silk, thyine wood (from an African coniferous tree yielding the resin sandarac, once used in varnish); vessels of ivory, brass, iron and marble; cinnamon, frankincense; fine flour, wheat; various perfumes, ointments. The city is also characterised by the "smell of beasts".

The destruction of Babylon paves the way for the new Jerusalem. If the city has gone soft then it no longer bears the leading edge. A city of clarity replaces the overly-sensual and chaotic Babylon. A city with new purpose, the new Jerusalem is a representation of the divine intellect — *ratio* — the mind of God on Earth. Priest replaces priestess, and the blood sacrifice of an animal replaces the menstrual sacrifice of the woman. Rules imposed from without, local authority regulations and bye-laws, replace the inner rhythms of the city, its self-regulation. The whore of Babylon now becomes the scapegoat for Babel's downfall, for, from the ascetic viewpoint she is overly sensual, the unacceptable face of tantra.

From the sensual textures, the smells and tastes of Babylon, focus is shifted to a city made entirely of precious gems, devoid of smell, avoiding the animal smell — the new Jerusalem. There is a shift also to the cultivated eye that carries the museum mentality of look-but-don't-touch, and the world of optics, of distancing and objectivity: "...the city was...like unto clear glass" says the Bible of the new Jerusalem. The senses have become transparent, see-through, transcending smell, lifting away from contact to appreciation at a distance, by eye — a shift from Aphrodite to Apollo. But we are already in danger of opposing Babylon and the new Jerusalem, when we could re-vision both cities as a soul-spirit tandem, Babylon the soul, Jerusalem its spiritual aspect. John Michell[14] says of the two cities, "Babylon is destroyed, Jerusalem is revealed. But these are not two different cities...they are identical..."

Jerusalem is then logos to Babylon as eros. As the 'city of glass', Jerusalem is the place of clear sight, Caer Arianrhod of the Celts, which is the turning castle of the stars about the north pole — the 'silver wheel'. The Celtic grail, the bubbling, chaotic cauldron of Cerridwen which is the fount of all life and sustenance, is kept in the turning castle of Arianrhod, where souls were said to await a new bodily incarnation. The feminine rhythm and sensuality and the animal heart then beating within the walls of glass, within an imposed discipline. There is an outer meaning to the inner rhythm; a warm sense of interiority to the Ice Queen's outer realm; the trance that shows in the glassy stare of the eyes is represented internally as a relaxation that warms as it spreads, like the result of a shot of Teyside malt. The warming, rich spirit of the grain is contained by the cold, austere glass.

So the fall of Babylon to reveal the new Jerusalem is also a predictable shift in consciousness — the discovery of clarity within feeling, within relating; and the discovery of feeling at the heart of clarity. Then there is a sudden need for distancing in a close relationship; or a sudden intimacy in what was previously just a friendship. Mind is discovered at the centre of the heart, giving a logic to love; and secret desire and passion is the undisclosed centre of an outer coldness, where logic is about to be dissolved by love. The tension thus disclosed may be unbearable of course, and surely characterises both the replacement of city 'villages' — homely communities — with glass-and-steel cities; and the disintegration of the sacred sexuality of Babylon (eros in health) to the seediness and alienation of Soho's peep-shows (eros as invalid). Eros is then mechanised also, an emptied-out relationship achieved through one-way mirror in an invalidating voyeurism.

One of Calvino's "invisible cities" is Chloe, where "...the

people who move through the streets are all strangers. At each encounter, they imagine a thousand things about one another; meetings which could take place between them, conversations, surprises, caresses, bites. But no one greets anyone; eyes lock for a second, then dart away, seeking other eyes, never stopping." So this is a city of ice and fire in uneasy relationship, where, ". . . meetings, seductions, copulations, orgies are consummated among them without a word exchanged, without a finger touching anything, almost without an eye raised. A voluptuous vibration constantly stirs Chloe, the most chaste of cities." [15]

The crystalline and ordered geometry of the new Jerusalem, that ". . . lieth foursquare. . . the length as large as the breadth. . . The length and breadth and the height of it are equal", may be a revelation of Apollonic *aritmos* which is the given order and harmony of the cosmos according to number. And this may be fire-in-ice, eros as the grail, cauldron and heart caught within an Apollonic structure, a given logos or meaning. Then, as John Michell says in *City of Revelation*, "The essential feature of the legend of the new Jerusalem is that the City is not a creation of the intellect, but a revelation of the pre-existent order. . . "

Calvino's [16] imaginary Eudoxia is such a 'city of revelation', and metaphor for the logic of love, where the chaotic life and smells of Babylon marry the more clinical architecture of the new Jerusalem, a *kosmos*, or ordered universe, where everything has its place against what Calvino calls ". . . a stain that spreads out shapelessly . . ." Thus, "In Eudoxia. . . a carpet is preserved in which you can observe the city's true form. . . laid out in symmetrical motives whose patterns are repeated along straight and circular lines. . . " But here too is "All of Eudoxia's confusion, the mule's braying, the lampblack stains, the fish smell. . . ", like the confusions of Babylon listed in *Revelations*. There is a powerful logic in this chaos, for ". . . the true map of the universe is in the city of Eudoxia, just as it is, a stain that spreads out shapelessly, with crooked streets, houses that crumble upon one another amid clouds of dust, fires, screams in the darkness".

Drawing the two cities apart once more, if we were to identify the suffering of Babylon's soul as a neurosis, we might call her hysterical, over-eroticised. The new Jerusalem, in contrast, is paranoid, afraid of succumbing to eros' touch.

212

The Tower and the Winding Stair: Twin Aspects of Babylon

The man, a raking telescopic searcher bleary-eyed from looking. A cloud-buster fingering into weather in uncertain ways, worrying after the deluge he believes he has caused. The man's body a weather tower like a lighthouse upping stone-stiff into cloud, the winding stairway his stepped-up senses that gather in deeply bowled eyes. The woman's body a deepwater well with moss-soft skin polished on the inside by the coming and going of waters, knows the weather by touch, its timely round, its outcries. The man's tower and the woman's winding stair meeting in one building (like the lighthouse), provides a metaphor for the deepening of the senses through imagination that is the gift of a circulation between partners. Then the rain is seen as a sustained applause; and sheet lightning is the gods' laundry hung crackling, hung dry, across a giant bowl of cloud unweighting itself by the gallon. This building and metaphor, the microcosm of the macrocosmic ensouled city, joins earth and sky, and roots in underworld, for it carries with it a closeness to death, as the lighthouse is a symbol of imminent danger.

The lighthouse is a guide to sailors who would otherwise wreck on the cliffs or rocks. Yet at night we see only the winking light, not the full body of the lighthouse. The body is the vehicle by which the light gains height, a perfect metaphor for mind and spirit standing on the shoulders of body and soul, and of spiritual illumination out of image-sense, out of bodily form and function. Knowledge of the shadow of the body — an 'invisible city' at night — raised to awareness, is to crown the invisible with a visible indicator, a warning light. Raised consciousness of the body, seeing through its literalisms while not losing its presence, provides the warning lights for maintenance of appropriate health. Once we know how to read the warning light, it is our choice whether or not to wreck ourselves on the rocks — whisky and ice for breakfast an obvious, literal sign of a spirit washed up; wrung out; on-the-rocks.

We began with a starched king, the sun-baked warrior, who builds a city and its temple — a tower — to invite the presence of the deities. 'Babylon' as 'gate of god' is the portal, the entry-place of the divine, the city housing the divine because the deities are explicitly called into its houses. But possibly the biblical Nimrod, the first great warrior, thinks he is a god, inflates, and becomes a tyrant. Tyranny is one form of stiffness, the containing city of crystal is another. In one, the ruler is stiff and the city gone soft. In the other, the city if stiff, and its coming ruler, Christ, is the warrior of the heart, the soft one, the vulnerable turner of cheeks. Within the soft city, Nimrod, as the masculine tyrannical ruler, is in permanent erection, and erects a permanent phallus, the tower of Babel, to the inseminating god Marduk. The new Jerusalem however is a priapian city, the gemstone walls always hard; and its inhabitants, its carers, are gardeners, tenders of soft fruit, caring for the poor and unfortunate, the outcast, the sick.

In these cities, logos and eros may mingle — the starched warriors of Babylon washed and softened in the babble and confusion of the soulful town; the prayerful inhabitants of the new Jerusalem walking the walls of a town modelled on an image of perfection, an harmonic universe. Today however, both city and inhabitants may lean more to logos than eros. The city gone hard may have frozen to the planner's touch; may have lost its soul while the inhabitants try to regain theirs in therapy; may crystallise in the face of materialism and utilitarianism, losing its explicit aesthetic. As we have said, such a city may be dominated by a single architectural theme such as Le Corbusier's right-angled architecture, a geometric grid of steel and glass, of straight roads, a monotheism of form. The buildings scrape the skies, moving people out of the alleys, breaking up the wider nexus of relationships in moving people who were once together on the ground, close to earth.

Jehovah views the tower built by Nimrod and contemplates the single language spoken by all people. He brings down a confusion of tongues, so that the people may spread themselves far and wide. This may be a gift, a polytheism of language, a genesis of variety from a common set of rules. This is a variety of self-presentation, variation of living form for the sake of it; an explicit aesthetic. The word 'babel' has entered our popular language as 'babble'. The Oxford English Dictionary defines it as "a visionary scheme", "a sense of confusion", "a confused turbulent medley of sounds". This cacophony, from the point of view of logos, is a chaos. From psyche's perspective it is a richness, the multiple voice and vision of imagination.

However, perhaps Jehovah's interference in Babylon's growth may have been a cure in disguise, the single male god homeopathically treating a monotheism of the singular great goddess Ishtar, and out of this cure may have come the multiple tongues, the babble that was Babel. Alternatively, he may have destroyed the common root-language of soul — dreaming and myth — to make way for the language of ego perception. The latter is a language of literalisms, and of self-referential dogma, characterised by the forgotten speeches of so many politicians. These are so often hollow sermons, flowering briefly with transcendental spirit, but with no nourishing root in soul to guarantee permanence.

A legend says that no dew will ever form on the tomb of Nimrod, although its surrounds are saturated. (Alchemical texts say that properly collected dew is an essential ingredient in the Work, through which the sun and moon may be married). Such a sulphurous, dry king brings forth the familiar picture of the herculean hero, and the jaded, burned-out Arthur, parted from his land, which has dried out, has become a waste land. We are also reminded of the puer Phaeton, who scorched the earth with Helios' sun-chariot, and was blasted by Zeus' thunderbolt before he could cause any more damage; and of Icarus, who flew too close to the sun. When Babylon fell, perhaps its soul had been lost through the inflation or insensitivity of a dessicate king parted from his land, or out of touch with the ways that encourage Earth's embrace, an artist without a Muse.

If Nimrod had been following traditional worship, perhaps the dew would have rested upon his grave, symbolising his embrace of eros. For in the Babylon of warrior-kings, the religious outlook stressed the priestess as experiencer of the epiphany. In fact, every woman had, at least once in her life, to spend a day as a temple prostitute. The priestesses of Ishtar embraced the god Marduk, who would step into her temple on the ziggurat, and then walk to earth, descending the seven levels of the winding stair. So the sky-god would meet the goddess of earth.

The god descends and ascends the winding stair that is the drawing out, the slowing down, the softening of the phallic tower, its inner meaning slowly revealed, like the winding staircase within a lighthouse that forces a circuitous route. The same stairway is represented by the seven levels of the path surrounding the tor at Glastonbury, said to have once been a maze.[17]

The temple at the top of the ziggurat of Etemenanki was said to be furnished simply with an opulent couch and a golden table. A priestess was always present. The man who comes to her in tantric rite throws a silver coin in her lap and says, "The goddess Ishtar prosper thee". She is the lap of the goddess, who has also come to earth, the starry goddess Ishtar, Astarte, Ashtoreth; the Queen of the heavens who rules the souls raised to starry brightness; and who comes to earth to animate the grove, the hanging garden, the mount. Her teaching is to look to the intrinsic light of darkness, to value image.

We have met the temple prostitute as the whore of Babylon that *Revelations* scapegoats as the rotten core of the debauched city. She carries its sins, and is associated with its canonical seven hills, and rides upon the seven-headed beast. This is again the seven steps to heaven, the seven stars to the Dragon (the constellation *Draco*), whose head-star was once the pole star. Gerald Massey [18] says that the genetrix of the seven, *Ta-urt*, became Hes-ta-urt, then Ishtar, then Astarte. The biblical patriarchs say that she is the carrier of abominations; but the alchemists know that a secret nestles in her so-called filth.

Revelations identifies the city of Babylon with the whore herself: "And the woman which then... is that great city." The city is the starry firmament, the four quarters of heaven, brought to earth as the body of the goddess. Upon her forehead is written, "Mystery, Babylon the Great, The Mother of Harlots and Abominations of the Earth." She is the body of the genetrix that bleeds, the nether-side of creation, whom Massey [19] describes as, "... the buttocks, the hinder part, the feminine fundament of the northern heaven, represented by the genetrix Ta-Urtu..., the goddess of the seven stars, which are also called the hinder thigh..." She is the stairway to heaven, as the mount of the north pole, and her religious mystery is sensual. Tradition recognises the inner-thigh of the animal in these seven stars, with the polar centre as the birth-place.

The Indo-European root of 'whore', *kar*, appears in the Latin *carus*, 'a friend', 'beloved', 'a dear one'. The Latin *caritas* means 'dearness', 'affection'; also 'a high price'. She is, properly, an expensive whore, and there is a high price to pay for abusing her; a priestess nearest and dearest to the deities, their special friend. Recall that Jesus befriended the fallen woman Mary Magdalene. The priestess has befriended the god in sexual embrace and may bear his children. The temple prostitute was then known as a 'Grace', who dealt in both charity and beauty.

Let us stay with this embrace, with the sufferings of it also, the vulnerabilities and defences. And the paradox of the vulnerability of priapism, of suffering a permanent hardness or erection, which we met as the stiff shell of the new Jerusalem. The outer tower,

Babel, appears priapic, but has an inner softness, as the winding stair, the more feminine ascents and descents of orgasm, rather than the one-pointedness of ejaculation. Let us turn to Jung's daemon-dream[20], the earliest dream he could remember, that he claimed acted as a guide for the rest of his life. For this was a dream of a towering underground phallus, "twelve to fifteen feet high", in Jung's own words; skin-covered, one-eyed, erect. This was a seed image for Jung, the image of the tower that literally became his sanctuary, his temple, later in life. Yeats also retreated to a tower, and for both men the symbol of the tower became a guiding force.

When Jung built the tower at Bollingen, Zurich, as his retreat, he called it "...a kind of representation in stone of my innermost thoughts and of the knowledge I had acquired." Also, "...a confession of faith in stone."[21] Jung's tower was begun in 1923. Yeats' Norman tower, and family's summer home from 1919-29, Thoor Ballylee in County Galway, inspired his greatest collection, "The Tower" (1928), and many subsequent poems. In "Blood and the Moon", Yeats wrote, "I declare this tower is my symbol; I declare/ This winding, gyring, spiring treadmill of a stair is my/ ancestral stair;..."

For both Jung and Yeats, the tower, a place of retreat and isolation, was a place to contact the Ancestors. Jung wrote, "In the tower at Bollingen it was as if one dived into many centuries simultaneously."[22] Yeats saw the outer tower and its inner stair as separate symbolism, in tension, as we have outlined here, and devoted a collection, "The Winding Stair", to this tension. Marie-Louise von Franz[23] describes Jung's tower as "a mother symbol and a mandala in stone." However, in Jung's account in his autobiography, the tower started as "...the maternal hearth", but later, when he added an upper section, "I could no longer hide myself behind the 'maternal' (tower)." The tower now became an extension of his masculine ego, an erect phallus, returning him to the dream of his childhood. But this ego cannot escape the fact that, "There I live in my second personality and see life in the round, as something forever coming into being and passing on..."[24], the winding stair within the stiff phallus, its inner-sense and imaginal interiority, as well as the literal space within. The eros within a logos casing.

The tower is connected with the dead, as a rebirth in stone, and is then a womb, a hollow, where Jung has "...feelings of repose and renewal." So the stiff resurrects into new life, as Yeats'

217

"I declare this tower as my symbol; I declare this winding, gyring, spiring treadmill of a stair is my ancestral stair..." W B Yeats

"Hades' bobbin" unwinding "the winding path". Unlike Jung's optimistic acceptance of old age and certain death, Yeats feared and hated growing older, indeed underwent rejuvenation operations. The tower for him became tomb rather than womb. For a man who had trained so hard as a magician in the Golden Dawn, and wrote so passionately of "death-in-life and life-in-death", it is strange that Yeats feared so greatly the winding stairs to the stars, that is fateful ageing. The poems in "The Tower" are full of bitterness and anguish, and this lingers on into his subsequent "The Winding Stair and Other Poems", where the symbol of the tower dominates the early poems of this collection. The virility of youth is gone, for Yeats' life is literally more than half-finished, "Half dead at the top", so, "In mockery I have set/ A powerful emblem up,/ And sing rhyme upon rhyme/ In mockery of a time/ Half dead at the top." ("Blood and the Moon").

While Jung's tower blossoms, Yeats' seems to be crumbling, like Babel itself. We saw that the dictionary definition of 'Babel' includes a "confused turbulent medley of sounds". This latter cacophony is heard by Jung[25], as both melody and chaotic medley: "One evening — I can still remember it precisely — I was sitting by the fireplace and had put a big kettle on the fire to make hot water for washing up. The water began to boil and the kettle to sing. It sounded like many voices, or stringed instruments, or even like a whole orchestra. It was just like polyphonic music...It was as though there were one orchestra inside the Tower and another one outside. Now one dominated, now the other, as though they were responding to each other."

Jung's senex preoccupation, with the in-search of the latter part of life, does not bear the weariness of Yeats' swansong, which dwells on, "...the wreck of the body,/ slow decay of blood..." ("The Tower"). We do not find the quiet meditations of Jung, akin to Milton's "...let my lamp at midnight hour,/ Be seen in some high lonely Tower,/ Where I may oft out-watch the Bear..." (Milton: "Il Penseroso"). Rather, in "The Tower", Yeats writes, acidly, "It is time that I wrote my will;..." And, in a defeatist manner, "...of the hour/ When the swan must fix his eye/ Upon a fading gleam,/ Float out upon a long/ Last reach of glittering stream/ And there sing his last song."

The outer tower is senex-like: firm, rigid, with foundation, reminding a person of what he or she has achieved. The winding stair is puer-like, often an unrealised fantasy; sometimes an adventurous leap. The puer flies high but may plummet, returning to the ground, to senex consciousness, for 'plummet' is a plumb-line of lead, and lead is the metal of Saturn, senex ruler. But the outer tower could also be seen as the phallic puer, uninitiated and untrained in sexuality, wanting an uncomplicated, direct sexual encounter. While the winding stair is the woman within and without who wants extensive foreplay and gradual arousal. She is initiatrix into a more circuitous and satisfying sexuality. She indeed teaches us to screw, to follow the circular and winding patterns to a more penetrating experience, that does however keep to its point; a deeper orgasm or a mirroring between partners that deepens one to the other. And this initiatrix is in the tradition of the temple prostitute, Ishtar or Aphrodite's priestess, the courtesan who knows the sacredness of the heart; the tantric *suvasini* to whom every sensual encounter and sexual act is sacred.

The *hieros gamos* literalised in the temple prostitution of Babylon, imaged in the erotic dream, is also the coming together of the hard outer shell of the tower, and its inner softness, as the winding stair. This is respectively the particle and wave in light. Ejaculation is like the particle, while orgasm is like the wave. Hence the 'underground' story that Einstein's understanding of particle and wave operation in the motion of light happening simultaneously, came via a wet dream. The wave-like energy of orgasm as the winding stair, is also experienced in a different form in karezza, in sexual embrace that stimulates but does not lead to orgasm.

The outer tower finds its pathos in priapism, the suffering of an eternal hardness. The winding stair has its pathos in vertigo, where heights produce dizziness and fear. The hardened, macho male lover for whom every sexual act is a conquest, and the anxious woman who stifles her sexual potential in repressive role-play and pretends orgasm to please her man, reduce sex to an event rather than an experience. Then a sacred act is de-souled.

A logos-dominated society such as ours is in permanent erection, is priapic, and attempts to tower, to dominate, over nature's eros. Our current social outlook is repressively manipulative of eros, literalised in a sexually manipulative and sexually menacing culture. Returning eros to the world, as an aesthetic, is to shift focus from the obvious phallus of Priapus, to his occupation — a gardener who specialises in pears. Cultivation of eros in the world (in Marcuse's [26] and Norman O. Brown's [27] terms, the revolutionary eroticising of society), requires the

220

gardener's touch, fork rather than gun; green fingers rather than green berets. When D.H. Lawrence created an erotic hero out of a gardener, the gamekeeper Mellors in Lady Chatterley's Lover, his book caused an outcry in a society that applauded and applauds the heroics of warfare. Lawrence would have a social revolution without literalised violence, an aesthetic revolution, the cultivation of sense-awareness, Bachelard's "material imagination", that sees through ugliness, with senses tuned to the poetics of space[28]; of fire and illumination[29]; of concrete form; and of the motion, depth and reflectivity of waters.[30] (As Bachelard's[31] startling study of violent animal images in poetry, Lautréamont, shows however, this aesthetic revolution recognises and honours the violence of *image*, the pathos given with psyche. The open acceptance of such violent image, rather than its repression, then negating ego's need to literalise such image in violent acts).

Then our values shift, as did Yeats' in the opening poem of "The Winding Stair", away from the deadening cynicism of a fear of growing old, or never being open to Earth's embrace, to a more joyful acceptance of equality in the world, where we meet "Two girls in silk kimonos, both/ Beautiful, one a gazelle." ("In Memory of Eva Gore-Booth and Con Markievicz"); and "Bodies of holy men and women exude/ Miraculous oil, odour of violet." ("Oil and Blood"). Then we are reminded of the sensuous treasures of Babylon that is the deity's 'gate', Ishtar's portal. We walk through this gate in every act of direct perception — in soul making — in prayer, in lovemaking, in dreaming, when the stars appear within the dark of the dream as Yeats' "Babylonian mathematical starlight".[32]

In this night air we smell more clearly the odours of the hanging Gardens. Our descent to dreaming is the slow climb up the winding seven steps of the ziggurat, where we touch the stars at its rooftop temple, and face the gods. Here we ask the question Yeats poses in "A Dialogue of Self and Soul": "I summon to the winding ancient stair;/ Set all your mind upon the steep ascent,/ Upon the broken, crumbling battlement,/ Upon the breathless starlit air,/ Upon the star that marks the hidden pole;/ Fix every wandering thought upon/ That quarter where all thought is done :/ Who can distinguish darkness from the soul?"

Bibliography

Chapter 1
1 Hillman, J. "Peaks and Vales", in Hillman J. et al. *Puer Papers*, 1979, Spring.
2 Jung, C.G. quoted in Cobb,N. *Prospero's Island*, 1984, Coventure.
3 Wiener, H. "Human Exocrinology: The Olfactory Component of Non-verbal Communication", in Weitz, S. (Ed.) *Non Verbal Communication*, 2nd ed. 1979, OUP.
4 Hillman, J. *Archetypal Psychology: A Brief Account*, 1983, Spring.
5 Hillman, J. *The Thought of the Heart* (Eranos Lectures: 2), 1981, Spring.
6 Kugler,P. *The Alchemy of Discourse*, Bucknell Univ. Press.
7 Gombrich, E.H. *The Image and the Eye*, 1982, Phaidon. (See also: Hillman, J. *Egalitarian Typologies Versus the Perception of the Unique* (Eranos Lectures: 1980, Spring.)
8 Hillman, J. 1981, op.cit
9 See especially Gooch, S. *Total Man*, 1972, Allen Lane.
10 Hillman, J. *Re-visioning Psychology*, 1975, Harper-Colophon.
11 Delaney, F. *The Celts*, 1986, BBC: Hodder and Stoughton.
12 Blake, W. "Vala, or the Four Zoas", in *William Blake: The Complete Poems*, 1977, Penguin.
13 Morgan, M.O. *The Mabin of the Mabinogion*, 1984, R.I.L.K.O.
14 Baker, R. *Human Navigation and the Sixth Sense*, 1981, Hodder.
15 Lockhart, R. *Words as Eggs*, 1983, Spring.
16 Graves, R. *Mammon and the Black Goddess*, 1962, Cassell.
17 Massey, G. *The Natural Genesis*, 1974(a), Weiser.
18 Merry, E.C. *The Flaming Door*, 2nd ed., 1962, Floris Books.
19 Graves, R. *The White Goddess*,1961, Faber; also Bleakley, A. *Fruits of the Moon Tree*, 1984, Gateway.
20 Morton Nance, R. *A Glossary of Cornish Sea-Words*, 1963, The Federation of Old Cornwall Societies.

Chapter 2
1 Otto, W.F. *The Homeric Gods*, 1955, Thames & Hudson.
   See also Stroud, J. & Thomas, G. (Eds.) *Images of the Untouched*, 1982, Spring.
2 See Kerenyi, C. in Hillman, J. (Ed.) *Facing the Gods*, 1980, Spring.
3 Hillman, J. *Healing Fiction*, 1983, Station Hill.
4 Spignesi, A. *Starving Women*, 1983, Spring.

223

5 Hillman, J. *The Dream and the Underworld*, 1979, Harper-Colophon.
6 Boer, C. (trs.) *The Homeric Hymns*, 2nd ed., 1979, Spring.
7 Hillman, J. 1979, op.cit.
8 Lockhart, R. 1983, op.cit.
9 Guggenbuhl, A. *Eros on Crutches*, 1980, Spring.
10 Hillman, J. "Salt : A Chapter in Alchemical Psychology", in Stroud, J. and Thomas, G. (Eds.) 1982, op.cit.
11 Spignesi, A. 1983, op.cit.
12 Hillman, J. "On the Necessity of Abnormal Psychology", in *Loose Ends*, 1975, Spring.
13 See Ziegler, A. *Archetypal Medicine*, 1983, Spring.
14 Graves, R. *The Greek Myths: Vols. 1 & 2*, 1960, Penguin.
15 Campbell, J. *The Way of the Animal Powers*, 1984, Times Books.
16 Kerenyi, C. in Hillman, J. (Ed.) 1980, op.cit.
17 Jencks, B. *Your Body: Biofeedback at its Best*, 1977, Nelson Hall.
18 Knight, C. "Levi-Strauss and the Dragon", *Man* Vol. 18 No. 1, March 1983; also recent research quoted in Shuttle, P. and Redgrove, P. *The Wise Wound*, (2nd ed.), 1986, Paladin.
19 Hillman, J. *Anima*, 1985, Spring.
20 Otto, W. 1955, op.cit.
21 Bleakley, A. 1984, op.cit.
22 Woodman, M. *The Owl Was a Baker's Daughter*, 1980, Inner City.
23 Yates, F. *The Occult Philosophy in the Elizabethan Age*, 1979, RKP.
24 See Ferrucci, P. *What We May Be*, 1982, Turnstone.
25 See Perera, S.B. *Descent to the Goddess*, 1981, Inner City.
26 Underwood, G. *Pattern of the Past*, 1970, Pitman.
27 Graves, R. 1960, op.cit.
28 Mott, F.J. *The Universal Design of the Oedipus Complex*, 1950, McKay.
29 Wolfram von Eschenbach, *Parzival*, (trs. Hatto), 1980, Penguin.
30 Yates, F. *The Art of Memory*, 1966, RKP.

Chapter 3
1 Campbell, J. *Creative Mythology*, (*The Masks of God Part IV*), 1976, Penguin.
2 Kerenyi, C. *Dionysos*, 1976, RKP.
3 Hillman, J. 1981, op.cit.
4 ibid.
5 ibid.
6 Massey, G. 1974(a), op.cit.
7 See research of Sidney Jourard quoted in Open University D102, section on non-verbal communication.
8 Bachelard, G. *Water and Dreams*, 1983, Pegasus Fndtn.
9 Hillman, J. "Image-Sense", *Spring*, 1979.
10 Graves, R. 1961, op.cit.
11 Graves, R. 1962, op.cit.
12 ibid.
13 ibid.
14 ibid.
15 See Hillman on Ficino in Hillman, J. 1975, op.cit.
16 Baker, R. op.cit.
17 Douglas, N. & Slinger, P. *Sexual Secrets*, 1979, Hutchison.
18 Wiener, H. 1979, op.cit.
19 Joseph Conrad, *Heart of Darkness*, Penguin.

Chapter 4
1 Bremmer, J. (Ed.) *Interpretations of Greek Mythology*, 1987, Croom Helm.
2 von Franz, M-L. *On Dreams and Death*, 1986, Shambhala.
3 Massey, G. 1974(a), op.cit.
4 Jung, C.G. *Symbols of Transformation*, Vol. 5 in Collected Works, 1956, RKP.
5 Christian, R. *Old English Customs*, 1972, David & Charles.
6 Mott, F.J. 1950, op.cit.
7 ibid.
8 Berry, P. "The Dogma of Gender", in *Echo's Subtle Body*, 1982, Spring.
9 Rohrbaugh, J.B. *Women: Psychology's Puzzle*, 1981, Sphere.
10 Thornton, E.M. *The Freudian Fallacy*, 1986, Palladin.
11 Massey, G. 1974(a), op.cit.
12 Harrison, J.E. *Themis*, 1963, Merlin.
13 Spignesi, A. 1983, op.cit.
14 Harrison, J.E. 1963, op.cit.
15 Shuttle. P. & Redgrove, P. 1986, op.cit; Bleakley, A. 1984, op.cit.
16 Knight, C. 1983, op.cit.
17 Campbell, J. 1984, op.cit.
18 Bettelheim, B. *Symbolic Wounds*, 1955, Thames & Hudson.
19 Massey, G. 1974(a), op.cit.
20 Quoted in Stein, M. *In Midlife*, 1983, Spring.
21 Hillman, J. *Inter-Views*, 1983, Harper-Colophon.
22 Hillman, J. *In-Search: Psychology & Religion*, 1979, Spring.
23 Stein, M. 1983, op.cit.
24 Mott, F.J. 1950, op.cit.
25 Quoted in La Fontaine, J.S. *Initiation*, 1985, Penguin.
26 ibid.
27 Massey, G. 1974(a), op.cit.
28 Moore, T. *Rituals of the Imagination*, 1983, Pegasus Fndtn.
29 Massey, G. *Gerald Massey's Lectures*, 1974(b), Weiser.
30 Hillman, J. "On the Necessity of Abnormal Psychology", 1975, op.cit.
31 Freud, S. *Two Short Accounts of Psychoanalysis*.
32 Freud, S. *Introductory Lectures on Psychoanalysis*, 1952, Allen & Unwin.
33 Bremmer, J. 1987, op.cit.
34 Graves, R. 1960, op.cit.
35 ibid.
36 Kerenyi, C. *The Heroes of the Greeks*, 1959, Thames & Hudson.

Chapter 5
1 See especially Hillman, J. 1975, op.cit.; and "An Inquiry into Image", Spring, 1977.
2 Casey, E. "Getting Placed: Soul in Space", Spring, 1982.
3 See especially Heron, J. *Co-counselling*, 1975, University of Surrey.
4 Hillman, J. 1975, op.cit.
5 Lowen, A. *Betrayal of the Body*, 1969, Collier-Macmillan.
6 Lowen, A. *Bioenergetics*, 1979, Penguin.
7 Watkins, M. *Waking Dreams*, 1972, Harper.
8 Hudson, L. *Human Beings*, 1975, Jonathan Cape.
9 Hillman, J. 1975, op.cit.

10 Ficino, M. *The Book of Life* (trs. Boer), 1980, Spring.
11 Casey, E. "Towards an Archetypal Imagination", Spring, 1974.
12 Hillman, J. 1983, op.cit.
13 Avens, R. *The New Gnosis*, 1984, Spring.

Chapter 6
 1 Hillman, J. 1979, op.cit.
 2 Rogers, C. "on person-centred communities", in Villoldo, A. &
     Dytchwald, K. *Millenium*, 1981, J.P. Tarcher.
 3 Guggenbuhl, A. *Marriage Dead or Alive*, 1977, Spring.
 4 Massey, G. 1974(a), op.cit.
 5 Adler quoted in Ansbacher, H.L. & Ansbacher, R.R. *The Individual
     Psychology of Alfred Adler*, 1967, Harper & Row.
 6 Freud, S. *Beyond the Pleasure Principle*, 1984, Penguin.
 7 Graves, R. 1960, op.cit.
 8 Guggenbuhl, A. 1980, op.cit.
 9 ibid.
10 Sardello, R. "Beauty and Violence: The Play of Imagination in the
     World", *Dragonflies*, Vol.2 No.1, Winter 1980.
11 Hillman, J. *City & Soul*, 1978, Dallas.
12 "The Men Who Built the Tower of Babel", in *The World's Last Mysteries*,
     1977, Reader's Digest; see also Holroyd, S. & Lambert, D. *Mysteries of the
     Past*, 1979, Aldus Books (ch. 6).
13 Hillman, J. "Alchemical Blue and the *Unio Mentalis*", *Sulfur*, 1981.
14 Michell, J. *City of Revelation*, 1972, Garnstone.
15 Calvino, I. *Invisible Cities*.
16 ibid.
17 Ashe, G. *The Glastonbury Tor Maze*, 1979, Gothic Image.
18 Massey, G. 1974(a), op.cit.
19 ibid.
20 Jung, C.G. *Memories, Dreams, Reflections*, 1963, Collins/ RKP.
21 ibid.
22 ibid.
23 von Franz, M-L. *C.G. Jung: His Myth in Our Time*, 1975, Analytical
     Psychology, Inc., N.Y.
24 Jung, C.G. 1963, op.cit.
25 ibid.
26 Marcuse, H. *Eros and Civilisation*, 1969, Sphere.
27 Brown, N.O. *Love's Body*, 1966, Random House.
28 Bachelard, G. *The Poetics of Space*, 1964, Orion Press.
29 Bachelard, G. *The Psychoanalysis of Fire*, 1964, Beacon.
30 Bachelard, G. 1983, op.cit.
31 Bachelard, G. *Lautréamont*, 1986, Pegasus Foundation.
32 Yeats, W.B. *A Vision*.

Subject Index

Index of Historical Persons and Mythological Names